Fodor's 96 Pocket London

Reprinted from Fodor's *London '96*

Fodor's Travel Publications, Inc.
New York • Toronto • London • Sydney • Auckland

Fodor's Pocket London '96

Editors: Caroline Haberfeld, Lara Edelbaum
Author: Kate Sekules
Editorial Contributors: Robert Andrews, Robert Blake, Laura M. Kidder, Jane Moss, Ann Saunders, Mary Ellen Schultz, M. T. Schwartzman, Dinah Spritzer
Creative Director: Fabrizio La Rocca
Cartographer: David Lindroth
Cover Photograph: Brian Yarvin/Peter Arnold, Inc.
Design: Between the Covers

Copyright

ISBN 0-679-03061-1

Special Sales

Fodor's Travel Publications are available at special discounts for bulk purchases for sales promotions or premiums. Special editions, including personalized covers, excerpts of existing guides, and corporate imprints, can be created in large quantities for special needs. For more information contact your local bookseller or write to Special Markets, Fodor's Travel Publications, 201 East 50th Street, New York, NY 10022. Inquiries from Canada should be directed to your local Canadian bookseller or sent to Random House of Canada, Ltd., Marketing Department, 1265 Aerowood Drive, Mississauga, Ontario L4W 1B9. Inquiries from the United Kingdom should be sent to Fodor's Travel Publications, 20 Vauxhall Bridge Road, London, England SW1V 2SA.

MANUFACTURED IN THE UNITED STATES OF AMERICA

10 9 8 7 6 5 4 3 2 1

CONTENTS

ON THE ROAD WITH FODOR'S

A GOOD TRAVEL GUIDE is like a wonderful traveling companion. It's charming, it's brimming with sound recommendations and solid ideas, it pulls no punches in describing lodging and dining establishments, and it's consistently full of fascinating facts that make you view what you've traveled to see in a rich new light. In the creation of *Pocket London '96* we at Fodor's have gone to great lengths to provide you with the very best of all possible traveling companions—and to make your trip the best of all possible vacations.

What's New

A New Design

If this is not the first Fodor's guide you've purchased, you'll immediately notice our new look. More readable and easier to use than ever? We think so—and we hope you do, too.

How to Use this Guide

Organization

The first chapter is called Essential Information, comprising two sections that are chock-full of information about traveling within your destination and traveling in general. Important Contacts gives addresses and telephone numbers of organizations and companies that offer destination-related services and detailed information or publications. Here's where you'll find information about how to get to London from wherever you are. Smart Travel Tips, the second section, gives specific tips on how to get the most out of your travels, as well as information on how to accomplish what you need to in London.

Stars

Stars in the margin are used to denote highly recommended sights, attractions, hotels, and restaurants.

Credit Cards

The following abbreviations are used: **AE,** American Express; **DC,** Diners Club; **MC,** MasterCard; and **V,** Visa. Discover is not accepted outside the United States.

Please Write to Us

Everyone who has contributed to *Pocket London '96* has worked hard to make the text accurate. All prices and opening times are based on information supplied to us at press time, and the publisher cannot accept responsibility for any errors that may have occurred. The passage of time will bring changes, so it's always a good idea to call ahead and confirm information when it matters—particularly if you're making a detour to visit specific sights or attractions. When making reservations at a hotel or inn, be sure to speak up if you have a disability or are traveling with children, if you prefer a private bath or a certain type of bed, or if you have specific dietary needs or any other concerns.

Were the restaurants we recommended as described? Did our hotel picks exceed your expectations? Did you find a museum we recommended a waste of time? We would love your feedback, positive and negative. If you have complaints, we'll look into them and revise our entries when the facts warrant it. If you've happened upon a special place that we haven't included, we'll pass the information along to the writers so they can check it out. So please send us a letter or postcard (we're at 201 East 50th Street, New York, New York 10022). We'll look forward to hearing from you. And in the meantime, have a wonderful trip!

Karen Cure
Editorial Director

London Underground
West Ruislip
Uxbridge
Amersham
Harrow & Wealdstone
Stanmore
Edgware
High Barnet
Mill Hill East
Cockfosters
Walthamstow Central
Ongar
Epping
Hainault
Ruislip Gardens
South Ruislip
Northolt
Greenford
Perivale
Hanger Lane
Rayners Lane
West Harrow
South Harrow
Sudbury Hill
Sudbury Town
Alperton
Park Royal
North Ealing
Ealing Broadway
Ealing Common
West Acton
North Acton
Acton Central
East Acton
White City
Harrow-on-the-Hill
South Kenton
North Wembley
Wembley Central
Stonebridge Park
Harlesden
Willesden Junction
Kensal Green
Queen's Park
Kilburn Park
Maida Vale
Warwick Avenue
Royal Oak
Westbourne Park
Ladbroke Grove
Latimer Road
Goldhawk Road
Shepherd's Bush
Kensington (Olympia)
Holland Park
Wembley Park
Neasden
Dollis Hill
Willesden Green
Kilburn
West Hampstead
Finchley Road
Swiss Cottage
St. John's Wood
Kensal Rise
Brondesbury Park
Brondesbury
Finchley Road & Frognal
Hampstead Heath
Gospel Oak
Kentish Town West
Belsize Park
Chalk Farm
Camden Town
Kentish Town
Camden Road
Mornington Crescent
Euston
King's Cross St. Pancras
Caledonian Road
Holloway Road
Arsenal
Finsbury Park
Seven Sisters
Tottenham Hale
Blackhorse Road
Highbury & Islington
Drayton Park
Caledonian Road & Barnsbury
Canonbury
Dalston Kingsland
Hackney Central
Hackney Wick
Homerton
Essex Road
Angel
Old Street
Farringdon
Barbican
Moorgate
Liverpool Street
Shoreditch
Bethnal Green
Mile End
Stratford
Leyton
Leytonstone
Snaresbrook
South Woodford
Wanstead
Redbridge
Gants Hill
Barkingside
Fairlop
Newbury Park
Upminster
Upminster Bridge
Hornchurch
Elm Park
Dagenham East
Dagenham Heathway
Becontree
Upney
Barking
East Ham
Upton Park
Plaistow
West Ham
Bromley-by-Bow
Bow Road
Bow Church
Stepney Green
Whitechapel
Aldgate East
Aldgate
Tower Hill
Tower Gateway
Devons Road
All Saints
Poplar
Limehouse
Shadwell
Wapping
Rotherhithe
Surrey Quays
New Cross Gate
New Cross
Westferry
West India Quay
Heron Quays
South Quay
Crossharbour
Mudchute
Island Gardens
Canary Wharf
Blackwall
Brunswick Wharf
Canning Town
Royal Victoria
Prince Regent
Royal Albert
Beckton Park
Cyprus
Gallions Reach
Beckton
Custom House
Silvertown & London City Airport
North Woolwich
Paddington
Edgware Road
Marylebone
Baker Street
Great Portland Street
Regent's Park
Warren Street
Euston Square
Goodge Street
Russell Square
Tottenham Court Road
Oxford Circus
Bond Street
Marble Arch
Lancaster Gate
Queensway
Bayswater
Notting Hill Gate
High Street Kensington
Holborn
Chancery Lane
St. Paul's
Bank
Monument
Cannon Street
Mansion House
Blackfriars
Temple
Aldwych
Covent Garden
Leicester Square
Charing Cross
Embankment
Piccadilly Circus
Green Park
Hyde Park Corner
Knightsbridge
Sloane Square
Victoria
St. James's Park
Westminster
Waterloo
Lambeth North
Elephant & Castle
Borough
London Bridge
Kennington
Oval
Stockwell
Brixton
Vauxhall
Pimlico
Clapham North
Clapham Common
Clapham South
Balham
Morden
Gloucester Road
South Kensington
Earl's Court
West Brompton
Fulham Broadway
Parsons Green
Putney Bridge
East Putney
Southfields
Wimbledon Park
Wimbledon
West Kensington
Barons Court
Hammersmith
Ravenscourt Park
Stamford Brook
Turnham Green
Chiswick Park
Gunnersbury
Kew Gardens
Richmond
Acton Town
South Acton
South Ealing
Northfields
Boston Manor
Osterley
Hounslow East
Hounslow Central
Hounslow West
Hatton Cross
Heathrow Terminals 1, 2, 3
Heathrow Terminal 4
River Thames
Key to lines
Bakerloo
Central
Circle
District
East London
Hammersmith & City
Jubilee
Metropolitan
Northern
Piccadilly
Victoria
Docklands Light Railway †
Network SouthEast
Interchange stations
Connections with British Rail
Connections within walking distance
Closed Sundays
Closed Saturdays and Sundays
Served by Piccadilly line early mornings and late evenings Monday to Saturday and all day Sundays
For opening times see poster journey planners
Certain stations are closed during public holidays
UNDERGROUND
Travel Information 071-222-1234
Travelcheck 071-222-1200
Diary 2D 9/90
© Copyright London Regional Transport

Central London Exploring *(Boxes Refer to Detail Maps)*

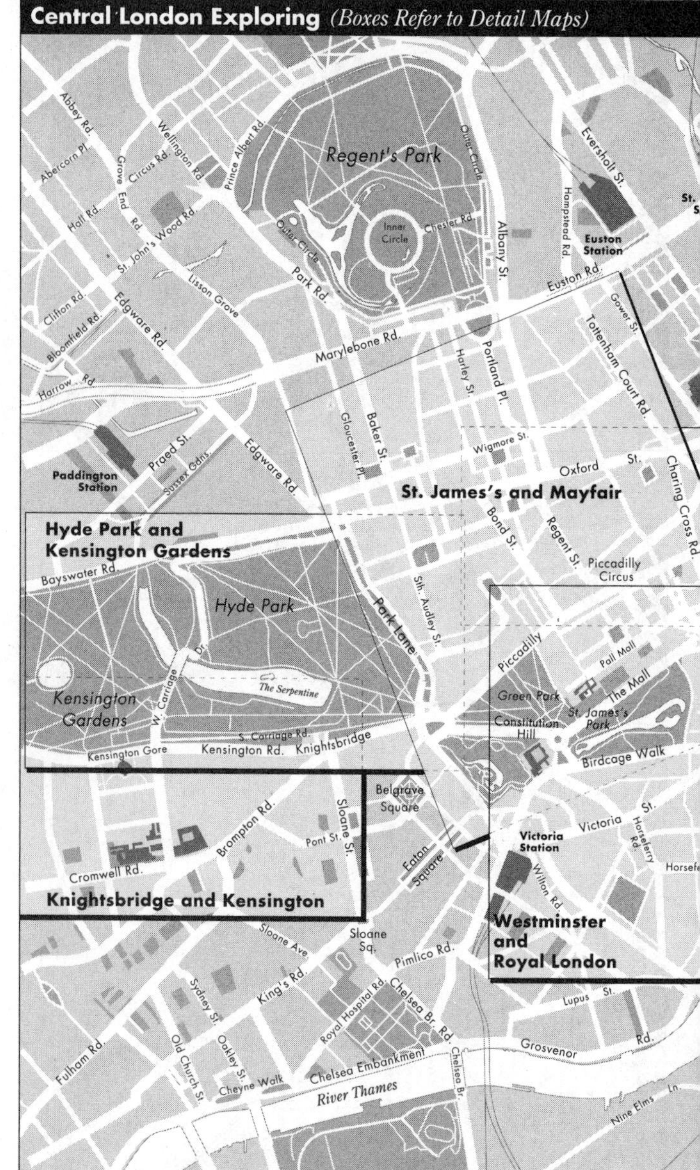

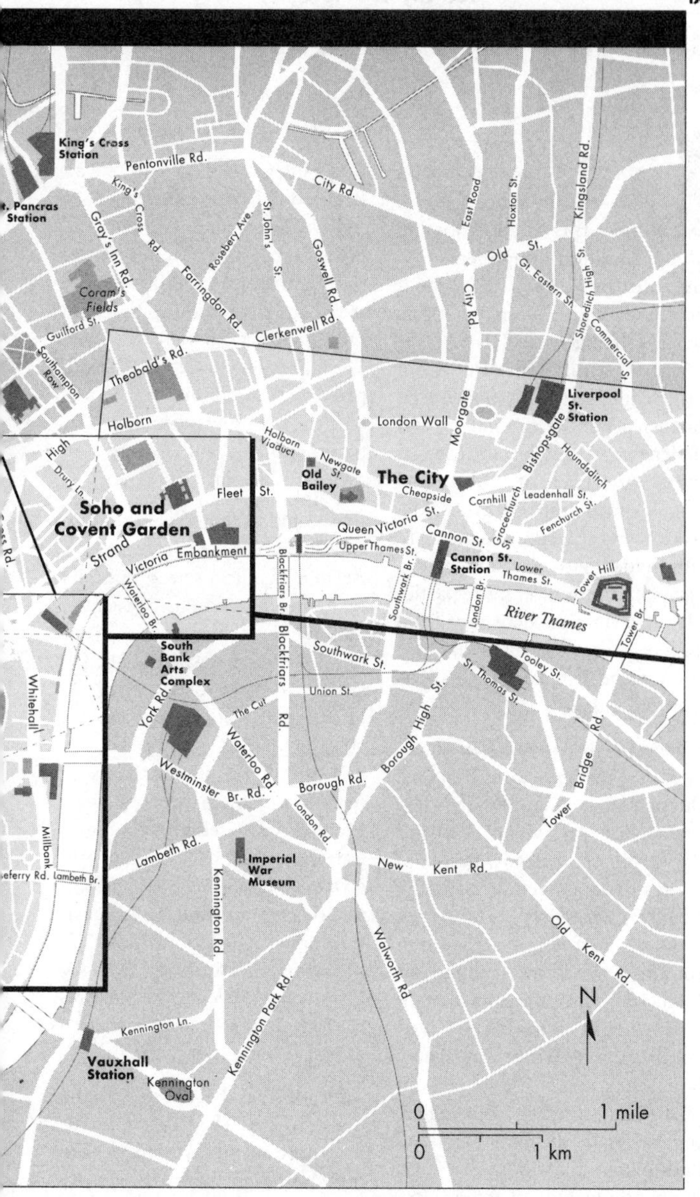
King's Cross Station
Pentonville Rd.
St. Pancras Station
King's Cross Rd.
Gray's Inn Rd.
City Rd.
St. John's St.
Rosebery Ave.
Goswell Rd.
Farringdon Rd.
East Road
Hoxton St.
Kingsland Rd.
Old St.
Gt. Eastern St.
Shoreditch High St.
Coram's Fields
Guilford St.
Southampton Row
Clerkenwell Rd.
Commercial St.
Theobald's Rd.
Holborn
London Wall
Moorgate
Liverpool St. Station
High
Drury Ln.
Holborn Viaduct
Newgate St.
Old Bailey
The City
Bishopsgate
Houndsditch
Soho and Covent Garden
Fleet St.
Cheapside
Cornhill
Leadenhall St.
Queen Victoria St.
Cannon St.
Gracechurch St.
Fenchurch St.
Strand
Victoria Embankment
Upper Thames St.
Cannon St. Station
Lower Thames St.
Tower Hill
Waterloo Br.
Blackfriars Br.
Southwark Br.
London Br.
River Thames
Tower Br.
South Bank Arts Complex
Blackfriars Rd.
Southwark St.
Tooley St.
St. Thomas St.
Union St.
Whitehall
York Rd.
The Cut
Borough High St.
Waterloo Rd.
Westminster Br. Rd.
Borough Rd.
Tower Bridge Rd.
London Rd.
Millbank
Lambeth Rd.
Imperial War Museum
New Kent Rd.
Lambeth Br.
Kennington Rd.
Walworth Rd.
Old Kent Rd.
Kennington Park Rd.
N
Kennington Ln.
Vauxhall Station
Kennington Oval
0
1 mile
0
1 km

THE CITY OF VILLAGES

LONDON IS AN ENORMOUS city—600 square miles—on a tiny island, hosting about 7 million Londoners, ⅛ of the entire population of England, Scotland, and Wales; but it has never felt big to me. It is fashioned on a different scale from other capital cities, as if, given the English penchant for modesty and understatement, it felt embarrassed by its size. Each of the 32 boroughs that comprise the whole has its own attitude, and most are subdivided into yet smaller enclaves exhibiting yet more particular behaviors, so there is really no such person as a generic Londoner. It's a cliché, but London really is a city of villages.

I have lived in several of these, and am, through long practice, fluent in the language of a few others, but "my" village, Holland Park, is the one I know best, and it illustrates as well as any how London is changing. Holland Park is small—just a few streets surrounding the former grounds of Holland House, a Jacobean mansion whose remains (it was bombed during World War II) now house a restaurant, a gallery, an open-air theater, and a youth hostel. North of the park, Holland Park Avenue metamorphoses into the windy local high street, Notting Hill Gate, then into bleak Bayswater Road, abutted on its right by Kensington Gardens and Hyde Park before breaking, where the main London gallows once stood, into irritating, commercial Oxford Street. But here, for a few West 11 moments, it is a broad, plane tree–lined boulevard, strung with vast, white-stucco, late-Victorian houses and looking an awful lot like Paris.

In our sophisticated age, the European ambience of Holland Park Avenue has been seized upon by niche-marketeers, and we now have two French patisseries, three international newsstands, a BMW showroom, and a candlelit Provençale restaurant within a couple of blocks. The history racket is doing similar things all over town, history being what London has to sell now that it no longer cuts much ice in the world economy. It would be sentimental to prefer the avenue's old hardware store and late-night family grocer (open till 9!) to the fancy Continental shops that have replaced them—London has to move with the times, after all.

Both good and bad come with the new territory. The Pakistani family whose members used to take turns minding the grocery store bought the block a decade later. Those Patels are now a well-known London dynasty, with most of the capital's newsstands in their empire—a satisfying reversal of roles from the British Raj days. Meanwhile, homeless Londoners (the number is about 100,000, and rising) work the overpriced yuppie supermarket threshold selling their magazine, *The Big Issue,* for a profit of 25p per guilty conscience. As one of the many villages built during Victoria's reign, Holland Park is a neighborhood unaccustomed to urban blight. But much of London has weathered several centuries of coping with the indigent population.

That's one of the best things about the city: Everything has been seen before, and history is forever poking its nose in. Whatever you're doing, you're doing it on top of a past layered like striated rock. You can see the cross sections clearly sometimes, as in the City, where lumps of Roman wall nest in the postmodern blocks of the street helpfully named London Wall. Walk toward the Thames to Cheapside, which you can tell was the medieval marketplace if you know the meaning of "ceap" ("to barter"), and there's the little Norman church of St. Mary-le-Bow, rebuilt by Wren and then again after the Blitz, but still ringing the Bow Bells. Then look to your right, and you'll be gobsmacked by the dome of St. Paul's. Of course, all you really wanted was to find a place for lunch—nearly impossible on a weekend in this office wasteland.

Instead of going weak-kneed at the sights, Londoners are apt to complain about such privations, while pretending simultaneously that no other city in the United Kingdom exists. Edinburghers and Liverpudlians can complain till Big Ben tolls 13, but Londoners continue to pull rank with a complacency that amuses and infuriates visitors in about equal measure. London definitely *used* to be important. The vein of water running through its center has always linked the city with the sea, and it once gave British mariners a head start in the race to mine the world's riches and bring them home. The river proved convenient for building not only palaces (at Westminster, Whitehall, Hampton Court, Richmond, and Greenwich) but an empire, too.

The empire dissolved, but the first Thames Bridge is still there, in almost the same spot that the emperor Claudius picked in AD 43, and although the current drab concrete incarnation dates only from 1972, it's still called London Bridge. The Tudor one was much better—something I learned before I was 10 from visits to the Museum of London, which used to live nearby in Kensington Palace. I liked the old bridge because of the row of decapitated heads stuck on poles above the gatehouse, which you could see on the model. It added a frisson to history, which more recent exhibitions, like the amazingly popular London Dungeon, have rather cynically packaged.

The old London Bridge lasted 600 years. Lined with shops and houses, it presided over a string of fairs *on* the Thames, when winters were colder and the water froze thick. Nowadays we're lucky to see a single snowfall come winter—and the operative word *is* "lucky." We are genuinely obsessed by the weather, because we have so much of it, though most of it is damp. Snow varies the scenery, stops any tube train with an above-ground route, makes kids of everyone who owns a makeshift toboggan and has access to a park, and fosters a community spirit normally proscribed by the city's geography and its citizens' cool.

The corollary to our temperate winter, though, is a fresh confidence in summer sufficient to support herds of sidewalk tables. Holland Park Avenue no longer has the monopoly on Parisian ambience. All over town, an epidemic of Continental-style café chains serving croissants and *salade frisée* has devoured the traditional tobacco-stained pubs serving warm bitter and bags of pork scratchings. Most of the remaining pubs have turned into faux-Edwardian parlors with coffee machines and etchings. The change has been going on for about a decade, and it suits London, as does its yet more recent (and momentous) discovery that restaurants are allowed to serve good food in smart surroundings and not charge the earth.

London is increasingly a European city, as if England were no longer stranded alone in the sea. In fact, ever since airplanes superseded ships, this island race has been undergoing an identity crisis, which reached its apogee in the '70s when Prime Minister Edward Heath sailed us irrevocably into the Common Market. Occasionally Britain still holds out against some European Union legislation or other, attempting to reassert differences that are following executions at the Tower and British Colonial supremacy into history. But however much the social climate changes, London is built on a firm foundation. Until the ravens desert the Tower of London—which is when, they say, the kingdom will fall—we have Westminster Abbey and St. Paul's and the Houses of Parliament, the Georgian squares and grand Victorian houses, the green miles of parks, the river, the museums and galleries and theaters, and 32 boroughs of villages to keep us going.

— by Kate Sekules

1 Essential Information

IMPORTANT CONTACTS

An Alphabetical Listing of Publications, Organizations, and Companies That Will Help You Before, During, and After Your Trip

AIR TRAVEL

The major gateways to London are Heathrow and Gatwick (☎ 181/759–2525 for both). Flying time is 6½ hours from New York, 7½ hours from Chicago, and 10 hours from Los Angeles.

CARRIERS

Carriers serving London include **American Airlines** (☎ 800/433–7300), **British Airways** (☎ 800/247–9297), **Continental** (☎ 800/231–0856); **Delta** (☎ 800/241–4141), **Northwest Airlines** (☎ 800/447–4747), **TWA** (☎ 800/892–4141), **United** (☎ 800/241–6522), **USAir** (☎ 800/428–4322), and **Virgin Atlantic** (☎ 800/862–8621).

BUS TRAVEL

For details on bus service within London, contact **London Transport** (☎ 0171/222–1234). Travelcards (*see* Underground *below*) are good for both the tube and the bus.

CAR RENTAL

Major car-rental companies represented in London include **Alamo** (☎ 800/327–9633, 0800/272–2000 in the United Kingdom); **Avis** (☎ 800/331–1084, 800/879–2847 in Canada); **Budget** (☎ 800/527–0700, 0800/181181 in the United Kingdom); **Hertz** (☎ 800/654–3001, 800/263–0600 in Canada, 0181/679–1799 in the United Kingdom); and **National** (sometimes known as Europcar InterRent outside North America; ☎ 800/227–3876, 0181/950–5050 in the United Kingdom). Rates in London begin at $21 a day and $126 a week for an economy car. This does not include tax, which in London is 17.5% on car rentals.

RENTAL WHOLESALERS

Contact **Auto Europe** (Box 7006, Portland, ME 04112, ☎ 207/828–2525 or 800/223–5555); **Europe by Car** in New York City (write 1 Rockefeller Plaza, 10020; visit 14 W. 49th St.; or call 212/581–3040, 212/245–1713, or 800/223–1516) or Los Angeles (9000 Sunset Blvd., 90069, ☎ 800/252–9401 or 213/272–0424 in CA); or **Foremost Euro-Car** (5658 Sepulveda Blvd., Suite 201, Van Nuys, CA 91411, ☎ 818/786–1960 or 800/272–3299).

THE CHANNEL TUNNEL

For information, contact **Le Shuttle** (☎ 01345/353535 in the

United Kingdom, 800/388–3876 in the United States), which transports cars, or **Eurostar** (☎ 0171/922–4486 in the United Kingdom, 800/942–4866 in the United States), the high-speed train service between London (Waterloo) and Paris (Gare du Nord). Eurostar tickets are available in the United Kingdom through **InterCity Europe,** the international wing of BritRail (London, Victoria Station, ☎ 0171/834–2345 or 0171/828–8092 for credit-card bookings), and in the United States through **Rail Europe** (☎ 800/942–4866) and **BritRail Travel** (1500 Broadway, New York, NY 10036, ☎ 800/677–8585 or 212/575–2667).

CUSTOMS

U.S. CITIZENS

The **U.S. Customs Service** (Box 7407, Washington, DC 20044, ☎ 202/927–6724) can answer questions on duty-free limits and publishes a helpful brochure, **"Know Before You Go."** For information on registering foreign-made articles, call 202/927–0540.

CANADIANS

Contact **Revenue Canada** (2265 St. Laurent Blvd. S, Ottawa, Ontario, K1G 4K3, ☎ 613/993–0534) for a copy of the free brochure **"I Declare/Je Déclare"** and for details on duties that exceed the standard duty-free limit.

FOR TRAVELERS WITH DISABILITIES

IN THE U.K.

For brochures and further information, contact the **Royal Association for Disability and Rehabilitation** (RADAR, 12 City Forum, 250 City Rd., London EC1V 8AF, ☎ 0171/250–3222) or **Mobility International** (rue de Manchester 25, B–1070 Brussels, Belgium, ☎ 00–322–410–6297), an international clearinghouse of travel information for people with disabilities.

Contact **London Transport's Unit for Disabled Passengers** (55 Broadway, London SW1H OBD, ☎ 0171/222–5600, Minicom 0171/918–3051) for details on **Stationlink,** a wheelchair-accessible "midibus" service as well as other access information. **Artsline** (☎ 0171/388–2227) provides information on accessibility of arts events.

EMBASSIES AND CONSULATES

U.S. Embassy (24 Grosvenor Sq., W1A 1AE, ☎ 0171/499–9000). Inside the embassy is the American Aid Society, a charity set up to help Americans in distress. Dial the embassy number and ask for extension 570 or 571.

Canadian High Commission (Canada House, Trafalgar Sq., London SW1Y 5BJ, ☎ 0171/629–9492).

EMERGENCIES

For police, fire department, or ambulance, dial 999.

The following hospitals have 24-hour emergency wards: **Charing Cross** (Fulham Palace Rd., Hammersmith W6, ☎ 0181/846–1234); **Guys** (St. Thomas St., SE1, ☎ 0171/407–7600); **Royal Free** (Pond St., Hampstead, NW3, ☎ 0171/794–0500); **St. Bartholomew's** (West Smithfield, EC1, ☎ 0171/600–9000); **St. Thomas's** (Lambeth Palace Rd., SE1, ☎ 0171/928–9292); **Westminster** (Dean Ryle St., Horseferry Rd., SW1, ☎ 0171/828–9811).

CREDIT CARDS

Here are the numbers to call for assistance should your credit cards be lost or stolen: **Access** (MasterCard, ☎ 01702/352255); **American Express** (☎ 0171/222–9633 for credit cards or 01800/521313 for traveler's checks); **Barclaycard** (Visa, ☎ 01704/230230); **Diners Club** (☎ 01252/516261).

PHARMACIES

Chemists (drugstores) with late opening hours include **Bliss Chemist** (50–56 Willesden La., NW6, ☎ 0171/624–8000; 5 Marble Arch, W1, ☎ 0171/723–6116), open daily 9 AM–midnight, and **Boots** (439 Oxford St., W1, ☎ 0171/409–2857), open Thursday 8:30–7.

GAY AND LESBIAN TRAVEL

The **International Gay Travel Association** (Box 4974, Key West, FL 33041, ☎ 800/448–8550), a consortium of 800 businesses, can supply names of travel agents and tour operators.

INSURANCE

Travel insurance covering baggage, health, and trip cancellation or interruptions is available from **Access America** (Box 90315, Richmond, VA 23286, ☎ 804/285–3300 or 800/284–8300); **Carefree Travel Insurance** (Box 9366, 100 Garden City Plaza, Garden City, NY 11530, ☎ 516/294–0220 or 800/323–3149); **Near Travel Services** (Box 1339, Calumet City, IL 60409, ☎ 708/868–6700 or 800/654–6700); **Tele-Trip** (Mutual of Omaha Plaza, Box 31716, Omaha, NE 68131, ☎ 800/228–9792); **Travel Insured International** (Box 280568, East Hartford, CT 06128, ☎ 203/528–7663 or 800/243–3174); **Travel Guard International** (1145 Clark St., Stevens Point, WI 54481, ☎ 715/345–0505 or 800/826–1300); and **Wallach & Company** (107 W. Federal St., Box 480, Middleburg, VA 22117, ☎ 703/687–3166 or 800/237–6615).

IN THE U.K.

The **Association of British Insurers** (51 Gresham St., London EC2V 7HQ, ☎ 0171/600–3333; 30

Gordon St., Glasgow G1 3PU, ☎ 0141/226–3905; Scottish Provident Bldg., Donegall Sq. W, Belfast BT1 6JE, ☎ 01232/249176; call for other locations) gives advice by phone.

MAIL

The **London Chief Post Office** (King Edward St., EC1A 1AA, ☎ 0171/239–5047) is open weekdays 8:30–6. The **Trafalgar Square Post Office** (24–28 William IV St., WC2N 4DL, ☎ 0171/930–9580) is open Monday–Saturday 8–8. Most other post offices are open weekdays 9–5:30, Saturday 9–12:30 or 1.

MONEY MATTERS

ATMS

For specific foreign **Cirrus** locations, call 800/424–7787; for foreign Plus locations, consult the **Plus** directory at your local bank.

CURRENCY EXCHANGE

If your bank doesn't exchange currency, contact **Thomas Cook Currency Services** (41 E. 42nd St., New York, NY 10017; 511 Madison Ave., New York, NY 10022, ☎ 212/757–6915 or 800/223–7373 for locations) or **Ruesch International** (☎ 800/424–2923 for locations).

WIRING FUNDS

Funds can be wired via **American Express MoneyGram℠** (☎ 800/926–9400 from the United States and Canada for locations and information) or **Western Union** (☎ 800/325–6000 for agent locations or to send using MasterCard or Visa, 800/321–2923 in Canada).

PASSPORTS AND VISAS

U.S. CITIZENS

For fees, documentation requirements, and other information, call the **Office of Passport Services** information line (☎ 202/647–0518).

CANADIANS

For fees, documentation requirements, and other information, call the Ministry of Foreign Affairs and International Trade's **Passport Office** (☎ 819/994–3500 or 800/567–6868).

PHONE MATTERS

The country code for Britain is 44. There are two area codes in London, 0171 for inner London and 0181 for outer London. You don't have to dial either if calling inside the same zone. Drop the 0 from the prefix and dial only 171 or 181 when calling from overseas. For local access numbers abroad, contact **AT&T** USADirect (☎ 800/874–4000), **MCI** Call USA (☎ 800/444–4444), or **Sprint** Express (☎ 800/793–1153).

RAIL TRAVEL

If you plan to travel a lot in Britain, you might consider purchasing a **BritRail Pass,** which gives unlimited travel over the entire British Rail network.

You *must* purchase the **BritRail Pass** before you leave home. It is available from most travel agents throughout the world, or from **BritRail Travel International** offices (1500 Broadway, New York, NY 10036, ☏ 212/575–2667; 94 Cumberland St., Toronto, Ontario M5R 1A3, ☏ 416/482–1777). (*see* The Channel Tunnel, *above*)

SIGHTSEEING

BY BOAT

In summer, narrow boats and barges cruise London's two canals, the Grand Union and Regent's Canal; most vessels (they seat about 60) operate on the latter, which runs between Little Venice in the west (nearest tube: Warwick Ave. on the Bakerloo Line) and Camden Lock (about 200 yards north of Camden Town tube station). **Jason's Trip** (☏ 0171/286–3428) operates one-way and round-trip narrow-boat cruises on this route. During April, May, and September, there are two cruises per day; from June to August, there are four. Trips last 1½ hours and cost £3.75 for adults, £2.50 for children and senior citizens round-trip.

London Waterbus Co. (☏ 0171/482–2550) offers the Zoo Waterbus service daily from March to September, on weekends in winter. A round-trip canal cruise, London Zoo–Camden Lock, costs £3.20 adults, £1.90 children. Combined zoo entrance–waterbus tickets are also available.

Canal Cruises (☏ 0171/485–4433) also offers cruises from March to October on the *Jenny Wren* (£3.90 adults, £1.80 children and senior citizens), and all year on the floating restaurant *My Fair Lady* (Tues.–Sat. dinner, £24.95; Sun. lunch, £16.95).

From April to October, boats cruise the Thames and offer a different view of the London skyline. Most leave from Westminster Pier (☏ 0171/930–4097); Charing Cross Pier (Victoria Embankment, ☏ 0171/839–3312); and Tower Pier (☏ 0171/488–0344). Downstream routes go to the Tower of London, Greenwich, and the Thames Barrier; upstream destinations include Kew, Richmond, and Hampton Court. Most of the launches seat between 100 and 250 passengers, have a public-address system, and provide a running commentary on passing points of interest. Depending upon the destination, river trips may last from one to four hours. For more information, call **Catamaran Cruisers** (☏ 0171/839–3572), **Tidal Cruises** (☏ 0171/928–9009), or **Westminster Passenger Services Association** (☏ 0171/930–4097).

BY BUS

London Transport's London Plus guided tours (☏ 0171/828–6449) offer passengers a good introduction to the city from double-decker buses, which are open-topped in summer. Tours run daily every half hour, or more frequently during summer, 10–5, from Marble Arch, Victoria, Piccadilly, Harrods, Trafalgar Square, and some 30 other places of interest. Tickets (£12 adults, £6 children) may be bought from the driver. Other agencies offering half- and full-day bus tours include **Evan Evans** (☎ 0171/837–3111), **Frames Rickards** (☎ 0171/837–3111), **Travellers Check-In** (☎ 0171/580–8284), and **The Big Bus Company** (☎ 0181/944–7810). Prices and pickup points vary according to the sights visited, but many pickup points are at major hotels.

ON FOOT

One of the best ways to get to know London is on foot, and there are many guided walking tours from which to choose. **The Original London Walks** (☎ 0171/624–3978) has a very wide selection and takes justifiable pride in the infectious enthusiasm of its guides. **City Walks** (☎ 0171/700–6931), **Streets of London** (☎ 0181/346–9255), and **Citisights** (☎ 0181/806–4325) are some of the better-known firms, but you can investigate more tours at the London Tourist Information Centre at Victoria Station. The lengths of walks vary (usually one to three hours), and you can generally find one to suit even the most specific interests–Shakespeare's London, say, or a Jack the Ripper tour. Prices range around £4 for adults.

For those who would rather explore on their own, the City of London Corporation has laid out a **Heritage Walk** leading through Bank, Leadenhall, and Monument streets. A map of this walk may be found in *A Visitor's Guide to the City of London,* available from the City Information Centre across from St. Paul's Cathedral. Another option is to follow the **Silver Jubilee Walkway,** created in 1977 in honor of the 25th anniversary of the accession of the present queen. The entire route covers 10 miles and is marked by a series of silver crowns set into the sidewalks; Parliament Square makes a good starting point. Books available from the British Travel Centre (12 Regent St., W1) list other London Regional Transport walks.

UNDERGROUND

PASSES

In London, the transportation system is known as the Underground or more affectionately the "Tube." Several passes for tube and bus travel are available at tube and rail stations, as well as some newsstands. The **One Day Travelcard** allows unrestricted travel on both bus and tube and is valid weekdays after 9:30 AM, weekends, and all national holidays (cost: £2.80–£3.80; children £1.50). The **LT Card** is the same as the One Day Travelcard, but without the time restrictions (cost: £3.90–£6.50, children £1.90–£2.70).

There are also weekly and monthly **Travelcards** valid for bus and tube travel; the cost varies according to the period of time and the number of zones covered. The **Visitor's Travelcard** may be bought in the United States and Canada for three, four, and seven days' travel; it is the same as the LT Card and has a booklet of discount vouchers to London attractions. In the United States, the Visitor's Travelcard costs $25, $32, and $49, respectively ($11, $13, and $21 for children); in Canada, C$29, C$36, and C$55, respectively (C$13, C$15, and C$25 for children). Apply to travel agents or, in the United States, to **BritRail Travel** (*see* The Channel Tunnel, *above*).

VISITOR INFO

Contact the **British Tourist Authority** (BTA) in the United States at 551 Fifth Avenue, Suite 701, New York, NY 10176, ☎ 212/986–2200 or 800/462–2748; 625 North Michigan Avenue, Suite 1510, Chicago, IL 60611, ☎ 312/787–0490; World Trade Center, 350 South Figueroa Street, Suite 450, Los Angeles, CA 90071, ☎ 213/628–3525; 2580 Cumberland Parkway, Suite 470, Atlanta, GA 30339, ☎ 404/432–9635; in Canada at 111 Avenue Road, 4th Floor, Toronto, Ontario M5R 3J8, ☎ 416/925–6326; and in Britain, by mail at Thames Tower, Black's Road, London W6 9EL.

In London, go in person to the **London Tourist Information Centre** at Victoria Station Forecourt for general information (Mon.–Sat., 8–7, Sun. 8–5) or to the **British Travel Centre** (12 Regent St.) for travel, hotel, and entertainment information (weekdays 9–6:30, Sat. 10–4). The **London Travel Service** (Bridge House, Ware, Hertfordshire SG12 9DE, ☎ 01992/456187) offers travel, hotel, and tour reservations (weekdays 9–5:30, Sat. 9–5).

The London Tourist Board's **Visitorcall** phone guide to London (☎ 01839/123456) gives information about events, theater, museums, transportation, shopping, restaurants, and so forth. A three-month events calendar (☎ 01839/401279), or annual version (☎ 01839/401278), is available by fax (set fax machine to polling mode, or press start/receive after the tone). Visitorcall charges a rate of 39p–49p per minute, depending on the time of day you call.

WEATHER

For current conditions and forecasts, plus the local time and helpful travel tips, call the **Weather Channel Connection** (☎ 900/932–8437; 95¢ per minute) from a Touch-Tone phone.

SMART TRAVEL TIPS

Basic Information on Traveling in London and Savvy Tips to Make Your Trip a Breeze

AIR TRAVEL

If time is an issue, **always look for nonstop flights,** which require no change of plane. If possible, **avoid connecting flights,** which stop at least once and can involve a change of plane, although the flight number remains the same; if the first leg is late, the second waits.

AIRPORT TRANSFERS

The Piccadilly Line of the Underground connects with Heathrow (all terminals). Trains run every four to eight minutes; journey time is roughly 50 minutes, and the price is £3 one-way. London Transport's *Airbus* shuttle service (☎ 0181/897–3305) also runs to Heathrow; two routes stop at many central locations, including most major hotels; travel time is about an hour and 20 minutes, and the cost for each route is £5 one-way.

An alternative to the *Airbus* is Bus 390, which departs Stand 8, Buckingham Palace Road. Journey time is about an hour, and the fare is £4 one-way.

By car, the most direct route to Heathrow from central London is via the M4. By taxi, the fare from downtown should be about £25 plus tip, though this and the journey time will depend on the traffic.

Fast, nonstop trains leave Victoria Station from every 15 minutes to once an hour, depending on time of travel; the journey time varies from 30 to 39 minutes, and the price is £8.60 one-way.

Regular bus services to Gatwick are provided by Green Line Coaches (☎ 181/668–7261), including the *Flightline* 777, which leaves Victoria Coach Station hourly until midnight. Travel time is about 70 minutes, and a one-way ticket costs £6.

To get to Gatwick by car, take the A23 and then the M23 from central London. Taxis from Gatwick to the city are prohibitively expensive—you may find that it is much more reasonable to take the train.

BUS TRAVEL

London's bus system consists of bright red double- and single-deckers, plus other buses of various colors. Destinations are displayed on the front and back, and the bus number is on the front, back, and side. Not all buses run the full length of their route at all times. Some buses still have a conductor whom you pay after finding a seat, but there are a lot of "one-man" buses on the road, in which you pay the driver upon boarding.

Buses stop only at clearly indicated stops. Main stops—at which the bus *should* stop automatically—have a plain white background with a red *LT* symbol on it. There are also request stops with red signs, a white symbol, and the word "request" added; at these you must hail the bus to make it stop. Smoking is not allowed on any bus. Although you can see much of the town from a bus, *don't* take one if you want to get anywhere in a hurry; traffic often slows to a crawl, and during rush hour you may find yourself waiting 40 minutes for a bus and then not being able to get on it once it arrives. If you do go by bus, ask at a London Travel Information Centre for a free "London Bus Map".

FARES

One-way fares start at 90p in the central zone. Travelcards (*see* Important Contacts, *above*) are good for both the tube and the bus.

THE CHANNEL TUNNEL

Le Shuttle, a special car, bus, and truck train, operates continuously, with trains departing every 15 minutes at peak times and at least once an hour through the night. No reservations are necessary, although tickets may be purchased in advance from travel agents. Most passengers travel in their own car, staying with the vehicle throughout the "crossing," with progress updates via radio and display screens. Motorcyclists park their bikes in a separate section with its own passenger compartment, and foot passengers must book passage by coach. At press time (summer 1995), prices for a one-day round-trip ticket began at £107–£154 for a car and its occupants. Prices for a five-day round-trip ticket began at £115.

Eurostar operates high-speed passenger-only trains, which whisk riders between stations in Paris (Gare du Nord) and London (Waterloo) in 3 hours and between London and Brussels (Midi) in 3¼ hours. At press time (summer 1995), fares were $154 for a one-way, first-class ticket and $123 for an economy fare.

The tunnel is reached from Exit 11a of the M20/A20. Tickets for either tunnel service can be purchased in advance (*see* Important Contacts, *above*).

CUSTOMS AND DUTIES

ENTERING LONDON

There are two levels of duty-free allowance for travelers entering Great Britain: one for goods bought outside the European Union (EU), the other for goods bought in the EU (Belgium, Greece, the Netherlands, Denmark, Italy, Portugal, France, the Irish Republic, Spain, Germany, or Luxembourg).

Of the first category, you may import duty-free: 200 cigarettes or 100 cigarillos or 50 cigars or 250 grams of tobacco; 2 liters of table wine and, in addition, (a) 1 liter of alcohol over 22% by volume (most spirits), (b) 2 liters of alcohol under 22% by volume (fortified or sparkling wine), or (c) 2 more liters of table wine; 50 milliliters of perfume; ¼ liter of toilet water; and other goods up to a value of £36, but not more than 50 liters of beer or 25 cigarette lighters.

Of the second category, the EU has set guidelines for the import of certain goods. Following side trips entirely within the EU, you no longer need to go through customs on your return to the United Kingdom; however, if you exceed the guideline amounts, you may be required to prove that the goods are for your personal use only ("personal use" includes gifts). The guideline levels are: 800 cigarettes, 400 cigarillos, 200 cigars, and 1 kilogram of smoking tobacco, plus 10 liters of spirits, 20 liters of fortified wine, 90 liters of wine, and 110 liters of beer. No animals or pets of any kind can be brought into the United Kingdom without a lengthy quarantine. The penalties are severe and strictly enforced. Similarly, fresh meats, plants and vegetables, controlled drugs, and firearms and ammunition may not be brought into Great Britain.

You will face no customs formalities if you enter Scotland or Wales from any other part of the United Kingdom, though anyone coming from Northern Ireland should expect a security check.

BACK HOME

All travelers flying out of the United Kingdom are subject to a £10 Airport Departure Tax.

IN THE U.S.➢ You may bring home $400 worth of foreign goods duty-free if you've been out of the country for at least 48 hours and haven't already used the $400 exemption, or any part of it, in the past 30 days.

Travelers 21 or older may bring back 1 liter of alcohol duty-free, provided the beverage laws of the state through which they reenter the United States allow it. In addition, 100 non-Cuban cigars and 200 cigarettes are allowed, regardless of your age. Antiques and works of art more than 100 years old are duty-free.

Duty-free, travelers may mail packages valued at up to $200 to themselves and up to $100 to others, with a limit of one parcel per addressee per day (and no alcohol or tobacco products or perfume valued at more than $5); outside, identify the package as being for personal use or an unsolicited gift, specifying the contents and their retail value. Mailed items do not count as part of your exemption.

IN CANADA➢ Once per calendar year, after having been out of Canada for at least seven days, you may bring in C$300 worth of goods duty-free. If you've been away less than seven days but more than 48 hours, the duty-free exemption drops to C$100 but can be claimed any number of times (as can a C$20 duty-free exemption for absences of 24 hours or more). You cannot combine the yearly and 48-hour exemptions, use the C$300 exemption only partially (to save the balance for a later trip), or pool exemptions with family members. Goods claimed under the C$300 exemption may follow you by mail; those claimed under the lesser exemptions must accompany you.

Alcohol and tobacco products may be included in the yearly and 48-hour exemptions but not in the 24-hour exemption. If you meet the age requirements of the province through which you reenter Canada, you may bring in, duty-free, 1.14 liters (40 imperial ounces) of wine or liquor *or* 24 12-ounce cans or bottles of beer or ale. If you are 16 or older, you may bring in, duty-free, 200 cigarettes, 50 cigars or cigarillos, and 400 tobacco sticks or 400 grams of manufactured tobacco. Alcohol and tobacco must accompany you on your return.

An unlimited number of gifts valued up to C$60 each may be mailed to Canada duty-free. These do not count as part of your exemption. Label the package "Unsolicited Gift—Value Under $60." Alcohol and tobacco are excluded.

FOR TRAVELERS WITH DISABILITIES

When discussing accessibility with an operator or reservationist, **ask hard questions.** Are there any stairs, inside *or* out? Are there grab bars next to the toilet *and* in the shower/tub? How wide is the doorway to the room? To the bathroom? For the most extensive facilities, meeting the latest legal specifications, **opt for newer accommodations,** which more often have been designed with access in mind. Older properties or ships must usually be retrofitted and may offer more limited facilities as a result. Be sure to **discuss your needs before booking.**

DRIVING

The best advice about driving in London is: **don't.** Because the capital grew up as a series of villages, there never was a central plan for London's streets, and the result is a winding mass of chaos, aggravated by a passion for one-way streets.

If you must risk life and limb, however, note that the speed limit is 30 mph in the royal parks, as well as (theoretically) in all streets—unless you see the large 40 mph signs (and small repeater signs attached to lampposts) found only in the suburbs.

Other basic rules: Pedestrians have right-of-way on "zebra" crossings (those black-and-white stripes that stretch across the street between two Belisha beacons—orange-flashing globe lights on posts). The curb on each side of the zebra crossing has zigzag markings. It is illegal to park within the zigzag area, or to pass another vehicle at a zebra crossing. On other crossings pedestrians must yield to traffic, but they do have right-of-way over traffic turning left at controlled crossings—if they have the nerve.

Traffic lights sometimes have arrow-style lights directing left or right turns; it is therefore important not to get into the turn lane if you mean to go straight ahead, so try to catch a glimpse of the road markings in time. The use of horns is prohibited between 11:30 PM and 7 AM.

LONDON DISTRICTS

Greater London is divided into 32 boroughs—33, counting the City of London, which has all the powers of a London borough. More useful for finding your way around, however, are the subdivisions of London into various postal districts. Throughout the guide we've listed the full postal code for places you're likely to be contacting by mail, although you'll find the first half of the code more important. The first one or two letters give the location: N=north, NW=northwest, etc. Don't expect the numbering to be logical, however. You won't, for example, find W2 next to W3.

MONEY AND EXPENSES

The monetary unit in Great Britain is the pound sterling (£), which is divided into 100 pence (p): There are £50, £20, £10, and £5 bills; £1 (100p), 50p, 20p, 10p, 5p, 2p, and 1p coins. At press time (summer 1995), the exchange rate was about U.S. $1.55 and Canadian $2 to the pound sterling.

ATMS

Cirrus, Plus and many other networks connecting automated teller machines operate internationally. Chances are that you can **use your bank card at ATMs** to withdraw money from an account and get cash advances on a credit-card account if your card has been programmed with a personal identification number, or PIN. Before leaving home, **check in on frequency limits** for withdrawals and cash advances. Also **ask whether your card's PIN must be reprogrammed** for use in London. Four digits are commonly used overseas. Note that Discover is accepted only in the United States.

On cash advances you are charged interest from the day you receive the money, whether from a teller or an ATM. Although transaction fees for ATM withdrawals abroad may be higher than fees for withdrawals at home, Cirrus and Plus exchange rates are excellent because they are based on wholesale rates only offered by major banks.

COSTS

A movie in the West End costs £5–£9.50 (less on Monday and at matinees); a theater seat, from £6 to about £20, more for hit shows; admission to a museum or gallery, around £3 (though many are free and others request a "voluntary contribution"); coffee, £1–£2; a pint of light (lager) beer in a pub, £1.70–£2.20 (stout usually costs a bit more); whiskey, gin, vodka, and so forth, by the glass in a pub, £1.50 and up (the measure is smaller than in the United States); house wine by the glass in a pub or wine bar, about £2, in a restaurant, £3.50 or more; a Coke, around 80p; a ham sandwich from a sandwich bar in the West End, £2; a 1-mile taxi ride, £4; an average Underground or bus ride, £1.30, a longer one, £2.30.

EXCHANGING CURRENCY

For the most favorable rates, **change money at banks.** You won't do as well at exchange booths in airports, rail, and bus stations, or in hotels, restaurants, and stores, although you may find their hours more convenient. To avoid lines at airport exchange booths, **get a small amount of currency before you leave home.**

VAT TAX

The British sales tax (VAT, Value Added Tax) is 17½%. The tax is almost always included in quoted prices in shops, hotels, and restaurants.

You can **get a VAT refund** by either the Over the Counter or the more cumbersome Direct Export method. Most larger stores provide these services, but only if you request them, and will handle the paperwork. For the Over the Counter method, you must spend more than £75 in one store. Ask the store for Form VAT 407 (you must have identification—passports are best), to be given to customs when you leave the country. (Lines at major airports can be long, so allow plenty of time.) The refund will be forwarded to you in about eight weeks, minus a small service charge, either in the form of a credit to your charge card or as a British check, which American banks usually charge you to convert. With the Direct Export method, the goods go directly to your home; you must have a Form VAT 407 certified by customs officials, the police, or a notary public when you get home and then sent back to the store, which will refund your money.

TRAVELER'S CHECKS

Whether or not to buy traveler's checks depends on where you are headed; **take cash to rural areas and small towns, traveler's checks to cities.** The most widely recognized are American Express, Citicorp, Thomas Cook, and Visa, which are sold by major commercial banks for 1%–3% of the checks' face value—it pays to **shop around.** Both American Express and Thomas Cook issue checks that can be countersigned and used by you or your traveling companion, and they both provide checks, at no extra charge, denominated in pounds. You can cash them in banks without paying a fee (which can be as much as 20%) and use them as readily as cash in many hotels, restaurants, and shops. So you won't be left with excess foreign currency, **buy a few checks in small denominations** to cash toward the end of your trip. Record the numbers of the checks, cross them off as you spend them, and keep this information separate from your checks.

WIRING MONEY

You don't have to be a cardholder to send or receive funds through MoneyGram℠ from American Express. Just go to a MoneyGram℠ agent, located in retail and convenience stores and in American Express Travel Offices. Pay up to $1,000 with cash or a credit card, anything over that in cash. The money can be picked up within 10 minutes in the form of U.S. dollar traveler's checks or local currency at the nearest MoneyGram℠ agent, or, abroad, the main **American Express Travel Office** (6 Haymarket, London SW1Y 4BS, ☎ 0171/930–4411). There are many other branches; check for the one nearest you. There's no limit, and the recipient need only present photo identification. The cost runs from 3% to 10%, depending on the amount sent, the destination, and how you pay.

You can also send money using Western Union. Money sent from the United States or Canada will be available for pickup at agent locations in 100 countries within 15 minutes. Once the money is in the system, it can be picked up at any one of 25,000 locations. Fees range from 4% to 10%, depending on the amount you send.

PACKING FOR LONDON

London can be cool, damp, and overcast, even in summer. You'll want a heavy coat for winter and a lightweight coat or warm jacket for summer. Always **bring a raincoat and umbrella.** Pack as you would for an American city: coats and ties for expensive restaurants and nightspots, casual clothes elsewhere. Jeans are popular in London and are perfectly acceptable for sightseeing and informal dining. Tweeds and sport jackets are popular here with men. For women, ordinary street dress is acceptable everywhere. If you plan to stay in budget hotels, take your own soap. Many do not provide it and some give guests only one tiny bar per room.

Bring an extra pair of eyeglasses or contact lenses in your carry-on luggage, and if you have a health problem, **pack enough medication** to last the trip or have your doctor write a prescription using the drug's generic name, because brand names vary from country to country (you'll then need a prescription from a doctor in the country you're visiting). **Don't put prescription drugs or valuables in luggage to be checked,** for it could go astray. To avoid problems with customs officials, carry medications in original packaging. Also don't forget the addresses of offices that handle refunds of lost traveler's checks.

ELECTRICITY

To use your U.S.-purchased electric-powered equipment, **bring a converter and an adapter.** The electrical current in London is 220 volts, 50 cycles alternating current (AC); wall outlets take plugs with three prongs.

If your appliances are dual voltage, you'll need only an adapter. Hotels sometimes have 110-volt outlets for low-wattage appliances marked "For Shavers Only" near the sink; don't use them for high-wattage appliances like blow-dryers. If your laptop computer is older, carry a converter; new laptops operate equally well on 110 and 220 volts, so you need only an adapter.

LUGGAGE

Free airline baggage allowances depend on the airline, the route, and the class of your ticket; ask in advance. In general, on domestic flights and on international flights between the United States and foreign destinations, you are entitled to check two bags—neither exceeding 62 inches, or 158 centimeters (length + width + height), or weighing more than 70 pounds (32 kilograms). A third piece may be brought aboard; its total dimensions are generally limited to less than 45 inches (114 centimeters), so it will fit easily under the seat in front of you or in the overhead compartment. In the United States, the Federal Aviation Administration (FAA) gives airlines broad latitude to limit carry-on allowances and tailor them to different aircraft and operational conditions. Charges for excess, oversize, or overweight pieces vary.

PASSPORTS AND VISAS

If you don't already have one, **get a passport.** While traveling, **keep one photocopy of the data page** separate from your wallet and leave another copy with someone at home. If you lose your passport, promptly call the nearest embassy or consulate and the local police; having the data page can speed replacement.

U.S. CITIZENS

All U.S. citizens, even infants, need a valid passport to enter Great

Britain for stays of up to three months. New and renewal application forms are available at any of the 13 U.S. Passport Agency offices and at some post offices and courthouses. (U.S. Passports are valid for 10 years.) Passports are usually mailed within four weeks; allow five weeks or more in spring and summer.

CANADIANS

You need a valid passport to enter Great Britain for stays of up to three months days. Application forms are available at 28 regional passport offices as well as post offices and travel agencies. Whether for a first or a renewal passport, you must apply in person. Children under 16 may be included on a parent's passport but must have their own to travel alone. Passports are valid for five years and are usually mailed within two to three weeks of application.

TAXIS

Those big black taxicabs are as much a part of the London streetscape as the red double-decker buses, yet many have been replaced by the new boxy, sharp-edge model, and the beauty of others is marred by the advertising they carry on their sides. Hotels and main tourist areas have cab stands (just take the first in line), but you can also flag a taxi down from the roadside. If the yellow "for hire" sign on the top is lit, then the taxi is available. Many cab drivers often cruise at night with their FOR HIRE signs unlit; this enables them to choose their passengers and avoid those they think might cause trouble. If you see an unlit, passengerless cab, hail it: You might be lucky.

FARES

Fares start at £1 for the first 582 yards and increase by units of 20p per 291 yards or 60 seconds. A 40p surcharge is added on weekday nights 8–midnight and Saturday up to 8 PM. The surcharge rises to 60p on Saturday night, Sunday, and national holidays—except over Christmas and on New Year's Eve, when it rises to £2. Fares are usually raised in June of each year.

TELEPHONES

There are three types of phones: Those that accept (a) only coins, (b) only British Telephone (BT) phone cards, or (c) both BT phone cards and credit cards.

The coin-operated phones are of the push-button variety; most take all but 1p coins. Insert the coins *before* dialing (minimum charge is 10p). If you hear a repeated single tone after dialing, the line is busy; a continuous tone means the number is unobtainable (or that you have dialed the wrong—or no—prefix). The indicator panel shows you how much money is left; add more whenever you like. If there is no answer, replace the receiver and your money will be returned.

Card phones operate with special cards that you can buy from post offices or newsstands. These cards, ideal for longer calls, are composed of units of 10p, and come in values of £2, £4, £10 and more. To use a card phone, lift the receiver, insert your card, and dial the number. An indicator panel shows the number of units used. At the end of your call, the card will be returned. Where credit cards are taken, slide the card through, as indicated.

For long-distance calls within Britain, dial the area code (which begins with a 01) followed by the number.

All calls are charged according to the time of day. Standard rate is weekdays 8 AM–6 PM; cheap rate is weekdays 6 PM–8 AM and all day on weekends.

INTERNATIONAL CALLS

The long-distance services of AT&T, MCI, and Sprint make calling home relatively convenient and let you avoid hotel surcharges; typically, you dial a local number abroad. Before you go, **find out the local access codes** for your destinations.

TIPPING

Restaurants: 10%–15% of the check for full meals if service is not already included; a small token if you're just having coffee or tea. **Taxis:** 10%–15%, or perhaps a little more for a short ride. **Porters:** 50p–£1 per bag. **Doormen:** £1 for hailing taxis or for carrying bags to check-in desk. **Bellhops:** £1 for carrying bags to rooms, £1 for room service. **Hairdressers:** 10%–15% of the bill, plus £1–£2 for the hair-washer.

UNDERGROUND

Known colloquially as the Tube, London's extensive Underground system is by far the most widely used form of city transportation. Trains run both below and above ground out into the suburbs, and **all stations are clearly marked** with the London Underground circular symbol. (In Britain, the word "subway" means "pedestrian underpass.") Trains are all one class; smoking is *not* allowed on board or in the stations.

There are 10 basic lines—all named—plus the East London line, which runs from Shoreditch and Whitechapel across the Thames and south to New Cross, and the Docklands Light Railway, which runs from Stratford in east London to Greenwich, with an extension to the Royal Docks that should be completed by the time you read this. The not-yet-built Metro Express, which will run from Haringey to Wimbledon underneath Soho and Fulham, may start appearing on maps, too—it's the light green line. The Central, District, Northern, Metropolitan, and Piccadilly lines all have branches, so **be sure to note which branch is needed for your particu-**

lar destination. Electronic platform signs tell you the final stop and route of the next train, and some signs conveniently indicate how many minutes you'll have to wait for the train to arrive.

FARES

For both buses and tube fares, London is divided into six concentric zones; the fare goes up the farther out you travel. Ask at Underground ticket counters for the London Transport booklets that give details of all the various ticket options for the tube. Traveling without a valid ticket makes you liable to an on-the-spot fine—£10 at press time (summer 1995)—so always pay your fare before you travel.

For one trip between any two stations, you can buy an ordinary single (one-way ticket) for travel anytime on the day of issue; if you're coming back on the same route the same day, then an ordinary return (round-trip ticket) costs twice the single fare. Singles vary in price from £1 to £3.10—expensive if you're making several journeys in a day. There are several passes good for both the tube and the bus; *see* Important Contacts, *above*.

HOURS

From Monday to Saturday, trains begin running just after 5 AM; the last services leave central London between midnight and 12:30 AM. On Sunday, trains start two hours later and stop running about an hour earlier. The frequency of the trains depends on the route and the time of day, but normally you should not have to wait more than 10 minutes in central areas.

INFORMATION

A pocket map of the entire tube network is available free from most Underground ticket counters. There is a large map on the wall of each platform.

There are LT (London Transport) Travel Information Centres at the following tube stations: Heathrow, daily, varying times at each terminal; Victoria, daily 8:15 AM–9:30 PM; Piccadilly Circus, daily 8:15–6; Oxford Circus, Monday–Saturday 8:15–6; Euston, Monday–Thursday and Saturday 7:15–6, Friday 7:15 AM–7:30 PM, Sunday 8:15–6; and King's Cross, Monday–Thursday 8:15–6, Friday 7:15 AM–7:30 PM, Saturday 7:15–6. For information on all London bus and tube times, fares, and so forth, call 0171/222–1234; the line is operated 24 hours.

WHEN TO GO

The heaviest tourist season in Britain runs from mid-April to mid-October, with another peak around Christmas—though the tide never really ebbs. Spring is the time to see the countryside and the London gardens at their freshest; early summer to catch the roses and full garden splendor; fall for near-ideal exploring conditions.

The British take their vacations mainly in July and August, when resorts are crowded. London in summer, however, though full of visitors, is also full of interesting things to see and do. But be warned: Air-conditioning is *very* rare in London, and in a hot summer you'll swelter. The winter can be rather dismal and is frequently wet and usually cold, but all the theaters, concerts, and exhibitions are going full speed.

CLIMATE

London's weather has always been contrary, and in recent years it has become positively erratic, with hot summers and mild winters proving the greenhouse effect is running affecting all of Britain. It is virtually impossible to forecast what the pattern might be, but you can be fairly certain that it will not be what you expect! The main feature of the British weather is that it is generally mild—with some savage exceptions, especially in summer. It is also fairly damp—though even that has been changing in recent years with recurring periods of drought.

What follows are the average daily maximum and minimum temperatures for London.

CLIMATE IN LONDON

Jan.	43F	6C	May	62F	17C	Sept.	65F	19C
	36	2		47	8		52	11
Feb.	44F	7C	June	69F	20C	Oct.	58F	14C
	36	2		53	12		46	8
Mar.	50F	10C	July	71F	22C	Nov.	50F	10C
	38	3		56	14		42	5
Apr.	56F	13C	Aug.	71F	21C	Dec.	45F	7C
	42	6		56	13		38	4

2 Exploring London

LONDON GREW FROM A WOODEN BRIDGE built over the Thames in the year AD 43 to its current 7 million souls and 600 square miles in haphazard fashion, meandering from its two official centers: Westminster, seat of government and royalty, and the City, site of finance and commerce. Many a tourist meanders the same way, and below are comprehensive sections on the famous parts of **Westminster and Royal London** and the **City.**

However, London's *un*official centers multiply and mutate year after year, and it would be a shame to stop only at the postcard views. Life is not lived in monuments, as the patrician patrons of the great Georgian architects understood when they commissioned the elegant squares and town houses of **St. James's** and **Mayfair** for newly rich merchants. Thanks to World War II bombs and today's newly rich merchants, the West End's elegance is patchy now. On its border, the once-seedy **Soho** is still pleasuring the flesh (gastronomically these days); and Westminster Abbey's original vegetable patch (or convent garden), which became the site of London's first square, **Covent Garden,** is now an unmissable stop on any agenda.

If the great, green parks (*see* Hyde Park and Kensington Gardens, *below*) are, as in Lord Chatham's phrase, "the lungs of London," then the River Thames is its backbone. The river underlay the commercial success that made London great, and along its banks stand reminders from every century. Though there was traffic as far east as the **Docklands** from Roman times, they had their first boom in the Victorian era; today they are undergoing a peculiar stop-start renaissance. It's said that only cockneys "born within the sound of Bow Bells" in the adjacent **East End** are authentic Londoners, and so our tour around one of London's most diverse and least known areas may be the quintessential local experience.

Back on the river, the **South Bank** section absorbs the Southwark stews of Shakespeare's day—and the current reconstruction of his original Globe theatre, the concert hall from the '50s Festival of Britain, the arts complex from the

'70s, and—farther downstream—the gorgeous 17th- and 18th-century symmetry of **Greenwich,** where the world's time is measured.

WESTMINSTER AND ROYAL LONDON

Numbers in the margin correspond to points of interest on the Westminster and Royal London map.

This tour is London For Beginners. If you went no farther than these few acres, you would see many of the famous sights, from the Houses of Parliament, Big Ben, Westminster Abbey, and Buckingham Palace, to two of the world's greatest art collections, the National and the Tate Galleries. It might be possible to do it all in a day, but picking a highlight or two is a better idea. The galleries alone deserve a day apiece, and if you're going to the Abbey in summer, queuing up will consume most of your stamina. This is concentrated sightseeing, so pace yourself.

Westminster is by far the younger of the capital's two centers, postdating the City by some 1,000 years. Edward the Confessor put it on the map when he packed up his court from its cramped City quarters and went west a couple of miles, founding the abbey church of Westminster—the minster west of the City—in 1050. Subsequent kings continued to hold court there until Henry VIII decamped to Whitehall Palace in 1512, leaving Westminster to the politicians. And there they still are, not in the palace, which was burned almost to the ground in 1834, but in the Victorian mock-Gothic Houses of Parliament, whose 320-foot Clock Tower is as much a symbol of London as the Eiffel Tower is of Paris.

Trafalgar Square and the National Gallery

Trafalgar Square is the obvious place to start for several reasons. It is the center of London, by dint of a plaque on the corner of the Strand and Charing Cross Road from which distances on U.K. signposts are measured. It is the home of the National Gallery and of one of London's most distinctive landmarks, Nelson's Column; also of many a political demonstration, a raucous New Year's party, and the highest concentration of bus stops and pigeons in the capital. In short, it is London's most famous square.

Keeping watch from his 145-foot granite perch is E. H. Baily's 1843 statue of Admiral Lord Horatio Nelson, one
❶ of England's favorite heroes. Around the foot of **Nelson's Column,** three bas-reliefs depict his victories at Cape St. Vincent, the Battle of the Nile, and Copenhagen, and a fourth his death at Trafalgar itself in 1805; all four were cast from cannons he captured. The four majestic lions, designed by the Victorian painter Sir Edwin Landseer, were added in 1867. The calling cards of generations of picturesque pigeons have been a corrosive problem for the statue, but it may have been finally solved by a 150th-birthday present of a pigeon-proof gel coating. You can read about the area on a plaque marking the anniversary. Street performers were licensed for the first time last year, and they now enhance the square's intermittent atmosphere of celebration. This is strongest in December, first when the lights on the gigantic Christmas tree (an annual gift from Norway to thank the British for harboring their royal family during World War II) are turned on, and then—less festively, especially during the recent year when two people were crushed to death by the crowds—when thousands see in the New Year.

The north side of the square is filled by the low, gray,
★ ❷ colonnaded neoclassical facade of the **National Gallery.** The institution was founded in 1824. By the end of the century, enthusiastic directors and generous patrons had turned the National Gallery into one of the world's foremost collections, with works from painters of the Italian Renaissance and earlier, from the Flemish and Dutch masters, the Spanish school, and of course the English tradition, including Hogarth, Gainsborough, Stubbs, and Constable.

In 1991, following years of wrangling and the rehanging of the entire collection, the Sainsbury Wing was opened. It had been financed by the eponymous British grocery dynasty to house the early Renaissance collection. Here, the **Micro Gallery,** a computer information center in the Sainsbury Wing, might be the place to start. You can access in-

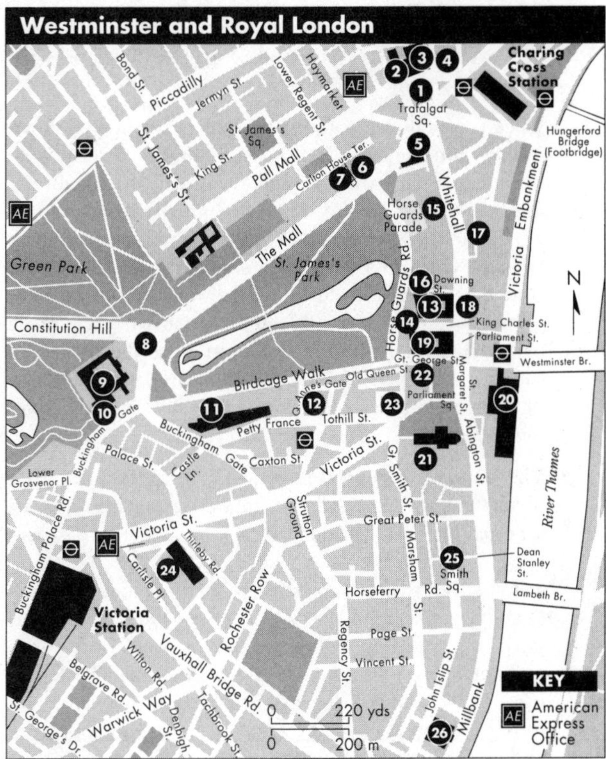

Admiralty Arch, **5**

Banqueting House, **17**

Buckingham Palace, **9**

Cabinet War Rooms, **14**

Cenotaph, **18**

Central Hall, **23**

Duke of York Steps, **7**

Foreign Office, **13**

Home Office, **19**

Horse Guards Parade, **15**

Houses of Parliament, **20**

Institute of Contemporary Arts (ICA), **6**

National Gallery, **2**

National Portrait Gallery, **3**

Nelson's Column, **1**

Queen Anne's Gate, **12**

Queen Victoria Memorial, **8**

Queen's Gallery, **10**

St. John's, Smith Square, **25**

St. Margaret's, **22**

St. Martin-in-the-Fields, **4**

Tate Gallery, **26**

10 Downing Street, **16**

Wellington Barracks, **11**

Westminster Abbey, **21**

Westminster Cathedral, **24**

depth information on any work here, choose your favorites, and print out a free personal tour map that marks the paintings you most want to see.

Once you're done exploring the gallery's contents, stop a moment on the steps in front and admire the view over Trafalgar Square toward Admiralty Arch, with the former Canada House on the west side and the former South Africa House on the east. On the sloping lawn in front is Grinling Gibbons's statue of James II, who failed to return Britain to Catholicism during his short reign (1685–8). Gibbons, "Master Carver in Wood to the Crown," was much in vogue at the end of the 17th century (see his choir-stall carvings at St Paul's). At the other end of the lawn is a bronze of George Washington presented to the British by the Commonwealth of Virginia in 1921.

3 The **National Portrait Gallery** just around the corner is a much smaller affair, an idiosyncratic collection that presents a potted history of Britain through its residents, past and present. As an art collection it is eccentric, since the subject, not the artist, is the point, and there are notable works (a Holbein portrait of Henry VIII, Stubbs and Hockney self-portraits) mixed up with photographs, busts, caricatures, and amateur paintings. (The miniature of Jane Austen by her sister Cassandra, for instance, is the only likeness we have of the great novelist). Many of the faces are obscure and will be just as unknown to English visitors, since the portraits outlasted their sitters' fame. But the annotation is comprehensive, and there is a new, separate research center for those who get hooked on particular personages—part of an expansion that has cleaned up the layout (still chronological, with the oldest at the top) and added a photography gallery. *St Martin's Pl., WC2,* ☎ *0171/306-0055.* ☛ *Free.* ⏲ *Weekdays 10–5, Sat. 10–6., Sun. 2–6. Closed public holidays. Tube: Charing Cross, Leicester Sq.*

Across the street, east of the National Gallery, is the
4 much-loved church of **St. Martin-in-the-Fields,** completed in 1726. James Gibbs's classical-temple-with-spire design, unusual at the time, has become familiar as the pattern for churches in early colonial America. Though it seems dwarfed by the surrounding structures, the spire is actu-

ally slightly taller than Nelson's Column. It is a welcome sight for the homeless, who have sought soup and shelter here since 1914. The church is also a haven for music lovers, since the internationally known Academy of St. Martin-in-the-Fields was founded here, and a popular program of lunchtime (free) and evening concerts continues today. St. Martin's is often called the royal parish church, partly because Charles II was christened here—not because his mistress, Nell Gwyn, lies under the stones, alongside William Hogarth, Thomas Chippendale (the cabinetmaker), and Jack Sheppard, the notorious highwayman. Also in the crypt is the **London Brass-Rubbing Centre,** where you can make your own souvenir knight from replica tomb brasses, with metallic waxes, paper, and instructions provided, and the **St. Martin's Gallery** showing contemporary work. There is also a crafts market in the courtyard behind the church. *St. Martin-in-the-Fields, Trafalgar Sq., ☎ 0171/930–0089. Credit card bookings for evening concerts, ☎ 0171/839–8362. Brass rubbing fee from £1. Church open daily 8–8; crypt open Mon.–Sat. 10–8, Sun. noon–6. Tube: Charing Cross, Leicester Sq.*

St. James's Park and the Mall

Leave Trafalgar Square from its southwest corner through
5 **Admiralty Arch,** designed in 1910 by Sir Aston Webb as part of a ceremonial route to Buckingham Palace and named after the adjacent Royal Navy headquarters. As you pass under the enormous triple archway—though not through the central arch, opened only for state occasions—the atmosphere changes along with the color of the road, for you are exiting frenetic Trafalgar Square and entering **The Mall** (rhymes with "shall"), which has nothing to do with shopping.

The original Mall was laid out around 1660 for the game that gave Pall Mall (*see* Pall Mall in St. James's and Mayfair, *below*) its name, and quickly became the place to be seen. Samuel Pepys, Jonathan Swift, and Alexander Pope all wrote about it, and it continued as the *beau monde*'s social playground into the early 19th century, long after the game of pall mall had gone out of vogue. Something of the former style survives on those summer days when the queen is throwing a Buckingham Palace garden party: The Mall is thronged with hundreds of her subjects, from the grand and titled to the humble and hardworking, all of whom have donned hat and frock to take afternoon tea with her—or somewhere near her—on the lawns of Buck House. The old Mall still runs alongside the graceful pink 115-foot-wide avenue that replaced it in 1904 for just such occasions.

St. James's Park, along the south side of the Mall, is London's smallest, most ornamental park, and the oldest of its royal ones. Henry VIII drained a marsh that festered here next to the lepers' hospital that St. James's Palace replaced, and bred his deer on the newly dry land. Later kings tinkered with it further, James I installing aviary and zoo (complete with crocodiles); Charles I laying formal gardens, which he then had to cross to his execution in 1649; and Charles II employing André Lenôtre, Louis XIV's Versailles landscaper, to remodel it completely with avenues, fruit orchards, and a canal. Its present shape more or less reflects what John Nash designed under George IV.

More than 30 species of birds—including flamingos, pelicans, geese, ducks, and swans (which belong to the queen)—now congregate on Duck Island at the east end of the lake, while on summer days the deck chairs are crammed with office lunchers being serenaded by music from the bandstands. The best time to stroll the leafy walkways, though, is after dark, with Westminster Abbey and the Houses of Parliament rising above the floodlit lake, and peace reigning.

Back on the Mall, look to the other (north) side for a more solid example of John Nash's genius, **Carlton House Terrace.** Between 1812 and 1830, under the patronage of George IV (Prince Regent until George III's death in 1820), Nash was responsible for a series of West End developments, of which these white-stucco facades and massive Corinthian columns may be the most imposing. It was a smart address, needless to say, and one that prime ministers Gladstone (1856) and Palmerston (1857–75) enjoyed. Today Carlton House Terrace is home to the Royal College of Pathologists,
6 the Royal Society, the Turf Club, and, at No. 12, the **Institute of Contemporary Arts,** better known as the **ICA.** Behind its incongruous facade, the ICA has provided a stage

for the avant-garde in performance, theater, dance, visual art, and music since it was established in 1947. There are two cinemas, an underused library of video artists' works, a bookshop, a café and a bar, and a team of adventurous curators. *The Mall,* ☎ *0171/930–3647. 1-day membership: £1.50 adults, children under 14 free. An additional charge is made for entry to specific events.* ⌚ *Daily noon–9:30, later for some events; closed Dec. 24–27, Jan. 1. Tube: Charing Cross.*

TIME OUT The **ICAfé** is windowless but brightly spotlit, with a self-service counter offering good hot dishes, salads, quiches, and desserts. The bar upstairs, which serves baguette sandwiches, has a picture window overlooking the Mall. Both are packed before popular performances, and are subject to the £1.50 one-day membership fee.

7 Bisecting Carlton House Terrace are the **Duke of York Steps,** surmounted by the 124-foot Duke of York's Column, from which an 1834 bronze of George III's second son, Frederick, gazes toward the Whitehall War Office. The Duke was popular among his troops until each man in the army had one day's pay extracted to fund this £25,000 tribute, which was perched so high, said the wits, to keep him away from creditors. He owed £2 million at his death.

Buckingham Palace to Parliament Square

8 Facing the palace from the traffic island at the west end of the Mall is the white marble **Queen Victoria Memorial.** The monument was conceived by Sir Aston Webb as the nucleus of his ceremonial Mall route and executed by the sculptor Thomas Brock, who was knighted on the spot when it was revealed to the world in 1911. Many wonder why he was, since the thing is Victoriana incarnate: The frumpy queen glares down the Mall, with golden-winged Victory overhead and her siblings Truth, Justice, and Charity, plus Manufacture, Progress-and-Peace, War-and-Shipbuilding, and so on—in Osbert Sitwell's words, "tons of allegorical females . . . with whole litters of their cretinous children"—surrounding her. Climbing it is not encouraged, even though it's the best vantage point for viewing the daily **Changing**

of the Guard, which, with all the pomp and ceremony monarchists and children adore, remains one of London's best free shows. *Guard leaves Wellington Barracks 11 AM, arrives Buckingham Palace 11:30. Daily Apr.–July; alternate days Aug.–March. Tube: St James's Park, Victoria.*

9 **Buckingham Palace** tops the must-see lists, although the building itself is no masterpiece and has housed the monarch only since Victoria moved here from Kensington Palace at her accession in 1837. At that time the place was a mess. George IV, at *his* accession in 1820, had fancied the idea of moving to Buckingham House, his parents' former home, and had employed John Nash, as usual, to remodel it. The government authorized only "repair and improvement"; Nash, who had other ideas, overspent his budget by about half a million pounds. George died, Nash was dismissed, and Edward Blore finished the building, adding the now familiar east front (facing the Mall). Victoria arrived to faulty drains and sticky doors and windows nevertheless, but they did not mar her affection for the place, nor that of her son, Edward VII. The Portland stone facade dates only from 1913 (it, too, was part of the Aston Webb scheme), and the interior was renovated and redecorated only after World War II bomb damage.

The palace contains some 600 rooms, including the State Ballroom and, of course, the Throne Room. The royal apartments are in the north wing; when the queen is in, the royal standard flies at the masthead. Until recently all were off limits to the public, but a 1992 fire at Windsor Castle created an urgent need for cash. And so the state rooms are now on show—on something of an experimental basis through 1997—for eight weeks in August and September, when the royal family is away. Without an invitation to one of the queen's garden parties, however, you won't see much of the magnificent 45-acre grounds. *Buckingham Palace Rd., ☎ 0171/799–2331. ☛ £8 adults, £5.50 senior citizens, £4 children under 17. Call for hours, which had not been set at press time. Tube: St James's Park, Victoria.*

The former chapel at the south side, on the other hand,
10 has been open to visitors since 1962 as the **Queen's Gallery.**
On display here are paintings from her majesty's collec-

tion—the country's largest—including works by Vermeer, Leonardo, Rubens, Rembrandt, Canaletto . . . and Queen Victoria. Sign-of-the-times note: Now that she is a taxpayer, HRH's artworks, along with all her other possessions (for example, Buckingham Palace), are officially part of a business known as "Royal Collection Enterprises." *Buckingham Palace Rd., ☎ 0171/799–2331. ☛ £3 adults, £2 senior citizens, £1.50 children. ⏲ Tues.–Sat. 10–5, Sun. 2–5; closed Dec. 24–Mar. 4, Good Fri. Tube: St James's Park, Victoria.*

Nearly next door stand the Nash-designed **Royal Mews.** Mews were originally falcons' quarters (the name comes from their "mewing," or feather shedding), but horses gradually eclipsed birds of prey. Now some of the magnificent royal beasts live here alongside the fabulous bejeweled, glass, and golden coaches they draw on state occasions. The place is unmissable children's entertainment. *Buckingham Palace Rd., ☎ 0171/799–2331. ☛ £3 adults, £2 senior citizens, £1.50 children. Combined ticket for Queen's Gallery and Royal Mews: £5 adults, £3.50 senior citizens, £2.20 children. ⏲ Oct.–Mar., Wed. noon–4; Apr.–Oct., Tues.–Thurs. noon–4; closed Mar. 25–29, Oct. 1–5, Dec. 23–Jan. 5. Tube: St James's Park, Victoria.*

11 Turn back along Buckingham Palace Road, continue down Birdcage Walk, and on the right you'll soon see the **Wellington Barracks,** the headquarters of the Guards Division. Five regiments of elite foot guards (Grenadier, Coldstream, Scots, Irish, and Welsh) protect the sovereign and patrol the palace dressed in tunics of gold-purled scarlet and tall fur "busby" helmets of Canadian brown bearskin. (The two items cost more than £4,000 for the set.) If you want to learn more about the guards, you can visit the **Guards Museum**; the entrance is next to the Guards Chapel. *Wellington Barracks, Birdcage Walk, ☎ 0171/930–4466, ext. 3430. ☛ £2 adults, £1 children under 16 and senior citizens. ⏲ Sat.–Thurs. 10–4; closed national holidays. Tube: St James's Park.*

12 Past the barracks on the right is the entrance to **Queen Anne's Gate,** two pretty 18th-century closes, once separate but now linked by a statue of the last Stuart monarch. Have a look

at the Henry Moore bronze *Mother and Child,* then follow Dartmouth Street out of Queen Anne's Gate. Great
George Street, at the end, leads into Parliament Square. But
turn left at Storey's Gate for a detour down Horse Guard's
13 Road past the **Foreign Office,** built in the 1860s by Sir
Giles Gilbert Scott, who was better known for such fantastical Gothic Revival buildings as the House of Commons
(*see* The Houses of Parliament, *below*)

Make a right before the Foreign Office into King Charles
14 Street to find the **Cabinet War Rooms**—an essential visit for
World War II buffs. During air raids the War Cabinet met
in this warren of 17 bomb-proof chambers. The Cabinet
Room is still arranged as if a meeting were about to con-
vene; in the Map Room, the Allied campaign is charted; the
Prime Minister's Room holds the desk from which Churchill
made his morale-boosting broadcasts; and the Telephone
Room has his hot line to FDR. *Clive Steps, King Charles
St.,* ☎ *0171/930–6961.* ☛ *£3.90 adults, £3 senior citizens,
£1.90 children under 16.* ⏲ *Daily 10–5:15; closed Good
Fri., May Day, Dec. 24–26, Jan. 1. Tube: Westminster.*

Farther along Horse Guards Road, opposite St. James's Park,
15 stands **Horse Guards Parade.** Once the tilt-yard of Whitehall Palace, where jousting tournaments were held, it is now
notable mainly for the annual Trooping the Colour ceremony, in which the queen takes the Royal Salute, her official birthday gift, on the second Saturday in June. (Like
Paddington Bear, the queen has two birthdays; her real one
is on April 21.) There is pageantry galore, with marching
bands and the occasional guardsman fainting clean away
in his busby, and throngs of people. The ceremony is televised and also broadcast on Radio 4. You can also attend
the queenless rehearsals on the preceding two Saturdays.

The quiet street barred by iron gates that you passed on
your right before coming to Horse Guards Parade is **Downing Street,** which contains London's modest version of the
16 White House at **10 Downing Street.** Only three houses remain of the terrace built circa 1680 by Sir George Downing, who spent enough of his youth in America to graduate
from Harvard—the second man ever to do so. No. 11 is
the residence of the chancellor of the exchequer (secretary

of the treasury), No. 12 the party whips' office. No. 10 has officially housed the prime minister since 1732. (The gates were Margaret Thatcher's brainwave.)

At the other end of Downing Street (though, of course, you can't walk through—you have to go all the way around via King Charles Street) is the wide street called Whitehall. Bang in the middle is the other facade of Horse Guards, where two mounted sentries known as the Queen's Life Guard provide what may be London's most frequently taken photo opportunity. They change, quietly, at 11 AM Monday–Saturday, 10 on Sunday. On a site reaching from here to the Thames and from Trafalgar to Parliament squares once stood Whitehall Palace, established by Henry VIII, who married two of his six wives (Anne Boleyn and Jane Seymour) and breathed his last there. The sheer scale of this 2,000-room labyrinth in red Tudor brick must have been breathtaking, but we won't dwell on it, since it burned to the ground in 1698, thanks to a fire started by a Dutch laundress whose name has not made it to posterity.

17 All that remains today is **Banqueting House,** but if the rest was like this, we should weep for its loss. Actually, we know that it was quite different. (One foreign visitor accused the palace of being "ill-built, and nothing but a heap of houses.") James I had commissioned Inigo Jones to do a grand remodeling of the palace, and Banqueting House is the only part that got completed. Jones (1573–1652), one of England's great architects, had been influenced by Andrea Palladio's work during a sojourn in Tuscany and had brought that sophistication and purity back with him to London. The graceful and disciplined classical style of Banqueting House must have stunned its early occupants. James I's son, Charles I, enhanced the interior by employing the Flemish painter Peter Paul Rubens to glorify his father all over the ceiling. As it turned out, these allegorical paintings, depicting a wise monarch being received into heaven, were the last thing Charles saw before he was beheaded by Cromwell's Parliamentarians on a scaffold outside in 1649. But his son, Charles II, was able to celebrate the restoration of the monarchy here 20 years later. *Whitehall,* ☎ *0171/930–4179.* ☛ *£2.90 adults, £2.20 senior citizens, £1.90 children under 16.* ⏲ *Mon.–Sat. 10–5; closed Good Fri., Dec. 24–26, Jan.*

1, and at short notice for banquets, so call first. Tube: Westminster.

Walk south on Whitehall toward Parliament Square, and
18 in the middle of the street you'll see the **Cenotaph,** a stark white monolith designed in 1920 by Edward Lutyens to commemorate the 1918 armistice. On Remembrance Day (the Sunday nearest November 11) it is strewn with blood-red poppies to honor the dead of both world wars, with the first wreath laid by the queen.

The Houses of Parliament

Continue down Whitehall (which becomes Parliament
19 Street beside Gilbert Scott's Foreign Office), pass the **Home Office** on the right, bear left, and you will soon be confronted with London's most famous and photogenic sight: the
★ 20 **Houses of Parliament,** with the Clock Tower, which everyone mistakenly calls Big Ben, looming largest, and Westminster Abbey ahead of you across Parliament Square.

The Palace of Westminster, as the complex is still properly called, was established by Edward the Confessor in the 11th century, when he moved his court from the City, and has been the seat of English administrative power ever since. In 1512, Henry VIII abandoned it for Whitehall (*see* Whitehall Palace following 10 Downing Street, *above*). It ceased to be an official royal residence after 1547: At the Reformation, the Royal Chapel was secularized and became the first meeting place of the Commons. The Lords settled in the White Chamber.

These, along with everything but the **Jewel Tower** and **Westminster Hall,** were destroyed in 1834 when "the sticks"—the arcane abacus beneath the Lords' Chamber on which the court had kept its accounts until 1826—were incinerated and the fire got out of hand. The same cellar had seen an earlier attempt to raze the palace: the infamous Gunpowder Plot of November 5, 1605, perpetrated by the Catholic convert Guy Fawkes and his fellow conspirators. If you are in London in late October or early November, you may see children with dressed-up teddy bears demanding a "penny for the guy!" They do it because, to this day,

November 5 is Guy Fawkes Day (a.k.a. Bonfire Night), when fireworks bought with the pennies accompany pyres of these makeshift effigies of Guy Fawkes, and anyone who still knows it recites: "Remember, remember / The 5th of November, / The Gunpowder Treason and plot. / There isn't a reason/Why gunpowder treason / Should ever be forgot."

After the 1834 fire, architects were invited to submit plans for new Houses of Parliament in the grandiose "Gothic or Elizabethan style." Charles Barry's were selected from among 97 entries, partly because Barry had invited the architect and designer Augustus Pugin to add the requisite neo-Gothic curlicues to his own Renaissance-influenced style. As you can see, it was a happy collaboration, with Barry's classical proportions offset by Pugin's ornamental flourishes—although the latter were toned down by Gilbert Scott when he rebuilt the bomb-damaged House of Commons after World War II.

The two towers were Pugin's work. The **Clock Tower,** now virtually the symbol of London, was completed in 1858 after long delays due to bickering over the clock's design. (Barry designed the faces himself in the end.) It contains the 13-ton bell that chimes the hour (and the quarter) known as Big Ben. Some say Ben was "Big Ben" Caunt, heavyweight champ; others, Sir Benjamin Hall, the far-from-slim Westminster building works commissioner. At the other end is the 336-foot-high **Victoria Tower,** which contains the 3-million-document parliamentary archives and now gleams from its recent restoration and cleaning. The rest of the complex was scrubbed down some years ago.

There are two Houses, the Lords and the Commons. The House of Lords consists of more than 1,000 people, most of whom have recently bestowed titles and are known as "life peers," (in contrast to aristocrats); there are also 26 Anglican bishops who are "spiritual peers." The House of Commons consists of 650 elected Members of Parliament (MPs). The party with the most MPs forms the government, its leader becoming Prime Minister; other parties form the Opposition. Since 1642, when Charles I tried to have five MPs arrested, no monarch has been allowed into the House of Commons. The State Opening of Parliament in November consequently takes place in the House of Lords, after a ritual inspection of the cellars in case a modern Guy Fawkes lurks.

Visitors aren't allowed many places in the Houses of Parliament, though the Visitors' Galleries of the House of Commons do afford a fine view of the surprisingly cramped debating chambers. The opposing banks of green leather benches seat only 346 MPs—not that this is much of a problem, since absentees far outnumber the diligent. When MPs vote, they exit by the "Aye" or the "No" corridor, counted by the party "whips" (yes, it is a foxhunting term); when they speak, it is not directly to each other but through the Speaker, who also decides who will get the floor each day. Elaborate procedures notwithstanding, debate is often drowned out by the amazingly immature jeers and insults familiar to TV viewers since 1989, when cameras were first allowed into the House of Commons.

The House of Lords was televised first, perhaps because its procedures are more palatably dignified, with the Lord Chancellor, or Chief Justice, presiding from his official seat, the Woolsack (England's economy was once dependent on this commodity), over a few gently slumbering peers. Or perhaps the Lords were first because of their telegenic gold and scarlet chamber, Pugin's masterpiece. The Upper House remains the highest court of appeal in the land, though its parliamentary powers are restricted to delaying or suspending passage of a bill. It is separated from the Lower House by the octagonal **Central Lobby,** which is where constituents wait for their MPs and also where the press is received—hence the term "lobby correspondent" for a domestic political reporter. Other public areas of the 1,100-room labyrinth are rather magnificently got up in high neo-Gothic style and punctuated with stirring frescoes commissioned by Prince Albert. You pass these en route to the Visitors Galleries—if, that is, you are patient enough to wait in line for hours (the Lords line is shorter) or have applied in advance through your embassy. *St. Stephen's Entrance, St. Margaret St., SW1, ☎ 0171/219–3000. ☛ Free. Commons open Mon.–Thurs. 2:30–10, Fri. 9:30–3; Lords open Mon.–Thurs. 2:30–10. Closed Easter wk, May bank holiday, July–Oct., 3 wks at Christmas. Tube: Westminster.*

As you cross Parliament Square, have a look at the statues dotted around: Lord Palmerston and Benjamin Disraeli, prime ministers under Victoria; Sir Robert Peel, who formed the first Metropolitan Police Force (hence the nickname "bobbies"); a hulking, hunched Churchill in a 1973 bronze; Richard the Lionheart; Oliver Cromwell; and, on the far side (as if over the pond), Abraham Lincoln.

Westminster Abbey

Off the south side of Parliament Square, announced by the teeming human contents of herds of tour buses, stands
★ 21 **Westminster Abbey.** Nearly all of England's monarchs were crowned here, amid vast pomp and circumstance, and most are buried here, too. The place is crammed with spectacular medieval architecture and impressive and moving monuments. It is worth pointing out, though, that the Abbey is still a place of worship, and while attending a service is not something to undertake purely for sightseeing reasons, it provides a glimpse of the Abbey in its full majesty, accompanied by music from the Westminster choristers and the organ that Henry Purcell once played. Some parts are closed on Sunday except to worshipers.

The origins of Westminster Abbey are uncertain. The first church on the site may have been built as early as the 7th century by the Saxon King Sebert (who may be buried here, alongside his queen and his sister); a Benedictine abbey was established in the 10th century. There were certainly pre-existing foundations when Edward the Confessor was crowned in 1040, moved his palace to Westminster, and began building a church. Only traces have been found of that incarnation, which was consecrated eight days before Edward's death in 1065. (It appears in the Bayeaux Tapestry.) Edward's canonization in 1139 gave a succession of kings added incentive to shower the Abbey with attention and improvements. Henry III, full of ideas from his travels in France, pulled it down and started again with Amiens and Rheims in mind. In fact it was the master mason Henry de Reyns ("of Rheims") who, between 1245 and 1254, put up the transepts, north front, and rose windows, as well as part of the cloisters and Chapter House;

and it was his master plan that, funded by Richard II, was resumed 100 years later. Henry V (reigned 1413–1422) and Henry VII (1485–1509) were the chief succeeding benefactors. The Abbey was eventually completed in 1532. After that, Sir Christopher Wren had a hand in shaping the place; his West Towers were completed in 1745, 22 years after his death. The most riotous elements of the interior were, similarly, much later affairs.

The **Nave** is your first sight on entering; you need to look up to gain a perspective on the awe-inspiring scale of the church, since the eye-level view is obscured by the 19th- (and part 13th-) century choir screen, past which point an entry fee is charged. Before paying, look at the poignant **Tomb of the Unknown Warrior,** an anonymous World War I martyr who lies buried here in memory of the soldiers fallen in both world wars. Nearby is one of the very few tributes to a foreigner, a plaque to Franklin D. Roosevelt.

There is only one way around the Abbey, and as there will almost certainly be a crocodile of shuffling visitors at your heels, you'll need to be alert to catch the highlights. Pass through the **Choir,** with its mid–19th-century choir stalls, into the **North Transept.** Look up to your right to see the painted-glass **Rose Window,** the largest of its kind; left for the first of the extravagant 18th-century monuments in the North Transept chapels. You then proceed into the **Henry VII Chapel,** passing the huge white marble tomb of Elizabeth I, buried with her half sister, "Bloody" Mary I; then the tomb of Henry VII with his queen, Elizabeth of York, by the Renaissance master Torrigiano (otherwise known for having been banished from Florence after breaking Michelangelo's nose). All around are magnificent sculptures of saints, philosophers, and kings, with wild mermaids and monsters carved on the choir stall misericords (undersides), and exquisite fan vaulting above—one of the miracles of Western architecture.

Next you enter the **Chapel of Edward the Confessor,** where beside the royal saint's shrine stands the **Coronation Chair,** which has been briefly graced by nearly every regal posterior. Edward I ordered it around 1300, and it shelters the Stone of Scone (pronounced *skoon*), a brown sandstone block upon which Scottish kings had been crowned since time began, and which Edward I symbolically stole in 1296. Scottish Nationalists borrowed it back for about six months in 1950; otherwise, only Oliver Cromwell (who took it to Westminster Hall to "crown" himself Lord Protector) and wartime caution have removed it from here.

The tombs and monuments for which Westminster Abbey is probably best loved appeared at an accelerated rate starting in the 18th century. One earlier occupant, though, was Geoffrey Chaucer, who in 1400 became the first poet to be buried in **Poets' Corner.** Most of the other honored writers have only their memorials here, not their bones: William Shakespeare and William Blake (who both had a long wait before the dean deemed them holy enough to be here at all), John Milton, Jane Austen, Samuel Taylor Coleridge, William Wordsworth, Charles Dickens. All of Ben Jonson is here, though—buried upright in accord with his modest demand for a two-foot-by-two-foot grave. ("O rare Ben Jonson," reads his epitaph, in a modest pun on the Latin *orare,* "to pray for.") Sir Isaac Newton, James Watt, and Michael Faraday are among the scientists with memorials. There is only one painter: Godfrey Kneller, whose dying words were "By God, I will not be buried in Westminster."

After the elbow battle you are guaranteed in Poets' Corner, you exit the Abbey by a door from the South Transept. *Broad Sanctuary,* ☎ *0171/222–5152.* ☛ *To nave free, to Royal Chapels and Poets' Corner £4 adults, £2 students and senior citizens, £1 children under 15.* ⏲ *Mon., Tues., Thurs., and Fri. 9–4; Wed. 9–7:45; Sat. 9–2 and 3:45–5; Sun. all day for services only; closed weekdays to visitors during services. Tube: Westminster.*

Outside the west front is an archway into the quiet green **Dean's Yard** and the entrance to the **Cloisters,** where the monks strolled in contemplation. You may do the same, and catch a fine view of the massive flying buttresses above in the process. You may also, for a modest fee, take an impression from one of the tomb brasses in the **Brass-Rubbing Centre** (☎ 0171/222–2085). Also here is the entrance to **Westminster School,** formerly a monastic college, now one of Britain's finest public (which means the exact opposite) schools; Christopher Wren and Ben Jonson number among the old boys.

Also here are the Chapter House and the Norman Undercroft below. The **Chapter House,** a stunning octagonal room supported by a central column and adorned with 14th-century frescoes, is where the King's Council and, after that, an early version of the Commons met between 1257 and 1547. (The monks complained about the noise.) In the **Undercroft,** which survives from Edward the Confessor's original church, note the deliciously macabre effigies made from the death masks and actual clothing of Elizabeth I, Charles II, and Admiral Lord Nelson (complete with eye patch), among others. Finally, the **Pyx Chamber** next door contains the Abbey's treasure, just as it used to when it became the royal strongroom in the 13th century. *Undercroft, Pyx Chamber, Chapter House, ☏ 0171/222–5152. Joint ☛ £2.10 adults, £1.65 senior citizens, £1.05 children under 15. ⏲ Daily 10:30–4; closed Good Fri., Dec. 24–26. Tube: Westminster.*

Dwarfed by the Abbey is its northern neighbor, the church
22 of **St. Margaret's,** founded in the 12th century and rebuilt between 1486 and 1523. It is the parish church of the Houses of Parliament and much sought after for weddings; Samuel Pepys married here in 1655, Winston Churchill in 1908. The east Crucifixion window celebrates another union, the marriage of Prince Arthur and Catherine of Aragon. Unfortunately, it arrived so late that Arthur was dead and Catherine had married his brother, Henry VIII. Sir Walter Raleigh is among the notables buried here, but without his head, which had been removed at Old Palace Yard, Westminster.

23 Across the road from the Abbey's west front is **Central Hall,** headquarters of the Methodist Church in Britain. The building, now used mostly for concerts and meetings, was the site of the first General Assembly of the United Nations in 1948. Next door is the 1986 **Queen Elizabeth Conference Centre,** which hosts both official and commercial functions.

Westminster Cathedral and the Tate Gallery

From Parliament Square, you have a choice between more religion or modern art, with Westminster Cathedral to the southwest and the Tate Gallery along the Thames to the south.

Taking the shorter—and, frankly, less interesting—route to church first, turn your back on the Abbey and exit Parliament Square down **Victoria Street,** the unlovely road to Victoria Station. Though it dates from the early 1860s, most of its Victorian and Edwardian buildings have been replaced by depressing concrete. On the right, note the three-sided steel sign that announces NEW SCOTLAND YARD, which in 1967 replaced the granite-faced, turreted 1890 Thameside edifice (now called the Norman Shaw Building) that Sherlock Holmes knew so well.

24 You can't miss **Westminster Cathedral**—once you are almost upon it, that is. It's set back from the left side of the street in a 21-year-old paved square that has fallen on hard times. Westminster Council, the local authority, would like to turn it into the Piazza San Marco of London, but until funding is found, it remains the windy haunt of homeless people and pigeons.

The cathedral is the seat of the Cardinal of Westminster, head of the Roman Catholic Church in Britain; consequently it is London's principal Roman Catholic church. The asymmetrical redbrick Byzantine hulk, dating only from 1903, is banded with stripes of Portland stone and abutted by a 273-foot campanile at the northwest corner, which you can scale by elevator. Faced with the daunting proximity of the heavenly Abbey, the architect, John Francis Bentley, flew in the face of fashion by rejecting neo-Gothic in favor of the Byzantine idiom, which still provides maximum contrast today—not only with the great church, but with just about all of London.

The interior is partly unfinished but worth seeing for its atmosphere of broody mystery; for its walls, covered in mosaic of a hundred different marbles from all over the world; and for a majestic nave—the widest in England—distinguished by a series of Eric Gill reliefs depicting the Stations of the Cross. *Ashley Pl., ☎ 0171/834–7452. ☛ To tower: £2 adults, £1 senior citizens and children. Cathedral open daily, tower open daily Apr.–Sept.*

Retracing your steps east along Victoria Street, take a right in front of the Abbey into Great Smith Street, then the second left into Great Peter Street, and a right off there for a detour into **Smith Square.** This elegant enclave of perfectly preserved early 18th-century town houses still looks like the London of Dr. Johnson. The address is much sought-after by MPs, especially of the Tory persuasion, since No. 32 is the Conservative Party Headquarters. The Baroque
25 church of **St. John's, Smith Square,** completed around 1720, dominates charmingly. It is well known to Londoners as a chamber-music venue; its popular lunchtime concerts are often broadcast on the radio.

TIME OUT In the crypt of St. John's is **The Footstool**—about the only place to find refreshment around here. It has an interesting and reasonably priced lunchtime menu and also serves evening meals on concert nights.

Leave Smith Square by Dean Stanley Street, which brings you to traffic-laden Millbank along the river; turn right for a 10-minute walk to London's *other* world-class art mu-
26 seum, the **Tate Gallery.** The Tate Gallery of Modern British Art, to give it its full title, opened in 1897, funded by the sugar magnate Sir Henry Tate. "Modern" is slightly misleading, since one of the three collections here consists of British art from 1545 to the present, including works by William Hogarth, Thomas Gainsborough, Sir Joshua Reynolds, and George Stubbs from the 18th century, and by John Constable, William Blake (a mind-blowing collection of his visionary works), and the pre-Raphaelite painters from the 19th. Also from the 19th century is the second of the Tate's collections, the Turner Bequest, consisting of J. M. W. Turner's personal collection; he left it to the nation on condition that the works be displayed together. The James Stirling–designed **Clore Gallery** (to the right of the main gallery) has fulfilled his wish since 1987, and should not be missed.

The Tate's modern collection is international and so vast that it's never all on display at once. The current director, Nicholas Serota, instigated the strategy of annual rehanging, which goes some way toward solving the dilemma of the gallery's embarrassment of riches, but also means that a favorite work may not be on view; although the most famous and popular works are on permanent display. Come the year 2000, the Tate's space dilemma will be solved with the opening of the new gallery, opposite St. Paul's, in the former Bankside Power Station (*see* The South Bank, *above*), currently undergoing a £100m transformation to the plans of Swiss architects, Herzog & de Meuron. Even now, though, you can see work by an abundance of late 19th- and 20th-century artists, and a good deal more besides. Your tour will deal you multiple shocks of recognition (Rodin's *The Kiss,* Lichtenstein's *Whaam!*), and you can rent a "Tateinform" hand-held audio guide, with commentaries by curators, experts, and some of the artists themselves, to enhance the picture. Here's a short list of names: Matisse, Picasso, Braque, Léger, Kandinsky, Mondrian, Dali, Bacon, de Kooning, Pollock, Rothko, Moore, Hepworth, Warhol, Freud, Hockney. *Millbank,* ☏ *0171/821–1313 or 0171/821–7128 (recorded information).* ☛ *Free; personal audio guide rental, £2,* ☛ *charged for special exhibitions.* ⏲ *Mon.–Sat. 10–5:50, Sun. 2–5:50; closed Good Fri., May Day, Dec. 24–26, Jan. 1.*

ST. JAMES'S AND MAYFAIR

Numbers in the margin correspond to points of interest on the St. James's and Mayfair map.

These neighboring areas (together with part of the following section, Soho and Covent Garden) make up the West End, which is the real center of London nowadays. Here is the highest concentration of grand hotels, department stores, exclusive shops, glamorous restaurants, commercial art galleries, auction houses, swanky offices—all the accoutrements of a capital city.

The western boundaries of St. James's have already been grazed in the previous section, and you may have gotten the picture: This has been a fashionable part of town from the first, largely by dint of the eponymous palace, St. James's, which was a royal residence—if not *the* palace—from the time of Henry VIII until the beginning of the Victorian era. Mayfair, though it is younger than St. James's, is just as expensively patrician, from leafy squares on the grand scale to the jewels on display at Asprey's. Our jumping-off point is the familiar landmark of Trafalgar Square.

St. James's

A late-17th-century ghost in the streets of contemporary St. James's would not need to bother walking through walls, since practically none have moved since he knew them. Its boundaries, clockwise from the north, are Piccadilly, Haymarket, The Mall, and Green Park: a neat rectangle, with a protruding spur satisfyingly located at Cockspur Street. The rectangle used to describe "gentlemen's London," where Sir was outfitted head and foot (but not in between, since the tailors were, and still are, north of Piccadilly in Savile Row) before repairing to his club.

1 Starting in **Trafalgar Square,** you'll find Cockspur Street
on the left of former Canada House; follow it into St.
2 James's. At the foot of **Haymarket**—which got its name from
the horse fodder sold there until the 1830s—you'll find yourself facing streams of oncoming traffic. At the top is Piccadilly Circus; in between are two stray (from theaterland)
theaters, the Haymarket and Her Majesty's, where Lloyd-
Webber's *Phantom* has taken up residence. The **Design
Centre** at No. 28 is a showcase for British design, from interior to industrial, complete with a research library, gift
shop, and café. The American Express office is also here,
as are a couple of movie theaters—one very mall-like and
hawking every known Yankee snack. Back at the foot of
Haymarket, turn right into Pall Mall. Immediately on your
right, after the high-rise New Zealand House, is London's
3 earliest shopping arcade, the splendid Regency **Royal Opera
Arcade,** which John Nash finished in 1818.

Pall Mall, like its near-namesake, *the* Mall, rhymes with "shall" and derives its name from the cross between croquet and golf that the Italians, who invented it, called *pallo a maglio,* and the French, who made it chic, called *palle-*

St. James's and Mayfair

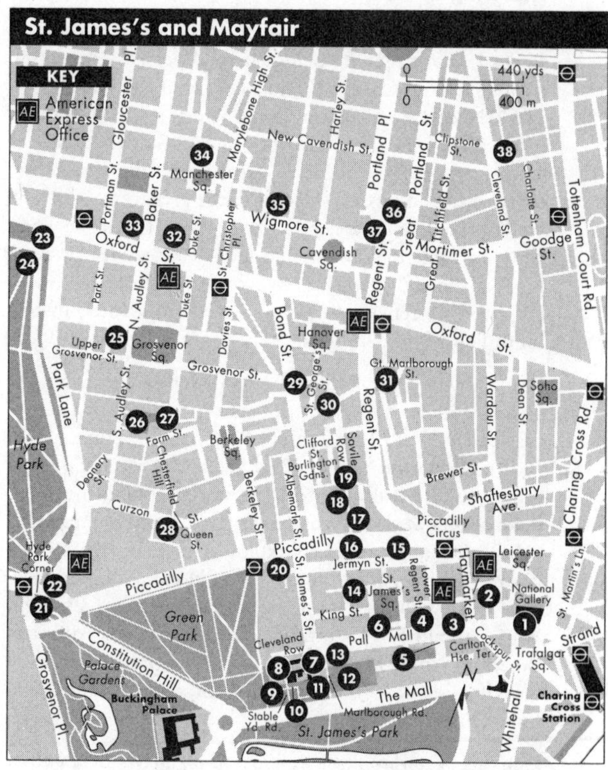

All Souls Church, **36**
Apsley House, **22**
Athenaeum, **5**
British Telecom Tower, **38**
Burlington Arcade, **18**
Burlington House, **17**
Church of the Immaculate Conception, **27**
Clarence House, **10**
Fortnum & Mason, **16**
Friary Court, **11**
Grosvenor Chapel, **26**
Grosvenor Square, **25**
Haymarket, **2**
Lancaster House, **9**
Langham Hotel, **37**
Liberty, **31**
London Library, **14**
Marble Arch, **23**
Marks and Spencer, **33**
Marlborough House, **12**
Museum of Mankind, **19**
Queen's Chapel, **13**
Reform Club, **6**
Ritz Hotel, **20**
Royal Opera Arcade, **3**
St. George's Church, **30**
St. James's Church, **15**
St. James's Palace, **7**
Selfridges, **32**
Shepherd Market, **28**
Sotheby's, **29**
Speakers' Corner, **24**
Trafalgar Square, **1**
Wallace Collection, **34**
Waterloo Place, **4**
Wellington Arch, **21**
Wigmore Hall, **35**
York House, **8**

maille. In England it was taken up with enthusiasm by James I, who called it "pell mell" and passed it down the royal line, until Charles II had a new road laid out for it in 1661. Needless to say, Catherine Street, as Pall Mall was officially named (after Charles's queen, Catherine of Braganza), was *very* fashionable. No. 79 must have been one of its livelier addresses, since Charles's gregarious mistress, Nell Gwyn, lived there. The king gave her the house when she complained about being a mere lease-holder, protesting that she had "always conveyed free under the Crown" (as it were); it remains, to this day, the only privately owned bit of Pall Mall's south side.

Stroll slowly down Pall Mall, the better to appreciate the creamy facades and perfect proportions along this showcase of 18th- and 19th-century British architecture. You'll
4 soon hit **Waterloo Place** on your left, a long rectangle punctuated by the **Duke of York memorial** column over the **Duke of York Steps,** which you may have seen from the other (Mall) side on the previous exploring tour. Waterloo Place is littered with statues, among them Florence Nightingale, the "Lady with the Lamp" nurse-heroine of the Crimean War; Captain R. F. Scott, who led a disastrous Antarctic expedition in 1911–12 and is here frozen in a bronze by his wife; Edward VII, mounted; George VI; and, as usual, Victoria, here in terra-cotta.

Flanking Waterloo Place looking onto Pall Mall are two of the gentlemen's clubs for which St. James's came to be
5 known as Clubland: the **Athenaeum** and the former United Service Club, now the **Institute of Directors.** The latter was built by John Nash in 1827–8 but was given a face-lift by Decimus Burton 30 years later to match it up with the Athenaeum, which he had designed across the way. It's fitting that you gaze on the Athenaeum first, since it was—and is—the most elite of all the societies. (It called itself "The Society" until 1830 just to rub it in.) Most prime ministers and cabinet ministers, archbishops, and bishops have belonged; the founder, John Wilson Croker (the first to call the British right-wingers "Conservatives"), decreed it the club for artists and writers, and so literary types have graced its lists, too (Sir Arthur Conan Doyle, Rudyard Kipling, J. M. Barrie—the posh ones). Women are barred. Most clubs will

tolerate female guests these days, but few admit women members, and anyway, even if your anatomy is correct it's almost impossible to become a member unless you have the connections—which, of course, is the whole point.

Next door are two James Barry–designed buildings, the **Trav-**
6 **ellers' Club** and the **Reform.** The latter is the most famous
club of all, thanks partly to Jules Verne's Phineas Fogg, who accepted the around-the-world-in-80-days bet in its smoking room, and was thus soon qualified to join the former. And—hallelujah—women can join the Reform. The **RAC Club** (for Royal Automobile Club, but it's never known as that), with its marble swimming pool, and the **Oxford and Cambridge Club** complete the Pall Mall quota; there are other, even older, establishments—Brooks's, the Carlton, Boodles, and White's (founded in 1736, and the oldest of all)—in St. James's Street around the corner, alongside *the* gentlemen's bespoke (custom) shoemaker, Lobb's, and *the* hatter, James Lock.

Instead of turning right into St. James's Street, stay on Pall
Mall until you are arrested by the surprisingly small Tudor
7 brick **St. James's Palace,** with its solitary sentry posted at
the gate. Matters to ponder as you look (you can't go in): It was named after a hospital for women lepers, which stood here in the 11th century; Henry VIII had it built; foreign ambassadors to Britain are still accredited to the Court of St. James's even though it has rarely been a primary royal residence; the present queen made her first speech here.

Continue along Cleveland Row by the side of the palace
to spy on a pair of current royal residences and a former
8 one. First on the left is **York House,** home of the duke and
duchess of Kent. A left turn into Stable Yard Road brings
9 you to **Lancaster House,** built for the Duke of York in the
1820s but more notable recently as the venue for the 1978
conference that led to the end of white rule in Rhode-
10 sia/Zimbabwe. On the other side of Stable Yard is **Clarence**
House, home to England's best-loved royal (and practically the only scandal-free one), the Queen Mother. It was designed by Nash and built in 1825 for the Duke of Clarence, who became William IV.

Now you come to the Mall. Look left to see the other facade of St. James's Palace, which was designed by Wren in
the 17th century. Then turn left up Marlborough Road and
11 you'll see the palace's open-sided **Friary Court.** Turn around,
12 and there is **Marlborough House,** designed by Wren in 1709
for the duchess of Marlborough, who asked for something
"strong plain and convenient" bearing no similarity to
Blenheim Palace. Judge for yourself, but she must have been
pleased with it, because she remained there until she died
13 in 1744. In front of the house is the **Queen's Chapel,** designed by Inigo Jones for the Infanta of Castille when she
was betrothed to Charles I in 1623. This was actually the
first classical church in England, and attending a service is
the only way you can get to delight in it. *Sun. services
Easter–July: Holy Communion 8:30* AM, *sung Eucharist or
morning prayer 11:15.*

Turn left, then right into St. James's Street, and right again
into King Street to penetrate to the heart of St. James's and
do a spot of shopping. You'd best stick to browsing at 8
King Street, though, which is **Christie's,** the fine-art auc-
tioneers who got £25 million for Van Gogh's *Sunflowers*;
ditto No. 7, **Spink & Son,** best known for selling money
(coins, banknotes, medals) but with an English and Asian
art gallery worth perusing. Coming up on the left, Duke
Street harbors further exclusive little art salons; but keep
going straight for now, into **St. James's Square,** one of London's oldest and leafiest. It was the most snobbish address
of all when it was laid out around 1670, with 14 resident
dukes and earls installed by 1720. Since 1841, No. 14—
one of the several 18th-century residences spared by World
14 War II bombs—has housed the **London Library,** which with
its million or so volumes is the best private humanities library in the land. You can go in and read the famous authors' complaints in the comments book—but not the
famous authors' books, unless you join, for £100 a year.

Leave the square via Duke of York Street to reach **Jermyn Street,** where the gentleman purchases his masculine paraphernalia. He buys his shaving sundries and hip flask from Geo. F. Trumper, briar pipe from Astley's, scent from Floris (for women too—both the Prince of Wales and his mother smell of Floris) or Czech & Speake, shirts from Turnbull

& Asser, deerstalker and panama from Bates the Hatter, and his cheeses from Paxton & Whitfield (founded in 1740 and a legend among dairies). Shop your way east along Jermyn Street, and you're practically in Piccadilly Circus, ready for the next leg of our tour.

Piccadilly

In the early 17th century, a humble tailor on the Strand called Robert Baker sold an awful lot of picadils—a collar ruff all the rage in courtly circles—and built a house with the proceeds. Snobs dubbed his new-money mansion Piccadilly ★ Hall, and the name stuck. As for the "Circus" of **Piccadilly Circus,** that refers not to the menagerie of backpackers and camera clickers clustered around the steps of **Eros,** but to the circular junction of five major roads.

Eros, London's favorite statue and symbol of the *Evening Standard* newspaper, is not in fact the Greek god of erotic love at all but the angel of Christian charity, commissioned in 1893 from the young sculptor Alfred Gilbert as a memorial to the philanthropic Earl of Shaftesbury. It cost Gilbert £7,000 to cast the statue he called his "missile of kindness" in the novel medium of aluminum, and since he was paid only £3,000, he promptly went bankrupt and fled the country. (Don't worry—he was knighted in the end.) Eros has lately done his best to bankrupt Westminster Council, too, owing to some urgent leg surgery and a new coat of protective microcrystalline synthetic wax.

Outside of Eros, there's not much to see in this sometime hub of London beyond a bank of neon advertisements, a very large branch of Tower Records, the tawdry Trocadero Centre (video arcades, food courts, chain stores, the Guinness World of Records), and a perpetual traffic jam. Look up to the east, though, for a glimpse of the curve of Regent Street, to which we'll return in due course.

South of Regent Street, opposite the neon, is the wide, straight road called **Piccadilly.** Walk west along it and you'll
15 soon reach **St. James's Church,** recessed from the street behind a courtyard filled, most days, with a crafts market. Completed in 1684, it was the last of Sir Christopher

Wren's London churches, and his own favorite. It also contains one of Grinling Gibbons's finest works, an ornate limewood reredos (the screen behind the altar). A 1940 bomb scored a direct hit here, but the church was completely restored, albeit with a fiberglass spire. It's a lively place, offering all manner of lecture series—many on incongruously New Age themes—and concerts, mostly Baroque, as well as a brass-rubbing center.

TIME OUT The Wren at St. James's, attached to the church, has not the faintest whiff of godliness, as the cake display proves. Hot dishes at lunchtime are vegetarian, very good, and very inexpensive. There are tables outside in spring and summer.

Stay on the south side of Piccadilly and you'll pass a succession of English emporia: **Simpson,** the gentlemen's outfitters (behind a disturbingly reflectionless window); **Swaine, Adeney & Brigg & Sons** for "umbrellas and whips"; **Hatchard's,** the booksellers, with an 18th-century front;
16 and **Fortnum & Mason,** the exclusive department store that supplies the queen's groceries. Legend has it that Fortnum's stocks chocolate-coated red ants alongside the glorious teas, marmalades, preserves, and tins of truffles and turtle soup. Try to pass by at the stroke of the hour so you can see the candy-colored automata of Mr. Fortnum and Mr. Mason bowing to a tinkly carillon above the main entrance.

17 Opposite Fortnum & Mason is **Burlington House,** built in the Palladian style for the Earl of Burlington around 1720, and one of the few surviving mansions from that period. It is home to the **Royal Academy of Arts,** which mounts major art exhibitions, usually years in the planning. The permanent collection (not all on show) includes at least one work by every academician past and present, including Gainsborough, Turner, and Constable, but its prize is, without doubt, a tondo (a sculpted disk) by Michelangelo of the Madonna and Child. It's up the glass staircase in the Sackler Galleries (opened in 1991 and designed by another academician, Sir Norman Foster), where temporary exhibitions are held. Every June, the RA mounts the **Summer Exhibition,** a mishmash of sculpture and painting, both amateur and professional, from abstract expressionist to photo-re-

alist (bias is toward the latter), with about 1,000 things crammed into every cranny—it's an institution. Art-weary now? Try the shop; it's one of the best museum stores in town. *Burlington House, Piccadilly,* ☎ *0171/439–7438 or 0171/439–4996 (recorded information).* ☛ *Varies according to exhibition. White Card (a group ticket to the three South Kensington museums and 10 additional ones; see South Kensington, below) accepted.* ⌚ *Daily 10–6; closed Good Fri., Dec. 24–26, Jan. 1.*

The two sides of the Burlington House courtyard are occupied by several other learned societies: the Geological Society, Chemistry Society, Society of Antiquaries, and the Royal Astronomical Society. Turning right as you exit, you'll find the entrance to one of Mayfair's enchanting cov-
18 ered shopping alleys, the **Burlington Arcade.** This one, built in 1819, is the second-oldest in London. It's still patrolled by top-hatted beadles, who prevent you from singing, running, or carrying open umbrellas or large parcels (to say nothing of lifting English fancy goods from the mahogany-fronted shops).

At the other end of the arcade, in an extension at the back of Burlington House, is a place you will often—who knows
19 why?—have practically to yourself, the **Museum of Mankind.** This overspill from the British Museum contains the best bits of the ethnographic collection, with amazing artifacts from Aztec, Mayan, African, and other unwestern civilizations beautifully displayed in miles of space. Long-running, imaginatively curated exhibitions are held on the first floor. When the long-awaited new British Library is up and running, the Department of Ethnography will be kicked back to the British Museum, so take advantage now. *6 Burlington Gardens,* ☎ *0171/437–2224.* ☛ *Free.* ⌚ *Mon.–Sat. 10–5, Sun. 2:30–6; closed Good Fri., May Day, Dec. 23–26, Jan. 1.*

TIME OUT The suitably themed **Café de Colombia** is usually as peaceful as the Museum of Mankind it inhabits—unless you collide with a school visit. Salads and pastries, Colombian coffee, and wine and beer are on the lunch menu.

Retrace your steps to Piccadilly, turn right, then turn right into Albermarle Street to travel back to the middle of the last century when electricity was young. In the basement of the Royal Institution is the **Faraday Museum,** a reconstruction of the laboratory where the physicist Michael Faraday discovered electromagnetic induction in 1831—with echoes of Frankenstein. *21 Albermarle St.,* ☏ *0171/409–2992.* ☛ *£1 adults, 50p children.* ⏲ *Weekdays 1–4; closed public holidays.*

Cross the road on Piccadilly, turn right, and soon you'll be
20 walking past the long, colonnaded front of the **Ritz** hotel, built in 1909, and meant to remind you of Paris. Beyond it is the 53-acre isosceles triangle of **Green Park,** the Mayfair hotel guests' jogging track. As with St. James's, Charles II made a public garden of the former royal hunting ground, and it too became fashionable—not least among duelists, highwaymen, and, the following century, hot-air balloonists. Nowadays you can see a tacky display of art on the railings, and a nice one of daffodils in spring.

The extreme west end of Piccadilly features the roaring traffic of **Hyde Park Corner,** the cyclist's nightmare. To cross here, you need to descend the pedestrian underpasses, fol-
21 lowing the signs to the **Wellington Arch** marooned on its central island. This 1828 Decimus Burton triumphal gateway almost wound up at the back door of Buckingham Palace, but here it stands instead, empty now of London's smallest police station, which occupied its cramped insides until 1992. A statue of Wellington also moved on, replaced by Adrian Jones's *Quadriga* in 1912.

Near the park, on the north side of Hyde Park Corner, is
22 **Apsley House**—built by Robert Adam in the 1770s and later refaced and extended—where Wellington lived from the 1820s until his death in 1852. As the **Wellington Museum,** it has been kept as the Iron Duke liked it: his uniforms and weapons, his porcelain and plate, and his extensive art collection, partially looted during military campaigns, displayed heroically. Unmissable, in every sense, is the gigantic Canova statue of a nude (but fig-leafed) Napoléon Bonaparte, Wellington's archenemy. Apsley House got iron shutters in 1830 after rioters, protesting the Duke's opposition

to the Reform Bill (he was briefly prime minister), broke the windows. Yes, the British loved him for defeating Napoléon, but mocked him with the name "Iron Duke"—it referred not to his military prowess, but to those shutters. *149 Piccadilly,* ☏ *0171/499–5676.* ☛ *£3 adults, £1.50 children and senior citizens.* ⌚ *Tues.–Sun. 11–5.*

Mayfair

Mayfair, like St. James's and Soho, is precisely delineated—a trapezoid contained by Oxford Street and Piccadilly on the north and south, Regent Street and Park Lane on the east and west. Within its boundaries are streets broad and narrow, but mostly unusually straight and grid-like for London, making it fairly easy to negotiate. Real estate here is exorbitant, so this is embassy country and the site of luxury shops and swank hotels.

Starting where we just left off, at Hyde Park Corner, head north along the boundary of Hyde Park, and risk your life crossing wide **Park Lane,** where drivers like to break the speed limit. You'll pass a succession of grand hotels: first the modern blocks of the Inter-Continental and the Hilton, then the triangular Art Deco Dorchester, followed by the "old lady of Park Lane," the Grosvenor House Hotel, on the site of the Earl of Grosvenor's 18th-century palace. After that, between Upper Grosvenor and Green streets, Nos. 93 to 99 plus No. 100, **Dudley House,** with their bow fronts and wrought-iron balconies, are the only survivors of Park Lane's early 19th-century glory days.

23 You have reached **Marble Arch,** the name of both the traffic whirlpool where Bayswater Road segues into Oxford Street and John Nash's 1827 arch, which moved here from Buckingham Palace in 1851. Search the sidewalk by the arch to find the stone plaque that marks (roughly) the place where the Tyburn Tree stood for four centuries, until 1783. This was London's central gallows, a huge wooden structure with hanging space for 21. Hanging days were holidays, the spectacle supposedly functioning as a crime deterrent to the hoi polloi. It didn't work, though. Oranges, gingerbread, and gin were sold, alongside ballads and "personal favors," to vast,

rowdy crowds, and the condemned, dressed in finery for his special moment, was treated more as hero than as villain.

Cross over (or under—there are signs to help in the labyrinth)
24 to the northeastern corner of Hyde Park, where **Speakers' Corner** harbors a late-20th-century public spectacle. Here, on Sunday afternoons, anyone is welcome to mount a soapbox and declaim upon any topic. It's an irresistible showcase of eccentricity, though sadly diminished since the death in 1994 of the "Protein Man," who thought meat, cheese, and peanuts led to uncontrollable acts of passion that would destroy western civilization.

Ignoring Oxford Street for now, retrace your steps south
25 along Park Lane and follow Upper Brook Street to **Grosvenor Square** (pronounced "Grove-na"), laid out 1725–31 and as desirable an address today as it was then. Americans certainly thought so—from John Adams, the second president, who as ambassador lived at No. 38, to Dwight D. Eisenhower, whose wartime headquarters was at No. 20. Now the ugly '50s block of the **U.S. Embassy** occupies the entire west side, and a British memorial to Franklin D. Roosevelt stands in the center. The little brick chapel used by
26 Eisenhower's men during World War II, the 1730 **Grosvenor Chapel,** stands a couple of blocks south of the square on South Audley Street, with the entrance to pretty **St. George's Gardens** to its left. Across the gardens is the headquarters
27 of the English Jesuits, the mid-19th-century **Church of the Immaculate Conception,** known as Farm Street because that is the name of the street on which it stands.

Continuing south toward Piccadilly, take Chesterfield Hill, then Queen Street, and cross Curzon Street to enter, via the
28 covered walkway at No. 47, **Shepherd Market.** This quaint and villagey tangle of streets was anything *but* quaint when Edward Shepherd laid it out in 1735 on the site of the orgiastic, fortnight-long May Fair (which gave the whole district its name). Now there are sandwich bars, pubs and restaurants, boutiques and nightclubs, and a (fading) redlight reputation in the narrow lanes.

Hit Curzon Street again and follow it east, taking Fitzmaurice Place left into **Berkeley Square** (pronounced to rhyme with "starkly"). Not many of its original mid-18th-century houses are left, but look at Nos. 42–46 (especially No. 44, which the architectural historian Sir Nikolaus Pevsner thought London's finest terraced house) and Nos. 49–52 to get some idea of why it was once London's top address—not that it's in the least humble now. The 200-year-old plane trees, which now dignify ugly showrooms and offices, presumably inspired that sentimental ballad about a nightingale singing here.

Leave via Bruton Street on the east side and continue on to **Bond Street,** divided into northern "New" (1710) and southern "Old" (1690) halves. The stretch of New Bond
29 Street you have entered boasts **Sotheby's,** the world-famous auction house, at No. 35, but there are other opportunities to flirt with financial ruin on Old Bond Street: the mirror-lined Chanel store, the vainglorious marble acres of Gianni Versace and the boutique of his more sophisticated compatriots Gucci, plus Tiffany's British outpost and art dealers Colnaghi, Léger, Thos. Agnew, and Marlborough Fine Arts. **Cork Street,** which parallels the top half of Old Bond Street, is where London's top dealers in contemporary art have their galleries—you're welcome to browse, but be dressed well. Royal personages buy baubles from Asprey & Co. at the beginning of New Bond Street, with many designers' shops (plus the more affordable fashion store, Fenwicks) continuing all the way up.

Before you reach Oxford Street, turn right into Brook Street (the composer Handel lived at No. 25), which leads to Hanover Square. Turning right down St. George Street
30 brings you to the porticos of **St. George's Church,** where Percy Shelley and George Eliot, among others, had their weddings. A right turn after the church down Mill Street brings you into the tailors' mecca of **Savile Row,** the fashionable spot for the bespoke suit since the mid-19th century.

Regent and Oxford Streets

John Nash and his patron, the Prince Regent—the future George IV—had grand plans for **Regent Street,** which was conceived as a kind of ultra-catwalk from the prince's palace, Carlton House, to Regent's Park (then called Marylebone Park). The section between Piccadilly and Oxford Street was to be called the Quadrant and lined with colonnaded purveyors of "articles of fashion and taste," in a big P.R. exercise to improve London's image as the provincial cousin of smarter European capitals. The scheme was never fully implemented, and what there was fell into such disrepair that, early this century, Aston Webb (of the Mall route) collaborated on the redesign you see today.

It is still a major shopping street, but one with a peculiar dearth of goods one wants to buy. Exceptions exist: **Hamley's,** the gigantic toy emporium, is fun; and since 1875 there
31 has been **Liberty,** which originally imported silks from the East, then diversified to other Asian goods, and is now best for its "Liberty print" cottons, its jewelry department, and—still—its high-class Asian imports. The stained-glass–lit mock-Tudor interior, with beams made from battleships, is worth a look.

Shopping continues to dominate as you reach **Oxford Circus** toward the north end of Regent Street. Turn left into **Oxford Street.** The reasons for this thoroughfare's reputation as London's main shopping drag may well elude you as you inch through the crowds and pass signs reading BANKRUPT! EVERYTHING MUST GO! and DESIGNER BARGAINS (don't bother—they're not). But two reasons to shop Ox-
32 33 ford Street remain, and they are called **Selfridges** and **Marks and Spencer.**

Harry Gordon Selfridge came to London from Chicago in 1906 and opened his store, with its row of massive Ionic columns, in 1909. Now British-run, Selfridges rivals Harrods in size and stock, but its image of lesser glamour has been tenacious. It stands toward the Marble Arch end of the street, close by the flagship branch of everyone's favorite chain store, Marks and Spencer (usually known by its pet names M&S or Marks & Sparks)—supplier of England's underwear—with by far the highest turnover of any shop in the land, so expect crowds at all times. Off Oxford Street near Bond Street tube station, to the south and north respectively, are **South Molton Street** and **St. Christopher's Place,** two little pedestrian-only streets that yield further goodies. (*See* Chapter 3, Shopping).

Take care not to exhaust yourself with consumer activities, because off Duke Street (to the right of Selfridges) in Man-
34 chester Square, the **Wallace Collection,** assembled by four generations of Marquesses of Hertford and given to the nation by the widow of Sir Richard Wallace, bastard son of the fourth, is important, exciting, undervisited—and free. As at the Frick Collection in New York, the setting here, Hertford House, is part of the show—a fine late-18th-century mansion, built for the Duke of Manchester.

The first marquess was a patron of Sir Joshua Reynolds, the second bought Hertford House, the third—a flamboyant socialite—favored Sèvres porcelain and 17th-century Dutch painting; but it was the eccentric fourth marquess who, from his self-imposed exile in Paris, really built the collection, snapping up Bouchers, Fragonards, Watteaus, and Lancrets for a song (the French Revolution having rendered them dangerously unfashionable), augmenting these with furniture and sculpture, and sending his son Richard out to do the deals. With 30 years of practice behind him, Richard Wallace continued acquiring treasures on his father's death, scouring Italy for majolica and Renaissance gold, then moving most of it to London. Look for Rembrandt's portrait of his son, the Rubens landscape, the Van Dycks, and Canalettos, the French rooms, and of course the porcelain, and don't forget to say hello to Frans Hals's *Laughing Cavalier* in the Big Gallery. *Hertford House, Manchester Sq.,* ☎ *0171/935-0687.* ☛ *Free.* ⌚ *Mon.–Sat. 10–5, Sun. 2–5; closed Good Fri., May Day, Dec. 24–26, Jan. 1.*

Take a left up Wigmore Street from Duke Street, passing
35 **Wigmore Hall,** the freshly renovated concert hall that the piano-maker Friedrich Bechstein built in 1901 (pick up a schedule for its excellent and varied concert series). Continue all the way back to Regent Street at the point where it becomes Portland Place.

Portland Place, the elegant throughway to Regent's Park, was London's widest street in the 1780s when the brothers Robert and James Adam designed it. The first sight to greet you there, drawing the eye around the awkward corner, is the succulently curvaceous portico and pointy Gothic
36 spire of **All Souls Church,** one part of Nash's Regent Street

scheme that remains. It is now the venue for innumerable concerts and Anglican services broadcast to the nation by the British Broadcasting Corporation. The 1931 block of **Broadcasting House** next door is home to the BBC's five radio stations. It curves too, if less beautifully, and features an Eric Gill sculpture of Shakespeare's Ariel (aerial—get it?) over the entrance, from which the playful sculptor was obliged to excise a portion of phallus lest it offend public decency—which the modified model did in any case.

37 The **Langham Hotel** across the street was built in 1864 to resemble a Florentine palace and duly played host to exiled royalty (Napoléon III of France, Haile Selassie of Ethiopia) and the beau monde the next 85 years until falling afoul of fashion (new luxury hotels were built farther west) and then, in 1940, a German land mine. Now it has been restored and reopened by the Hilton group.

Turn right about halfway up Portland Place into New Cavendish Street, left onto Great Portland Street, proceed as far as Clipstone Street, and look to your right. That giant
38 glass pencil is **British Telecom Tower,** imposed on London by the Post Office in 1965 (everyone still calls it the Post Office Tower) to field satellite phone calls and beam radio and TV signals around. It has a habit of popping up on the skyline from the most surprising locations, but here it reveals its full 620 feet. A terrorist bomb went off upstairs in 1975, and the great view from the top has been off-limits ever since.

SOHO AND COVENT GARDEN

Numbers in the margin correspond to points of interest on the Soho and Covent Garden map.

Yet another quadrilateral—this one described by Regent Street, Coventry/Cranbourn Streets, Charing Cross Road, and the eastern half of Oxford Street—encloses Soho, the most fun part of the West End. This appellation, unlike the New York neighborhood's similar one, is not an elision of anything, but a blast from the past—derived (as far as we know) from the shouts of "So-ho!" that royal huntsmen in Whitehall Palace's parklands were once heard to cry. One of Charles II's illegitimate sons, the Duke of Monmouth, was an early resident, his dubious pedigree setting the tone for the future: For many years Soho was London's strip show/peep show/clip joint/sex shop/brothel center. The mid-'80s brought legislation that granted expensive licenses to a few such establishments and closed down the rest; most prostitution had already been ousted by the 1959 Street Offences Act. Only a cosmetic smear of red-light activity remains now, plus a shop called "Condomania" and one or two purveyors of couture fetishwear for outfitting trendy club goers.

These clubs, which cluster around the Soho grid, are the diametric opposite of the St. James's gentlemen's museums—they cater to youth, change soundtrack every month, and have tyrannical fashion police at the door. Another breed of Soho club is the strictly members-only media haunts (the Groucho, the Academy, the Soho House, Fred's), salons for carefully segregated strata of high-income hipster.

It was after the First World War, when London households relinquished their resident cooks en masse, that Soho's gastronomic reputation was established. It had been a cosmopolitan area since the first immigrant wave of French Huguenots arrived in the 1680s. More French came fleeing the revolution in the late 18th century, then the Paris Commune of 1870, followed by Germans, Russians, Poles, Greeks, and (especially) Italians and, much later, Chinese. Pedestrianized Gerrard Street, south of Shaftesbury Avenue, is the hub of London's compact **Chinatown,** which boasts restaurants, dim sum houses, Chinese supermarkets, and February New Year's celebrations, plus a brace of scarlet pagoda-style archways and a pair of phone booths with pictogram dialing instructions.

Soho, being small, is easy to explore, though it's also easy to mistake one narrow, crowded street for another, and even Londoners get lost here. We enter from the northwest corner, **Oxford Circus.** From here, head south about 200 yards down Regent Street, turn left into Great Marlborough Street, and head to the top of Carnaby Street.

The '60s synonym for swinging London, **Carnaby Street** fell into a post-party depression, re-emerging sometime in the '80s as the main drag of a public-relations invention called West Soho. Blank stares would greet anyone asking directions to such a place, but it is geographically logical, and the tangle of streets—Foubert's Place, Broadwick Street, Marshall Street—do cohere, at least, in type of merchandise (youth accessories, mostly, with a smattering of designer boutiques). Broadwick Street is also notable as the birthplace, in 1758, of the great visionary poet and painter William Blake at No. 74.

Turn right off Broadwick Street into Berwick (pronounced
"Berrick") Street, famed as central London's best fruit and
vegetable market. Then step through tiny Walker's Court
(ignoring the notorious hookers' bulletin board); cross
Brewer Street, named for two extinct 18th-century breweries; and you'll have arrived at Soho's hip hangout, Old
Compton Street. From here, Wardour, Dean, Frith, and
Greek streets lead north, all of them bursting with the
aforementioned restaurants and clubs. Take either of the
1 latter two to **Soho Square,** laid out about 1680 and fashionable in the 18th century. Only two of the original houses
still stand, plus the 19th-century central garden.

In the other direction from Old Compton Street is a long-
standing Gallic outpost, recognizable by the tricolor flut-
2 tering outside on Dean Street, the **French House.** This pub
has been crammed with people ever since de Gaulle's Free
French Forces rendezvoused here during World War II.
Nowadays the crowd isn't French—it's Soho trendies and
peculiar bohemians. Opposite the French House is all that
3 remains of once-famous **St. Anne's Church,** probably the
work of Wren. A German bomb in 1940 spared only the
tower, and the graveyard behind it, on Wardour Street.

The street you now face is Shaftesbury Avenue, the heart of theaterland, and across which you'll find Chinatown.

TIME OUT Take any excuse you can think of to visit either of Soho's wonderful rival patisseries: **Maison Bertaux** (28 Greek St.) or **Pâtisserie Valerie** (44 Old Compton St.). Both serve divine gateaux, milles-feuilles, croissants, éclairs, etc., the former in an upstairs salon, the latter in a dark room behind the cake counters.

South of Shaftesbury Avenue and Gerrard Street is **Leicester Square** (no, not "lay-sess-ter" but "lester"), of which it is no compliment to say that it is showing no sign of its great age. Looking at the neon of the major movie houses, the fast-food outlets (plus a useful Häagen-Dazs café), and the disco entrances, you'd never guess it was laid out around 1630. By the 19th century it was already bustling and disreputable, and now it's usually the only place crowded after midnight—with suburban teenagers, Belgian backpackers, and London's swelling ranks of the homeless. That said, it is not a threatening place, and the liveliness can be quite cheering. In the middle are statues of Shakespeare, Hogarth,
Reynolds, and Charlie Chaplin. One landmark certainly
4 worth visiting is the **Society of London Theatre ticket kiosk,**
on the southwest corner, which sells half-price tickets for
many of that evening's performances (*see* Theater *in* Chapter 6, The Arts and Nightlife). On the northeast corner, in
5 Leicester Place, stands **Notre Dame de France,** with a wonderful mural by Jean Cocteau in one of its side chapels.

Charing Cross Road runs west of Leicester Square. A bibliophile's dream, it's lined with bookstores—new and second-hand, general and specialist. Although it does not qualify as a Soho street, check out little **Cecil Court,** running east off Charing Cross Road before it hits Trafalgar Square, for some of the best of the bookshops.

Covent Garden

The best place to begin your rounds of this ever-evolving
neighborhood is in its center, the former **Covent Garden Mar-**
6 **ket,** now often referred to as the **Piazza** that it became in
1980. It's very close to Covent Garden tube (just stroll south down James Street). The easiest way to find the market building from Charing Cross Road is to walk down Cranbourn Street, next to Leicester Square tube, then down Long Acre, and turn right at James Street.

This has always been the sort of neighborhood alluded to as "colorful." It was originally the "convent garden" belonging to the Abbey of St. Peter at Westminster (later Westminster Abbey). The land was given to the first Earl of Bedford by the Crown after the Dissolution of the

Soho and Covent Garden

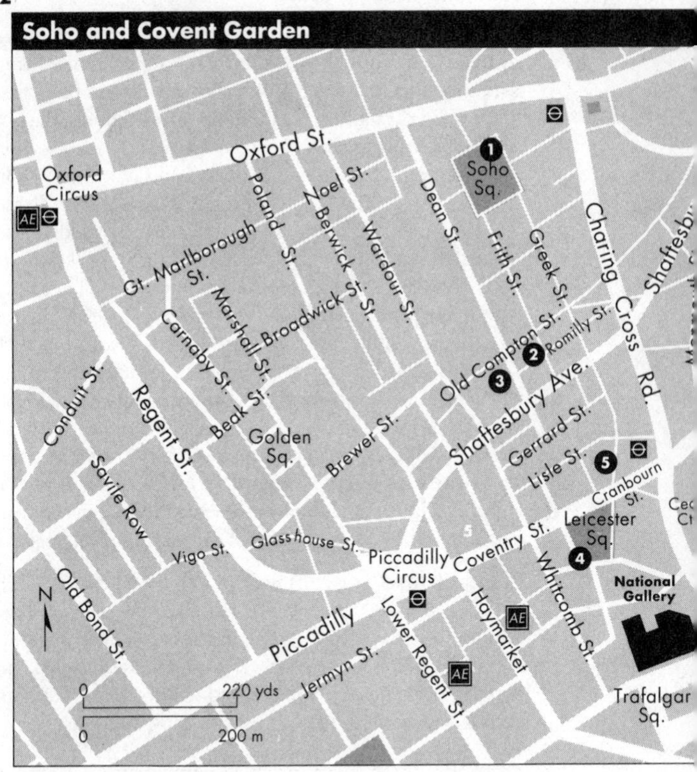

Adelphi, **20**

Bow Street Magistrates' Court, **15**

Bush House, **24**

Cleopatra's Needle, **19**

French House, **2**

Garrick Club, **12**

Jubilee Market, **9**

Lamb and Flag, **13**

London Transport Museum, **10**

Market building, **8**

Notre Dame de France, **5**

Piazza, **6**

Roman Bath, **23**

Royal Opera House, **14**

St. Anne's Church, **3**

St. Clement Danes, **26**

St. Mary-le Strand, **25**

St. Paul's Church, **7**

Society of London Theatre ticket kiosk, **4**

Soho Square, **1**

Somerset House, **22**

Theatre Museum, **11**

Theatre Royal, Drury Lane, **16**

Victoria Embankment Gardens, **18**

Waterloo Bridge, **21**

York Watergate, **17**

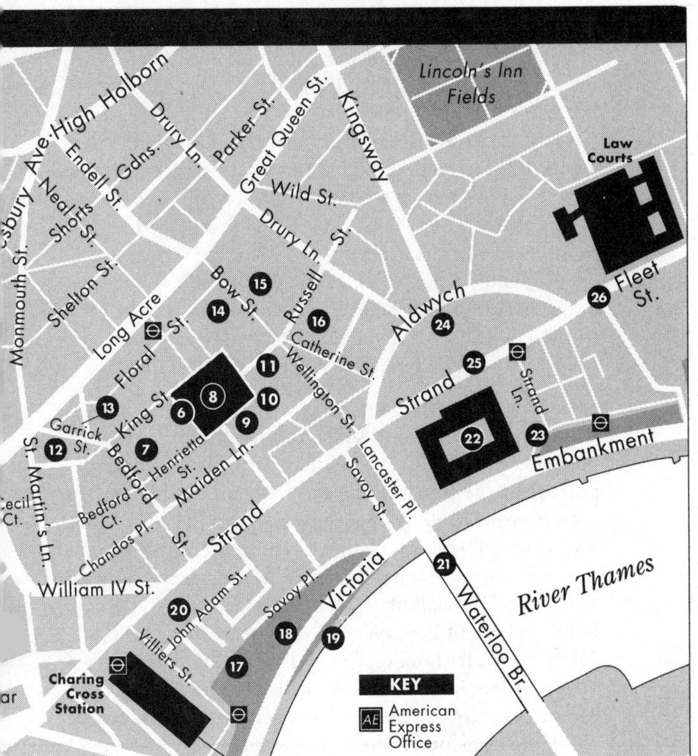

Lincoln's Inn Fields
Law Courts
High Holborn
Drury Ln.
Parker St.
Great Queen St.
Kingsway
Endell St.
Gdns.
Neal St.
Shorts
Wild St.
Drury Ln.
St.
Monmouth St.
Shelton St.
Bow St.
Russell
Long Acre
Floral St.
Catherine St.
Aldwych
Fleet St.
Wellington St.
Strand
Strand Ln.
Garrick St.
King St.
Henrietta St.
Maiden Ln.
Embankment
St. Martin's Ln.
Bedford St.
Bedford Ct.
Cecil Ct.
Chandos Pl.
Lancaster Pl.
Savoy St.
Strand
William IV St.
John Adam St.
Savoy Pl.
Victoria
Waterloo Br.
River Thames
Villiers St.
Charing Cross Station
KEY
American Express Office

Monasteries in 1536. The Earls—later promoted to Dukes—of Bedford held on to the place right up until 1918, when the eleventh Duke managed to offload what had by then become a liability. In between, the area enclosed by Long Acre, St. Martin's Lane, Drury Lane, and assorted streets north of the Strand had gone from the height of fashion (until the nobs moved west to brand-new St. James's) to a period of arty-literary bohemia in the 18th century, followed by an era of vice and mayhem, to become the vegetable supplier of London once more when the market building went up in the 1830s, followed by the Flower Market in 1870 (Eliza Dolittle's alma mater in Shaw's *Pygmalion* and Lerner and Loewe's musical version, *My Fair Lady*).

Still, it was no Mayfair, what with 1,000-odd market porters spending their 40-shillings-a-week in the alehouses, brothels, and gambling dens that had never quite disappeared. By the time the Covent Garden Estate Company took over the running of the market from the 11th Duke, it seemed as if seediness had set in for good, and when the fruit-and-veg trade moved out to the bigger, better Nine Elms Market in Vauxhall in 1974, it left a decrepit wasteland. But this is one of London's success stories: Now the (sadly defunct) Greater London Council stepped in with a dream of a rehabilitation scheme—not unlike the one that was tried, less successfully, in the Parisian equivalent, Les Halles. By 1980, the transformation was complete.

Go all the way through the market—we'll return in a
minute—exiting stage right to cross the Piazza (maybe pausing to watch the street entertainers, who have passed audi-
7 tions for this coveted spot) to **St. Paul's Church.** This 1633
work of the great Inigo Jones has always been known as "the
actors' church" thanks to the several theaters in its parish,
and well-known actors often read the lessons at services.

With your back to St. Paul's portico (the setting for *Pygmalion*'s opening scene), you get a good view of the restored
8 1840 **market building** around which Covent Garden piv-
ots. Inside, the shops are mostly higher-class clothing chains,
plus a couple of cafés and some knickknack stores that are
good for gifts. There's a superior crafts market on most days,
9 too. If you turn right, you'll reach the indoor **Jubilee Mar-**

ket, with stalls selling clothing, army surplus gear, more crafts, and more knickknacks.

Two entertaining museums stand at the southeastern corner of the square. First, in the old Flower Market, is the
10 **London Transport Museum,** which tells the story of mass transportation in the capital. It is particularly child-friendly, with lots of touch-screen interactive material, live actors in costume (including a Victorian horse-dung collector), old rolling-stock, period smells and sounds, and best of all, a tube driving simulator. *Piazza,* ☎ *0171/379–6344.* ☛ *£3.95 adults, £2.50 children 5–16 and senior citizens, children under 5 free. White Card accepted.* ⏲ *Daily 10–6; closed Dec. 24–26. Tube: Covent Garden.*

11 Next door is the **Theatre Museum,** which aims to re-create the excitement of theater itself. There are usually programs in progress allowing children to get in a mess with make-up or have a giant dressing-up session. Permanent exhibits attempt a history of the English stage from the 16th century to Mick Jagger's jumpsuit, with tens of thousands of theater playbills, and sections on such topics as Hamlet-through-the-ages and pantomime—the peculiar British theatrical tradition whereby men dress as ugly women (as distinct from RuPaul), and girls wear tights and play princes. There's a little theater in the bowels of the museum and a ticket desk for "real" theaters around town, plus a café and a good bookstore. *7 Russell St.,* ☎ *0171/836–7891.* ☛ *£3 adults, £1.50 children 5–14 and senior citizens.* ⏲ *Tues.–Sun. 11–7; closed Good Fri., Dec. 24–26, Jan. 1. Tube: Covent Garden.*

The best way to explore the little streets around the Piazza is to follow your nose, but here are a few suggested directions to point it in, with landmarks.

You could start off, wearing your shopping hat, on **Neal Street,** which begins north of Long Acre catercorner to the tube station, and is closed to traffic halfway down. To the left off Neal Street, on Earlham Street, is Thomas Neal's mall—named after the founder (in 1693) of the star-shaped cobbled junction of tiny streets just past there, called **Seven Dials.** Turning left into the next street off Neal Street, Shorts Gardens, you come to Neal's Yard (note the comical, water-operated wooden clock), originally just a whole-foods wholesaler, now an entire holistic village with therapy rooms, organic bakery and dairy, a great vegetarian café, and a medical herbalist's shop reminiscent of a medieval apothecary.

From Seven Dials, veer 45 degrees south into Mercer Street, turning right on Long Acre, then left into Garrick Street. Here stands a stray from clubland (the gents version), the
12 **Garrick Club.** Named for the 18th-century actor and theater manager David Garrick, it is, because of its literary-theatrical bent, more louche than its St. James's brothers, and famous actors, from Sir Laurence Olivier down, have always been proud to join—along with Dickens, Thackeray,
13 and Trollope, in their time. Find the **Lamb and Flag** down teeny Rose Street to the left. Dickens drank in this pub, better known in its 17th-century youth as the Bucket of Blood owing to the bare-knuckle boxing matches upstairs. (You'll find that many London pubs claim Dickens as an habitué, and it's unclear whether they lie or the author was the city's premier sot. (*See* Chapter 4, Restaurants and Pubs.)

From Rose Street, turn right into Floral Street, another shopping spot, especially good for high-fashion menswear and for the Sanctuary, a women-only day spa, with parrots, palms, and pool. At the other end you'll emerge onto Bow
14 Street, right next to the **Royal Opera House.** In fact, for the entire length of the block between James and Bow streets you've been walking past the theater's 1982 extension, which added much-needed rehearsal and dressing-room space to the building designed in 1858 by E. M. Barry, son of Sir Charles, the House of Commons architect. This one is the third theater on the site. The first opened in 1732 and burned down in 1808; the second opened a year later under the aegis of one John Anderson, only to succumb to fire in 1856. Anderson, who had lost two theaters already, had an appalling record when it came to keeping the limelights apart from the curtains.

Despite government subsidies, tickets for the Royal Opera are pricey, though the expense is unlikely to lead to riots as it did in 1763, 1792, and for *61 days* of protest in the Old Price Riots of 1809, when the cost of rebuilding inflated the cost of seats. (The public won.) Many British and world premiers have been staged here (including the world's first public piano recital in 1767), and the Royal Opera attracts all the glittering divas on the international circuit. Nowadays you can see some of them for free, when selected summer performances are relayed live to a giant screen in the Piazza.

15 Opposite the Royal Opera's Bow Street facade is the **Bow Street Magistrates' Court,** from which the prototype of the modern police force once operated. Known as the Bow Street Runners (because they chased thieves on foot), they were the brainchild of the second Bow Street magistrate—none other than Henry Fielding, the author of *Tom Jones* and *Joseph Andrews.*

Continuing on, and turning left into Russell Street, you reach Drury Lane, home to London's best-known auditorium and
16 almost its largest, the **Theatre Royal, Drury Lane**. It enjoys all the romantic accessories of a London theater—a history of fires (it burned down three times, once in a Wren-built incarnation), riots (in 1737, when a posse of footmen demanded free admission), attempted regicides (George II in 1716 and his grandson George III in 1800), and even sightings of a phantom (in the Circle, matinees).

The Strand and Embankment

South of Covent Garden, the ¾-mile-long traffic-clogged **Strand** is one of London's oldest streets. It was already lined with mansions seven centuries ago, when it was a mere Thames-side bridle path. In 1706 Thomas Twining, the tea tycoon, moved his shop into No. 216 (it's still there); it was closely followed by a slew of coffee houses, frequented by Boswell and Johnson, that persisted for most of that century, then music halls put the street on the map afresh in the early 1900s.

Starting at Charing Cross Station at the southern end of the Strand, take Villiers Street down to the Thames. On Watergate Walk at the western end of Victoria Embankment
17 stands the **York Watergate.** This was once the grand river entrance to York House, the Duke of Buckingham's man-

sion, built in 1625 and about the oldest building extant around here; it marks the place where the river used to flow before the road was built. A riverside road had seemed a good plan ever since Wren had come up with the idea after the Great Fire of 1666, but nobody got around to it until Sir Joseph Bazalgette set to work on the **Victoria Embankment** two centuries later. Bazalgette, incidentally, is better known for providing London with the sewer system still largely in use; he can be admired in effigy on the bronze bust right there by Hungerford Bridge.

Between the York Watergate and the Strand section of the
18 embankment is the triangular-handkerchief **Victoria Embankment Gardens,** where office sandwich-eaters and people who call it home coexist at lunchtime. If you walk
through to the river you come upon London's *very oldest
thing,* predating its arbitrary namesake, and London itself,
19 by centuries: **Cleopatra's Needle.** The 60-foot pink granite obelisk was erected at Heliopolis, in Lower Egypt, in
about 1475 BC, then moved to Alexandria, where in 1819
Mohammed Ali, the Turkish Viceroy of Egypt, rescued it
from its fallen state and presented it to the British. The British,
though grateful, had not the faintest idea how to get the
186-ton gift home, so they left it there for years until an
expatriate English engineer contrived an iron pontoon to
float it to London via Spain.

Cross the gardens northwest from there toward the Strand,
20 and you enter the **Adelphi.** This regal riverfront row was
the work of all four brothers Adam (John, Robert, James,
and William—hence the name, from the Greek *adelphoi,*
meaning brothers), London's Scottish architects. All the late-
18th-century design stars were roped in to beautify the in-
teriors, but the grandeur gradually eroded, and today very
few of the 24 houses remain; 7 Adam Street is the best.

Circumnavigate the Strand by sticking to the embankment
21 walk and you'll soon reach **Waterloo Bridge,** where (weather
permitting) you can catch some of London's most glamorous views, toward both the City and Westminster around
the Thames bend. Look past the bridge and there you'll see
22 the grand 18th-century classical river facade of **Somerset
House,** which houses the **Courtauld Institute Galleries.**

Founded in 1931 by the textile maven Samuel Courtauld, this is London's finest Impressionist and post-Impressionist collection, with bonus post-Renaissance works thrown in. Botticelli, Breughel, Tiepolo, and Rubens are represented, but the younger French painters (plus Van Gogh) are the stars—here, for example, are Manet's *Bar at the Folies-Bergère* and *Déjeuner sur l'Herbe* (a companion to the bigger version at the Musée d'Orsay in Paris). *The Strand,* ☎ *0171/873–2526.* ☛ *£3 adults, £1.50 children, students, and senior citizens. White Card accepted.* ⌚ *Mon.–Sat. 10–6, Sun. 2–6; closed public holidays. Tube: Temple, Embankment.*

Slinking north up narrow Strand Lane between Somerset
House and **King's College** (a branch of London University),
you'll come upon a curious little redbrick plunge-pool
23 known as the **Roman Bath.** It's probably about a thousand
years younger than Roman, but nobody is quite sure. To
see it, you have to peer in the window at No. 5. Dickens
may inadvertently have named it, in *David Copperfield,*
though nobody seems quite sure of that, either.

Now you're back on the Strand, with the main entrance of
Somerset House at your back, looking at the **Aldwych,** a great
big croissant of a potential traffic accident, with a central
island on which stand three hulking monoliths: India House,
24 Melbourne House, and the handsome 1935 neo-classical **Bush
House,** headquarters of the BBC World Service.

Dwarfed by Bush House but prettier by far, and stranded
(oops) in the traffic on islands in the Strand to the west,
25 are two churches. The 1717 **St. Mary-le-Strand,** James
Gibbs's (of St.-Martin-in-the-Fields fame) first public building, was inspired by the Baroque churches of Rome that
26 had impressed Gibbs during his studies there. Wren's **St.
Clement Danes** (with a tower appended by Gibbs) is dedicated to the Royal Air Force. Its 10 bells peal the tune of
the nursery rhyme "Oranges and lemons, / Say the bells of
St. Clements . . ." even though the bells in the rhyme belong to St. Clements, Eastcheap. Inside is a book listing 1,900
American airmen who were killed during World War II.

THE CITY

Numbers in the margin correspond to points of interest on the City map.

You may have assumed you had done this when your plane touched down at Heathrow, but note that capital letter: the City of London is not the same as the city of London. The capital-C City is an autonomous district, separately governed since William the Conqueror started building the Tower of London, and despite its compact size (you may hear it referred to as the "Square Mile," which is almost accurate), it remains the financial engine of Britain and one of the world's leading centers of trade.

The City is also London's most ancient part, although there is little remaining to remind you of that fact beyond a scattering of Roman stones. Not much is known about the period between AD 410, when the Roman legions left, and the 6th century, when the Saxons arrived, but it was really after Edward the Confessor moved his court to Westminster in 1060 that the City gathered momentum. As Westminster took over the administrative role, the City was free to develop the commercial heart that still beats strong.

The Romans had already found Londinium's position handy for trade—the river being navigable yet far enough inland to allow for its defense—but it was the establishment of crafts guilds in the Middle Ages, followed in Tudor and Stuart times by the proliferation of great trading companies (the Honourable East India Company, founded in 1600, was the star), that really started the cash flowing. King John had confirmed the City's autonomy by charter in 1215, and its commerce and government fed off each other, the leaders of the former electing the leaders of the latter. This is still largely the case: The Corporation of London has control over the Square Mile and elects a Lord Mayor just as it did in the Middle Ages, when the famous folk hero Richard Whittington was four times (not thrice, as in *Dick Whittington,* the pantomime) voted in.

Three times the City has faced devastation—and that's not counting the "Black Monday" of 1992, when sterling crashed. The Great Fire of 1666 spared practically none of

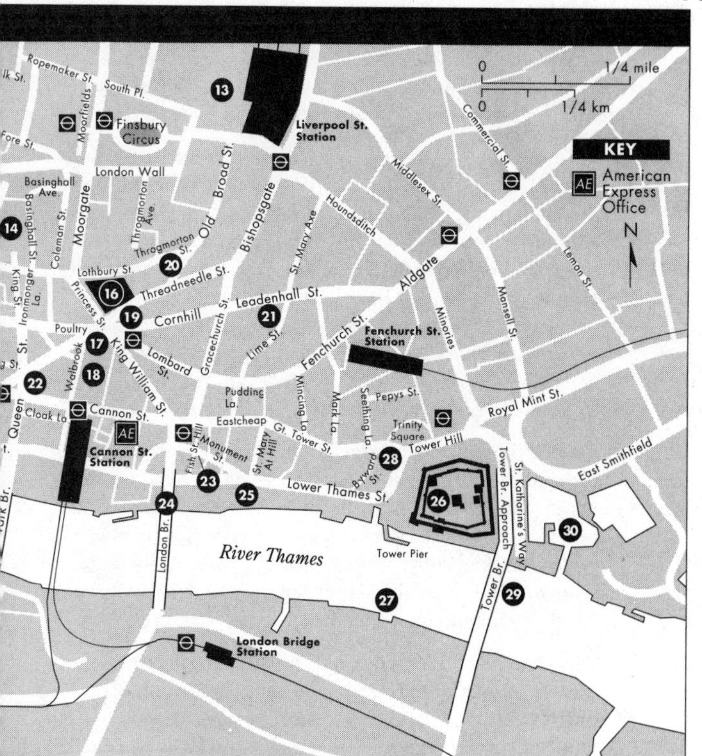

Ropemaker St.
South Pl.
Moorfields
Finsbury Circus
Fore St.
London Wall
Basinghall Ave.
Basinghall St.
Coleman St.
Moorgate
Throgmorton Ave.
Throgmorton St.
Old Broad St.
Bishopsgate
Liverpool St. Station
Houndsditch
St. Mary Axe
Middlesex St.
Commercial St.
Lothbury St.
Threadneedle St.
Princess St.
King St.
Ironmonger La.
Poultry
Cornhill
Leadenhall St.
Gracechurch St.
Lime St.
Aldgate
Fenchurch St.
Fenchurch St. Station
Minories
Mansell St.
Lemon St.
Lombard St.
King William St.
Walbrook
Queen St.
Cloak La.
Cannon St.
Cannon St. Station
Pudding La.
Eastcheap
Mincing La.
Mark La.
Seething La.
Pepys St.
Trinity Square
Gt. Tower St.
St. Mary At Hill
Fish St. Hill
Monument St.
Byward St.
Tower Hill
Royal Mint St.
East Smithfield
Lower Thames St.
Tower Br. Approach
St. Katharine's Way
River Thames
Tower Pier
London Br.
Tower Br.
London Bridge Station
0
1/4 mile
1/4 km
KEY
AE
American Express Office
N
13
14
16
17
18
19
20
21
22
23
24
25
26
27
28
29
30

Courant, moved in, followed by (literally) all the rest, "Fleet Street" has been synonymous with newspaper journalism. The papers themselves all moved out in the 1980s, but the British press is still collectively known as "Fleet Street."

Turn left on Bolt Court to reach Gough Square, where Samuel Johnson lived between 1746 and 1759, in the worst
2 of health, compiling his famous dictionary in the attic. **Dr. Johnson's House** is a shrine to the man possibly more attached to London than anyone else, ever, and includes a first edition of his dictionary among the Johnson-and-Boswell mementos. *17 Gough Sq.,* ☎ *0171/353–3745.* ☛ *£3 adults, £1 children under 18, and £2 senior citizens.* ⏲ *May–Sept., Mon.–Sat. 11–5:30; Oct.–Apr., Mon.–Sat. 11–5; closed national holidays. Tube: Chancery La., Temple.*

One of the places Dr. Johnson drank (like Dickens, he is claimed by many a pub) was his "local" around the cor-
3 ner in Wine Office Court, **Ye Olde Cheshire Cheese,** which retains a venerable open-fires-in-tiny-rooms charm when not too packed with tourists. Among 19th-century writers who followed Johnson's footsteps to the bar here were Mark Twain and, yes, Charles Dickens.

Back on Fleet Street, you come to the first of Wren's city churches—one of the bomb-damaged ones, reconsecrated
4 only in 1960 after a 17-year restoration: **St. Bride's.** As St. Paul's, Covent Garden is the actor's church, so St. Bride's belongs to journalists, many of whom have been buried or memorialized here, as reading the wall plaques will tell you. Even before the press moved in, it was a popular place to take the final rest. By 1664 the crypts were so crowded that Samuel Pepys had to bribe the grave digger to "justle together" some bodies to make room for his deceased brother. Now the crypts house a museum of the church's rich history, and a bit of Roman sidewalk. *Fleet St.,* ☎ *0171/353–1301.* ☛ *Free.* ⏲ *Mon.–Sat. 9–5, Sun. between the services at 11 and 6:30. Tube: Chancery La.*

The end of Fleet Street is marked by the messy traffic intersection called **Ludgate Circus,** which you should cross to Ludgate Hill to reach **Old Bailey,** second on the left. At the top, on the site of the courts we are about to visit, **Newgate Prison** stood from the 12th century right until the beginning of this one. Few survived for long in the version pulled down in 1770. Those who didn't starve were hanged, or pressed to death in the Press Yard, or they succumbed to the virulent gaol (the archaic British spelling of "jail") fever—any of which must have been preferable to a life in the stinking, subterranean, lightless Stone Hold, or to suffering the robberies, beatings, and general victimization endemic in what Henry Fielding called the "prototype of hell." The next model lasted only a couple of years before being torn down by insane mobs during the anti-Catholic Gordon Riots of 1780, to be replaced by the Newgate that Dickens visited several times (in between pubs) and used in several novels—Fagin ended up in the Condemned Hold here in *Oliver Twist,* from which he would have been taken to the public scaffold which replaced the Tyburn Tree and stood outside the prison until 1868.

Instead of a hanging, the modern visitor can watch a trial
5 by jury in the **Central Criminal Court,** better known as the Old Bailey, which replaced Newgate in 1907. The most famous, and most interesting, feature of the solid Edwardian building is the gilded statue of blind Justice perched on top, scales in her left hand, sword in her right. Ask the doorman which current trial is likely to prove juicy, if you're that kind of ghoul—you may catch the conviction of the next Crippen or Christie (England's most notorious wife-murderers, both tried here). *Public Gallery open weekdays 10–1 and 2–4; queue forms at the Newgate St. entrance. Check day's hearings on sign outside. Tube: Blackfriars.*

From mass murderers to stamp collectors . . . A right turn on Newgate Street at the top of Old Bailey, then a left onto
6 King Edward Street brings you to the **National Postal Museum.** This landmark for philatelists was founded in 1965, but the collection is as old as the postal service itself, and is one of the world's best. *King Edward Bldg., King Edward St., ☎ 0171/239–5420. ☛ Free. ⏲ Mon.–Thurs. 9:30–4:30, Fri. 9:30–4; closed national holidays. Tube: St. Paul's.*

The road turns into Little Britain farther along, then emerges
7 at **Smithfield,** London's main meat market. Nowadays the

meat is dead, but up to the middle of last century, it was livestock that was sold here. This "smooth field" was already a market in the 12th century, but the building you see today, modeled on the Victorian Crystal Palace, was not opened until 1868. Smithfield still bustles like nowhere else, frenetic porters (actor Michael Caine's father was one) slinging sides of beef about, dripping blood down their aprons, then repairing to pubs that have special early alcohol licenses for breakfast. Visitors, although welcome, had better (a) get up very early, because the show's over by 9:30, (b) keep out of the way, or get sworn at, and (c) not be vegetarian.

TIME OUT The **Fox and Anchor** (115 Charterhouse St.) serves beer alongside its famous Brobdingnagian mixed grills, from 6:30 AM.

Backtracking a few steps down Little Britain, you'll see on the left a perfect half-timbered gatehouse atop a 13th-century stone archway. Enter here to reach one of London's
8 oldest churches, the Norman **St. Bartholomew the Great.** Along with its namesake on the other side of the road, St. Bartholomew's Hospital, the church was founded by Rahere, Henry I's court jester. At the Dissolution of the Monasteries, Henry VIII had most of it torn down, so that the Romanesque choir is all that survives from the 12th century. The hospital across the street, although one of London's most famous, is in the process of "an orderly run-down and disposal" (despite protests) as part of a government reorganization of the National Health Service.

St. Paul's Cathedral

★ 9 Whichever way you approach **St. Paul's,** your first view of it will take your breath away. The cathedral is, of course, Sir Christopher Wren's masterpiece, completed in 1710 after 35 years of building and much argument with the royal commission, then, much later, miraculously (mostly) spared by the World War II bombs. Wren had originally been commissioned to restore Old St. Paul's, the Norman cathedral that had replaced, in its turn, three earlier versions, but the Great Fire left so little of it behind that a new cathedral was deemed necessary.

Wren's first plan, known as the New Model, did not make it past the drawing board, while the second, known as the Great Model, got as far as the 20-foot oak rendering you can see here today before being rejected, too, whereupon Wren is said to have burst into tears. The third, however, known as the **Warrant Design** (because it received the royal warrant), was accepted, with the fortunate coda that the architect be allowed to make changes as he saw fit. Without that, there would be no dome, since the approved design had featured a steeple. Parliament felt that building was proceeding too slowly (in fact, 35 years is lightning speed, as cathedrals go) and withheld half of Wren's pay for the last 13 years of work. He was pushing 80 when Queen Anne finally coughed up the arrears.

When you enter and see the **dome** from the inside, you may find that it seems smaller than you expected. You aren't imagining things; it *is* smaller, and 60 feet lower, than the lead-covered outer dome. Between the inner and outer domes is a brick cone, which supports the familiar 850-ton lantern, surmounted by its golden ball and cross. Nobody can resist making a beeline for the dome, so we'll start beneath it, standing dead center, on top of Wren's memorial, which his son composed and had set into the pavement, and which reads succinctly: *Lector, si monumentum requiris, circumspice*—"Reader, if you seek his monument, look around you."

Now climb the 259 spiral steps to the **Whispering Gallery.** This is the part of the cathedral with which you bribe children, who are fascinated by the acoustic phenomenon: Whisper something to the wall on one side, and a second later it transmits clearly to the other side, 107 feet away. The only problem is identifying "your" whisper from the cacophony of everyone else's, since this is a popular game. Look down onto the Nave from here, and up to the frescoes of St. Paul by Sir James Thornhill (who nearly fell off while painting them), before ascending farther to the **Stone Gallery,** which encircles the outside of the dome and affords a spectacular panorama of London. Up again (careful—you will have tackled 627 steps altogether) and you reach the **Golden Gallery,** from which you can view the lantern through a circular opening called the oculus.

Back downstairs there are the inevitable monuments and memorials to see, though fewer than one might expect, since Wren didn't want his masterpiece cluttered up. The poet John Donne, who had been Dean of St. Paul's for his final 10 years (he died in 1631), lies in the south choir aisle, his the only monument remaining from Old St. Paul's. The vivacious choir stall carvings nearby are the work of Grinling Gibbons, as is the organ, which Wren designed and Handel played. The painters Sir Joshua Reynolds and J. M. W. Turner are commemorated, as is George Washington. The American connection continues behind the high altar in the **American Memorial Chapel,** dedicated in 1958 to the 28,000 GIs stationed here who lost their lives in World War II.

A visit to the **crypt** brings you to Wren's tomb, the black marble sarcophagus containing Admiral Nelson (who was pickled in alcohol for his final voyage here from Trafalgar), and an equestrian statue of the Duke of Wellington on top of his grandiose tomb. ☎ *0171/248–2705.* ☛ *To cathedral, ambulatory (American Chapel), crypt, and treasury: £2.50 adults, £2 senior citizens, £1.50 children; to galleries: £3 adults, £2.50 senior citizens, £2 children; combined ticket: £5 adults, £4 senior citizens, £3 children. Cathedral open for sightseeing Mon.–Sat. 8:30–4:30 (closed occasionally for special services); ambulatory, crypt, and galleries open Mon.–Sat. 9:30–4:15. Tube: St. Paul's.*

Surrounding St. Paul's is . . . nothing. Various plans to redevelop the area, which was flattened by bombing and obviously rebuilt in a hurry, have been dogged by bickering and delay for decades. This is gradually going to change, however, when the ugly '60s building on Ludgate Hill, Juxon House, makes way for a more sensitive development that is nearly through the planning stage. The new St. Paul's approach will include the reinstallation of Sir Christopher Wren's 1672 Temple Bar gateway close to its original site as the City's western gateway. (At the moment, it's moldering in a suburban park.)

The Museum of London and the Barbican

Find Little Britain yet again, taking its right fork to cross Aldersgate Street to **London Wall,** named for the Roman rampart that stood along it. It's a dismal street, now dominated by post-modern architect Terry Farrell's late-'80s follies, but about halfway along you can see a section of 2nd-to-4th-century wall at St. Alphege Garden. There's another bit in an appropriate spot back at the start of London Wall, out-
10 side the **Museum of London,** which you can view better from a window inside the museum itself, near the Roman monumental arch the museum's archaeologists reconstructed a mere two decades ago. Anyone with the least interest in how this city evolved will adore the museum, especially said reconstructions and the dioramas—like one of the Great Fire (flickering flames! sound effects!), a 1940s air-raid shelter, a Georgian prison cell, and a Victorian street complete with fully stocked shops. There are plenty of treasures (the Cheapside Hoard of Jacobean jewelry shouldn't be missed), costumes, furniture, and domestic paraphernalia to flesh it all out, and galleries proceed chronologically for easy comprehension. *London Wall,* ☎ *0171/600–3699.* ☛ *£3.50 adults, £1.75 children under 18 and senior citizens, £8.50 family ticket (up to 2 adults and 3 children);* ☛ *Free 4:30–6. All tickets allow unlimited return visits for three months. White Card accepted.* ⏲ *Tues.–Sat. 10–6, Sun. noon–6; closed Good Fri., Dec. 24–25.*

North of the museum is the enormous concrete maze Lon-
11 doners love to hate—the **Barbican,** home of the Royal Shakespeare Company and its two theaters, the London Symphony Orchestra and its auditorium, the Guildhall School of Music and Drama, a major gallery for touring exhibitions, two cinemas, a convention center, and apartments for a hapless two-thirds of the City's residents (most part-time). The name comes from a defensive fortification of the City, and defensive is what Barbican apologists (including architects Chamberlain, Powell, and Bon) became when the complex was finally revealed in 1982, after 20 years as a building site. There ensued an epidemic of jokes about getting lost forever in the Barbican bowels. A hasty rethink of the contradictory signposts and nonsensical "levels" was performed, and navigatory yellow lines materialized,

Oz-like, on the floors, but it didn't help much—the Barbican remains difficult to navigate. Time has mellowed the elephant-gray concrete into a darker blotchy brownish-gray, and Londoners have come to accept the place, if not exactly love it, because of its contents. Actors rate the theater acoustics especially high, and the steep bank of the seating makes for a good stage view. The visiting exhibitions are often worth a trek, as are the free ones in the foyer.

Negotiating the windy walkways of the deserted residential section, then descending in elusive elevators to the lower depths of the Centre (where the studio auditorium, the aptly-named Pit, lives), spotting stray sculptures and water gardens, receiving electric shocks from the brass rails—all this has its perverse charm, but there is one unadulterated success in the Barbican, though unfortunately it's not often open to the public. Secreted on an upper floor is an enormous, lush conservatory in a towering glass palace, big enough for full-grown trees to flourish. *Silk St., ☎ 0171/638–4141. ☛ Free. ⏲ Mon.–Sat. 9 AM–11 PM, Sun. noon–11 PM. Gallery: ☛ £4.50 adults, £2.50 children and senior citizens. White Card accepted. ⏲ Mon.–Sat. 10–7:30, Sun. and national holidays noon–7:30. Conservatory: ☛ 80p adults, 60p children and senior citizens; open weekends noon–5:30 when not in use for private function (always call first). Tours (minimum 10 people; book in advance), ☎ 0171/628–0183; cost: £3.50 adults, £2.50 children and senior citizens. RSC backstage tours, ☎ 0171/628–3351. Tube: Moorgate, Barbican.*

TIME OUT The Barbican Centre's **Waterside Café** has salads, sandwiches, and pastries; they're unremarkable but are served in a tranquil enclosed concrete (naturally) waterside terrace.

South of the Barbican complex stands one of the only City
churches to have withstood the Great Fire, only to succumb
12 to the Blitz bombs three centuries later, **St. Giles without
Cripplegate.** The tower and a few walls survived; the rest
was rebuilt to the 16th-century plan in the 1950s, and now
the little church struggles hopelessly for attention amongst
the Barbican towers, whose parishioners it tends. Past

parishioners include Oliver Cromwell, married here in 1620, and John Milton, buried here in 1674.

Before heading south to the City's financial heart, detour east to see one of the more successful recent development
13 schemes, the **Broadgate Centre,** at the north end of Old Broad Street, hanging on the tails of the redeveloped **Liverpool Street Station.** In contrast to the Barbican, this collection of offices, shops, and restaurants got good notices as soon as it opened in 1987, especially for its circular courtyard surrounded by hanging gardens. The courtyard is iced over in winter to become London's only outdoor skating rink; it hosts bands and performers in summer.

The Guildhall and the Financial Center

Back on London Wall, turn south into Coleman Street, then right onto Masons Avenue to reach Basinghall Street and
14 the **Guildhall,** symbolic nerve center of the City. The Corporation of London ceremonially elects and installs its Lord Mayor here as it has done for 800 years. The Guildhall was built in 1411, and though it failed to avoid either the 1666 or 1940 flames, its core survived, with a new roof sensitively appended in the 1950s and further cosmetic embellishments added in the '70s.

The fabulous hall is a psychedelic patchwork of coats of arms and banners of the City Livery Companies, which inherited the mantle of the medieval trade guilds, which invented the City in the first place. Actually, this honor really belongs to two giants, Gog and Magog, the pair of mythical beings who founded ancient Albion, and who glower upon the prime minister's annual November banquet from their west gallery grandstand in 9-foot painted limewood form.

The 94 modern Livery Companies are more than symbolic banner-bearers, since they fund education and research in the trades they represent, and many offer apprenticeships. Most are modern and useful, like the Vintners', Plaisterers', Grocers', and Insurers' Companies. Other, older ones have had to move with the times and diversify—the Tallow Chandlers' Company has gone into the oil trade, and the Paviors' Company, no longer required to dispose of scavenging pigs, now concentrates on street construction. *Gresham St.,* ☎ *0171/606–3030.* ☛ *Free.* ⏲ *Mon.–Sat. 10–5; closed national holidays. Tube: St. Paul's, Moorgate, Bank, Mansion House.*

The 1970s west wing houses the **Guildhall Library**—mainly City-related books and documents, plus a collection belonging to one of the Livery Companies, **the Worshipful Company of Clockmakers,** with over 600 timepieces on show, including a skull-faced watch that belonged to Mary, Queen of Scots. ☎ *0171/606–3030.* ☛ *Free.* ⏲ *Weekdays 10–5; closed national holidays. Tube: St. Paul's, Moorgate, Bank, Mansion House.*

As you might guess, many streets around here were named for their own medieval craft guild, including the dairymen's lane, Milk Street, which you now follow south to **Cheapside.** Chepe being Old English for "market," you might also divine that this street was where the bakers of Bread Street, the cobblers of Cordwainers Street, the goldsmiths of Goldsmith Street, and all their brothers gathered to sell their wares.

15 You come now to another symbolic center of London, **St. Mary-le-Bow,** Wren's 1673 church—the spire survives intact. The bells are the symbolic part, since a Londoner must be born within the sound of them to qualify as a true cockney. The origin of that idea was probably the curfew rung on the Bow Bells during the 14th century, even though "cockney" only came to mean Londoner three centuries later, and then it was an insult.

TIME OUT **The Place Below** is literally below the church, in St. Mary-le-Bow's crypt, and gets packed with City workers weekday lunchtimes, since the self-service soup and quiche are particularly good. It's also open for breakfast, and Thursday and Friday evenings feature a posh and sophisticated vegetarian set dinner.

Walk to the east end of Cheapside. Here seven roads meet and financial institutions converge in a tornado of fiscal activity that is bereft of life on weekends. Turn to your left,
16 and you will be facing the citadel-like **Bank of England,**

known familiarly for the past couple of centuries as "The Old Lady of Threadneedle Street," after someone's parliamentary quip. The bank, which has been central to the British economy since 1694, manages the national debt and the foreign exchange reserves, issues banknotes, sets interest rates, looks after England's gold, and regulates its banking system. The history of all this is traced in the **Bank of England Museum.** *Bartholomew La., ☏ 0171/601–5545. ☛ Free. ⏲ Easter–Sept., weekdays 10–5, Sun. and public holidays 11–5; Oct.–Easter, weekdays 10–6; closed public holidays Oct.–Easter. Tube: Bank, Monument.*

17 With your back to the bank you will see the mid-18th-century Palladian facade of the Lord Mayor's abode, **Mansion House.** What you won't see is the colonnaded Egyptian Hall, or the cell where the suffragette Emmeline Pankhurst was held early in this century, or any of the state rooms where the mayor entertains his fellow dignitaries, since the building is closed to public scrutiny.

18 At the mayor's back door stands the parish church many think is Wren's best, **St. Stephen Walbrook,** on the street of the same name. Possibly you are beginning to think that *every* Wren church shares that distinction, but this one really does shine, by virtue of its practice dome, which predates the Big One at St. Paul's by some 30 years. Two inside sights warrant investigation: Henry Moore's 1987 central stone altar, which sits beneath the dome ("like a lump of Camembert," say critics), and, well, a telephone—an eloquent tribute to that genuine savior of souls, Rector Chad Varah, who founded the Samaritans, givers of phone help to the suicidal, here in 1953.

19 The third **Royal Exchange** to inhabit the isosceles triangle between Threadneedle Street and Cornhill was blessed by Queen Victoria at its 1844 opening. Sir William Tite designed the massive temple-like building, its pediment featuring 17 limestone figures (Commerce, plus merchants) supported by eight sizable Corinthian columns, to house the then thriving futures market. This has now moved on (*see* Cannon Bridge Station, *below*), leaving the Royal Exchange, which you may no longer enter, as a monument to money.

In back of the Bank of England at the start of Old Broad
Street is yet another venerable trading institution that has
20 completely changed, the **London Stock Exchange.** A mere
14 years after this building opened (again, the third on its
site), it was rendered practically useless, when the "Big
Bang," the stock market crash of late 1986, put a stop to
trading in equities on the floor. The London Traded Options Market persisted in one corner, which visitors could
spy on from the Viewing Gallery, until security-conscious-
ness following an IRA bomb in July 1990 closed *that* down.
It was due to close anyway, because in February 1992 that
last bastion of the jobbers and brokers of the stock exchange
floor merged with the London International Financial Futures Exchange (LIFFE, pronounced "life"), everyone
packed their phones, and they all decamped to deal at **Cannon Bridge Station** in nearby Cousin's Lane (☎ 0171/623–
0444; tours available by arrangement), leaving the dealing
floor at the Stock Exchange echoing with red-suspendered,
stripe-shirted '80s phantoms. All you can visit there now
is the reception desk, where a long-suffering security guard
says you can't go in and somewhat tetchily hands over an
information booklet.

Continue along Cornhill to Leadenhall Street. The final tale
of fiscal fortunes on this route is contained in what most
agree is the most exciting recent structure London can
21 boast, the **Lloyd's of London** tower, Richard Rogers's (of
Paris Pompidou Centre fame) 1986 masterpiece. The building is a fantastical steel-and-glass medium-rise of six towers around a vast atrium, with Rogers's trademark inside-out
ventilation shafts, stairwells, gantries, and so on partying
all over the facades. It is definitely best seen at night, when
cobalt and lime spotlights make it leap out of the deeply
boring gray skyline like Carmen Miranda at a funeral.

The institution that commissioned this fabulous £163-million fun house has been trading in insurance for two centuries and is famous the world over for several reasons: (1) having started in a coffee house; (2) insuring Marilyn Monroe's legs; (3) accepting no corporate responsibility for losses, which are carried by its investors; (4) having its "Names"—the rich people who underwrite Lloyd's losses; (5) seeming unassailable for a very long time . . . (6) until recently—losses in 1990 were £2.9 billion, (7) which caused the financial ruination of many Names.

The museum of Lloyd's history, containing the Lutine Bell, which heralds important announcements (one ring for bad news), have all been closed to the public—not on account of recent misfortunes, but as insurance against future ones, in the form of bombs. *1 Lime St., ☎ 0171/623–7100.*

TIME OUT **Lloyd's Coffee House,** despite its name and its position at the foot of the Lloyd's tower, has nothing to do with the 17th-century coffee house where the institution was born but serves British "caff" food all day long nevertheless.

Mithras, the Monument, and London Bridge

Now we leave the money markets and return briefly to Roman London, which you may have learned more about in the Museum of London. The museum funds an archaeological department, which—in 1954—unearthed in what was first taken for an early Christian church. In fact, wor-
22 shipers at the **Temple of Mithras** were not at all keen on Christ; they favored his chief rival during the 3rd and 4th centuries, Mithras, the Persian god of light. Mithraists aimed for all the big virtues, but still were not appreciated by early Christians, from whom their sculptures and treasures had to be concealed. These devotional objects are now on display back at the Museum of London, while here, on Queen Victoria Street, not far from the Bank of England, you can see the foundations of the temple itself.

Moving along a few centuries, the next shrine you pass, after a sharp left turn into Cannon Street, commemorates the "dreadful visitation" of the Great Fire of 1666. Known sim-
23 ply as **Monument,** this is the world's tallest isolated stone column—the work of Wren, who was asked to erect it "On or as neere unto the place where the said Fire soe unhappily began as conveniently may be." And so here it is—at 202 feet, exactly as tall as the distance it stands from Farriner's baking house in Pudding Lane, where the fire started. Above the viewing gallery (311 steps up—better than any StairMaster) is a flaming bronze urn, and around it a

cage for the prevention of suicide, which was a trend for a while in the 19th century. *Monument St.,* ☏ *0171/626-2717.* ☛ *£1 adults, 25p children.* ⊙ *Apr.–Sept., weekdays 9–5:30, weekends 2–5:30; Oct.–Mar., Mon.–Sat. 9–3:30. Tube: Monument.*

24 Just south of Monument is the latest **London Bridge.** This one dates from only 1972; it replaced the 1831 Sir John Rennie number that now graces Lake Havasu City, Arizona, the impulse purchase of someone at the McCulloch Oil Corporation, who (rumor has it) was under the impression that he'd bought the far more picturesque Tower Bridge. The version before that one, the first in stone and the most renowned of all, stood for 600 years after it was built in 1176, the focus of many a gathering thanks to the shops and houses crammed along its length, not to mention the boiled and tar-dipped heads of traitors that decorated its gatehouse after they were removed at the Tower of London. Before *that* the Saxons had put up a wooden bridge; it collapsed in 1014, which was probably the origin of "London bridge is falling down." Nobody is sure of the exact location of the very earliest London Bridge—the Roman version around which focus London grew—but it was certainly very close to the 100-foot-wide, three-span, prestressed concrete cantilever one that you see today.

Turn left onto Lower Thames Street and you'll come to
25 **Billingsgate,** London's principal fish market for 900 years—until 1982, when the fish moved to the Isle of Dogs farther east and the developers moved in here, leaving a sanitized, if pretty, shell, which at press time had yet to find a tenant. Next door is the Custom House, built early in the last century.

The Tower of London

You'll have spotted the most famous of the City's sights already, as it's an easy five-minute walk from the Custom
★ 26 House: the **Tower of London.** The Tower, as it's generally known, has top billing on every tourist itinerary for good reason. Nowhere else does London's history come to life so vividly as in this mini-city of melodramatic towers stuffed to bursting with heraldry and treasure, the intimate details

of lords and dukes and princes and sovereigns etched in the walls (literally in some places, as you'll see), and quite a few pints of royal blue blood spilled on the stones. Be warned that visitor traffic at the sight of sights is copious, meaning not only lines for the best bits, but a certain dilution of atmosphere, which can be disappointing if you've been fantasizing scenes from *Elizabeth and Essex*.

The Tower is still one of the royal palaces, although no monarch since Henry VIII has called it home. It has also housed the Royal Mint, the Public Records, the Royal Menagerie, and the Royal Observatory, although its most renowned and titillating function has been, of course, as a jail and place of torture and execution.

A person was mighty privileged to be beheaded in the peace and seclusion of **Tower Green** instead of before the mob at Tower Hill. In fact, only seven people were ever important enough—among them Anne Boleyn and Catherine Howard, wives two and five of Henry VIII's six; Elizabeth I's friend Robert Devereux, Earl of Essex; and the nine-days queen, Lady Jane Grey, aged 17. Tower Green's other function was as a corpse dumping ground when the chapel just got too full. You can see the executioner's block, with its charming forehead-sized dent, and his axe—along with the equally famous rack, where victims were stretched, and the more obscure scavenger's daughter, which pressed a body nearly to death, plus assorted thumbscrews, iron maidens, etc.—in the **Martin Tower,** which stands in the northeast corner.

Before we go any farther, you should know about the excellent free and fact-packed tours that depart every half hour or so from the Middle Tower. They are conducted by the 42 Yeoman Warders, better known as "Beefeaters"—ex-servicemen dressed in resplendent navy-and-red (scarlet-and-gold on special occasions) Tudor outfits.Beefeaters have been guarding the Tower since Henry VII appointed them in 1485. One of them, the Yeoman Ravenmaster, is responsible for making life comfortable for the eight ravens who live in the Tower—an important duty, since if they were to desert the Tower (goes the legend), the kingdom would fall.

In prime position stands the oldest part of the Tower and the most conspicuous of its buildings, the **White Tower.** This central keep was begun in 1078 by William the Conqueror; by the time it was completed, in 1097, it was the tallest building in London, underlining the might of those victorious Normans. Henry III (1207–1272) had it whitewashed, which is where the name comes from, then used it to house his menagerie.

The spiral staircase—winding clockwise to help the right-handed swordsman defend it—is the only way up, and here you'll find the **Royal Armouries,** Britain's national museum of arms and armor, with about 40,000 pieces on display. One of the Tower's original functions was as arsenal, supplying armor and weapons to the kings and their armies. Henry VIII started the collection in earnest, founding a workshop at Greenwich as a kind of bespoke tailor of armor to the gentry, but the public didn't get to see it until the second half of the 17th century, during Charles II's reign—which makes the Tower Armouries Britain's oldest public museum.

Here you can see weapons and armor from Britain and the Continent, dating from Saxon and Viking times right up to our own. Among the highlights are four of those armors Henry VIII commissioned to fit his ever-increasing bulk, plus one for his horse. Don't miss the tiny armors on the third floor—one belonging to Henry's son (who survived in it to become Edward VI), and another only just over 3 feet tall. In the **New Armouries,** added in the 17th century, are examples of almost every weapon made for the British soldier from the 17th to the 19th century.

Most of the interior of the White Tower has been much altered over the centuries, but the **Chapel of St. John,** downstairs from the armouries, is unadulterated 11th-century Norman—very rare, very simple, and very beautiful. Underneath it is "Little Ease," the cell where Guy Fawkes (*see* The Houses of Parliament *in* Westminster and Royal London, *above*) was held, chained to a ring in the floor.

The other fortifications and buildings surrounding the White Tower date from the 11th to the 19th century. Starting from the main entrance, you can't miss the **moat.** Until the Duke of Wellington had it drained in 1843, this was a stinking, stagnant mush, obstinately resisting all attempts to flush it with water from the Thames. Now there's a little raven graveyard in the grassed-over channel, with touching memorials to some of the old birds.

Across the moat, the **Middle Tower** and the **Byward Tower** form the principal landward entrance, with **Traitors' Gate** a little farther on to the right. This London equivalent of Venice's Bridge of Sighs was where the boats delivered prisoners to their cells, and so it was where those condemned to death got their last look at the outside world. During the period when the Thames was London's chief thoroughfare, this was the main entrance to the Tower.

Immediately opposite Traitors' Gate is the former Garden Tower, better known since about 1570 as the **Bloody Tower.** Its name comes from one of the most famous unsolved murders in history, the saga of the "little princes in the Tower." In 1483 the boy king, Edward V, and his brother Richard were left here by their uncle, Richard of Gloucester, after the death of their father, Edward I. They were never seen again, Gloucester was crowned Richard III, and in 1674 two little skeletons were found under the stairs to St. John's Chapel. The obvious conclusions have always been drawn—and were, in fact, even before the skeletons were discovered.

Another famous inmate was Sir Walter Raleigh, who was kept here from 1603 to 1616. It wasn't such an ordeal, as you'll see when you visit his spacious rooms, where he kept two servants, had his wife and two sons live with him, and wrote his *History of the World.* Unfortunately, he was less lucky on his second visit in 1618, which terminated in his execution at Whitehall.

Next to the Bloody Tower is the circular **Wakefield Tower,** which dates from the 13th century and once contained the king's private apartments. It was the scene of another royal murder in 1471, when Henry VI was killed mid-prayer. Henry founded Eton College and King's College, Cambridge, and they haven't forgotten: Every May 21, envoys from both institutions mark the anniversary of his murder by laying white lilies on the site.

The shiniest, the most expensive, and absolutely the most famous exhibits here are, of course, the **Crown Jewels,** now housed in the **Duke of Wellington's Barracks.** In their new setting you get so close that you could lick the gems (if it weren't for the wafers of bulletproof glass), and they are enhanced by new laser lighting, which almost hurts the eyes with sparkle. Before you meet them in person, you are given a high-definition-film preview along with a few scenes from Elizabeth's 1953 coronation.

It's a commonplace to call these baubles priceless, but it's impossible not to drop your jaw at the notion of their worth. Security is as fiendish as you'd expect, since the jewels—even though they would be literally impossible for thieves to sell—are *so* priceless that they're not insured.

A brief résumé of the top jewels: Finest of all is the **Royal Sceptre,** containing the earth's largest cut diamond, the 530-carat Star of Africa. This is also known as Cullinan I, having been cut from the South African Cullinan, which weighed 20 ounces when dug up from a De Beers mine at the beginning of the century. Another chip off the block, Cullinan II, lives on the **Imperial Crown of State** that Prince Charles is due to wear at his coronation—the same one that Elizabeth II wore in her coronation procession; it had been made for Victoria's in 1838. Aside from its 2,800 diamonds, it features the Black Prince's ruby, which Henry V was supposed to have worn at Agincourt, and is actually an imposter—it's no ruby, it's a semiprecious spinel. The other most famous gem is the Koh-i-noor, or "Mountain of Light" which adorns the **Queen Mother's crown.** When Victoria was presented with this gift horse in 1850, she looked it in the mouth, found it lacking in glitteriness, and had it chopped down to almost half its weight.

The little chapel of **St. Peter ad Vincula** can be visited only as part of a Yeoman Warder tour. The third church on the site, it conceals the remains of some 2,000 people executed at the Tower, Anne Boleyn and Catherine Howard among them. Being traitors, they were not so much buried as dumped under the flagstones, but the genteel Victorians had the courtesy to rebury their bones during renovations.

One of the more evocative towers is **Beauchamp Tower,** built west of Tower Green by Edward I (1272–1307). It was soon designated as a jail for the higher class of miscreant, including Lady Jane Grey, who is thought to have added her Latin graffiti to the many inscriptions carved by prisoners that you can see here.

Just south of the Beauchamp Tower is an L-shaped row of half-timbered Tudor houses, with the **Queen's House** at the center. Built for the governor of the Tower in 1530, this place saw the interrogation or incarceration of several of the more celebrated prisoners, including Anne Boleyn and the Gunpowder Plot conspirators. The Queen's House also played host to the Tower's last-ever prisoner, Rudolph Hess, the Nazi who parachuted into London in 1941 to seek asylum.

Don't forget to stroll along the battlements before you leave; from them, you get a wonderful overview of the whole Tower of London. *H. M. Tower of London,* ☎ *0171/709–0765.* ☛ *£7.95 adults, £5.95 senior citizens, £5.25 children under 15, £21.95 family (2 adults, 3 children, or 1 adult, 4 children). Small additional* ☛ *charge to the Fusiliers Museum.* ⏲ *Mar.–Oct., Mon.–Sat. 9:30–6:30, Sun. 2–6; Nov.–Feb., Mon.–Sat. 9:30–5; closed Good Fri., Dec. 24–26, Jan. 1. For tickets to Ceremony of the Keys (the locking of the main gates, nightly at 10), write well in advance to The Resident Governor and Keeper of the Jewel House, Queen's House, H. M. Tower of London, EC3. Give your name, the dates you wish to attend (including alternate dates), and number of people (up to 7), and enclose a self-addressed stamped envelope. Yeoman Warder guides leave daily from Middle Tower, subject to weather and availability, at no charge (but a tip is always appreciated), about every 30 min until 3:30 in summer, 2:30 in winter. Tube: Tower Hill.*

From the riverside, walk to the front of the Tower: There
27 is a good view across the river to ***HMS Belfast*** and the new
building developments along the south bank of the Thames.

To the west of the Tower is London's first "dark-ride" mu-
28 seum, the **Tower Hill Pageant,** where automated cars take
you past mock-ups of scenes from most periods of London's

past, complete with "people," sound effects, and even smells. There's also an archaeological museum with finds from the Thames, set up by the Museum of London. *Tower Hill Terrace, ☎ 0171/709–0081. ☛ £5.45 adults, £3.45 children under 16 and senior citizens. ⏲ Apr.–Oct., daily 9:30–5:30; Nov.–Mar., daily 9:30–4:30; closed Dec. 25. Tube: Tower Hill.*

Tower Bridge and St. Katharine's Dock

The eastern edge of the City is rich indeed in symbols of London, as you will gather when staggering out from the ★ 29 Tower only to be confronted with the aptly named **Tower Bridge.** Despite its venerable, nay medieval, appearance, Tower Bridge is a Victorian youngster that celebrated its centenary in June 1994. Constructed of steel, then clothed in Portland stone, it was deliberately styled in the Gothic persuasion to complement the Tower next door, and is famous for its enormous bascules—the "arms," which open to allow large ships through. Nowadays this rarely happens, but when river traffic was dense, the bascules were raised about five times a day.

The bridge's 100th-birthday gift was a new exhibition, one of London's most imaginative and fun. You are conducted in the company of "Harry Stoner," an animatronic bridge construction worker worthy of Disneyland, back in time to witness the birth of the Thames's last downstream bridge. History and engineering lessons are painlessly absorbed as you meet the ghost of the bridge's architect, Sir Horace Jones, see the bascules work, and wander the walkways with their grand upstream–downstream views annotated by interactive video displays. Be sure to hang on to your ticket and follow the signs to the Engine Rooms for part two, where the original steam-driven hydraulic engines gleam, and a cute rococo theater is the setting for an Edwardian music-hall production of the bridge's story. ☎ *0171/403–3761. ☛ £5 adults, £3.50 children under 15 and senior citizens. ⏲ Apr.–Oct., daily 10–6:30; Nov.–Mar., daily 10–5:15 (last entry 1¼ hrs before closing); closed Good Fri., Dec. 24–25, Jan. 1. Tube: Tower Hill.*

30 You've left the City now, but still worth a look is **St. Katharine's Dock,** which you reach from the wharf underneath Tower Bridge. Finished in 1828, St. Katharine's thrived until container ships and their cargoes grew too big for the little river docks to handle, and it was shut down in 1968. Developers moved in and created this enclave of shops and luxury apartments, whose inhabitants moor their luxury yachts in the marina alongside a few old Thames sailing barges (which you can charter) and the converted-warehouse Dickens Inn, with its waterside terrace. (Dickens did not drink here.)

KNIGHTSBRIDGE AND KENSINGTON

Numbers in the margin correspond to points of interest on the Knightsbridge and Kensington map.

Salubrious Knightsbridge has approximately equal doses of elite residential streets and ultra-shopping opportunities. To its east is one of the highest concentrations of important artifacts anywhere, the "museum mile" of South Kensington, with the rest of Kensington offering peaceful strolls, a noisy main street, and another palace. This is an all-weather tour—museums and shops for rainy days, grass and strolls for sunshine.

Knightsbridge

When you surface from the Knightsbridge tube station—one of London's deepest—you are immediately engulfed among the angry drivers, professional shoppers, and ladies-who-lunch who comprise the local population. If you're in a shopping mood, **Harvey Nichols**—right at the tube—has six floors of total fashion, and **Sloane Street,** leading south, is strung with the boutiques of big French and English designers. (*See* Chapter 3, Shopping.)

1 There's no point pretending you don't want to see **Harrods,** so we'll head there next, going west down Brompton Road and soon colliding with the store's domed terra-cotta Edwardian bulk, outlined in thousands of white

lights by night. The 15-acre Egyptian-owned store's sales weeks are world-class, and the store is as frenetic as a stock market floor, since its motto, *Omnia, omnibus, ubique* ("everything, for everyone, everywhere") is not too far from the truth. Visit the pet department, a highlight for children, and don't miss the extravagant **Food Hall,** with its stunning Art Nouveau tiling in the neighborhood of meat and poultry, which continues in the fishmonger's territory, where its glory is rivaled by displays of the sea produce itself. This is the place to acquire your green-and-gold souvenir Harrods bag, since food prices are surprisingly competitive. Go as early as you can to avoid the worst of the crowds. From Harrods, continue west down the Brompton Road, pausing at Beauchamp (Bee-chum) Place and Walton Street if shopping is your intention.

TIME OUT **Patisserie Valerie** (215 Brompton Rd., ☎ 0171/832-9971; open daily), just down the road from Harrods, offers light meals and a gorgeous array of pastries. It's perfect for breakfast, lunch, or tea.

Presently, at the junction of Brompton and Cromwell roads,
❷ you come to the pale, Italianate **Brompton Oratory,** a product of the English Roman Catholic revival of the late 19th century led by John Henry Cardinal Newman (1801–1890), who established this oratory in 1884 and whose statue you see outside.

South Kensington

You are now in museum territory. (The neighborhood's three large museums, incidentally, can be reached via a long underground passage from the South Kensington tube.) Since 1994, museum visiting has put less strain on the pocket with the launch of the **White Card**—a group ticket to the three South Kensington museums and 10 further ones.

The next building along, at the start of Cromwell Road, is the first of the colossal museums of South Kensington, the
★ ❸ **Victoria and Albert,** recognizable by the copy of Victoria's Imperial Crown it wears on the lantern above the central cupola, and always referred to as the V&A. It showcases the

applied arts of all disciplines, all periods, all nationalities, and all tastes, and is a wonderful, generous place to get lost in, full of innovation and completely devoid of pretension. The collections are *so* catholic that confusion is a hazard—one minute you're gazing on the Jacobean oak 12-foot-square four-poster **Great Bed of Ware** (one of the V&A's most prized possessions, given that Shakespeare immortalized it in *Twelfth Night*); the next, you're in the 20th-century end of the equally celebrated **Dress Collection,** coveting a Jean Muir frock you could actually buy at Harrods.

Prince Albert, Victoria's adored consort, was responsible for the genesis of this permanent version of the 1851 Great Exhibition, and his queen laid its foundation stone in her final public London appearance in 1899. From the start, the V&A had an important role as a research institution, and that role continues today, with many resources available to scholars, designers, artists, and conservators. Two of the latest are the **Textiles and Dress 20th Century Reference Centre,** with ingenious space-saving storage systems for thousands of bolts of cloth, and the **Textile Study Galleries,** which perform the same function for 2,000 years' worth of the past.

Follow your own whims around the 7 miles of gallery space, but try to reach the new and spectacular **Glass Gallery,** where a collection spanning four millennia is reflected between room-size mirrors, under young designer Danny Lane's breathtaking glass balustrade. *Cromwell Rd.,* ☎ *0171/938–8500. Suggested contribution: £4.50 adults, £1 children and senior citizens. White Card accepted.* ⏲ *Mon. noon–5:50, Tues.–Sun. 10–5:50; closed Good Fri., May Day, Dec. 24–26, Jan. 1. Tube: S. Kensington.*

❹ The **Natural History Museum** provides clues to its contents in relief panels scattered across its outrageously ornate French Romanesque–style terra-cotta facade. Alfred Waterhouse, the architect, carved living creatures to the left of the entrance, extinct ones to the right, a categorization that is sort of continued in reverse inside, with **Dinosaurs** on the left and the **Ecology Gallery** on the right. Both these newly renovated exhibits (the former with life-size *moving* dinosaurs, the latter complete with moonlit "rain forest")

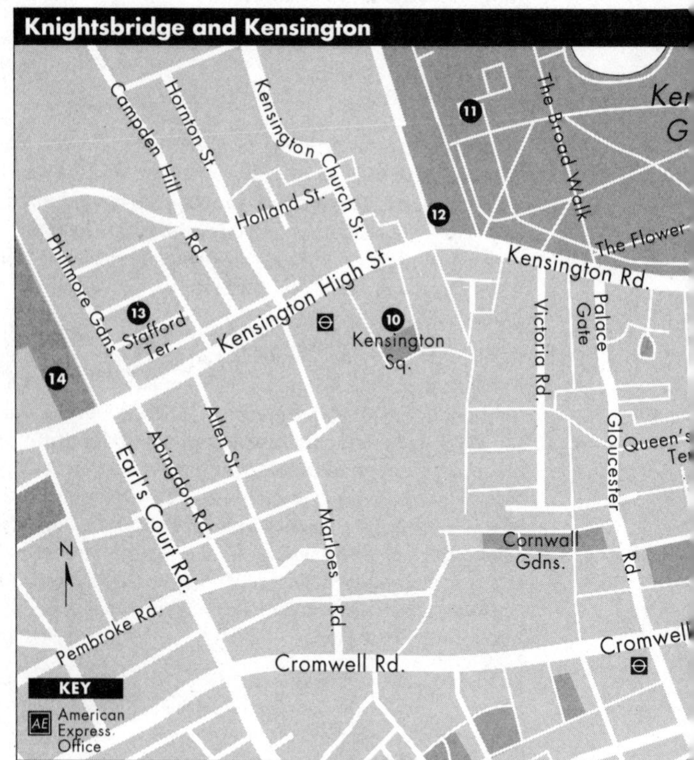

Albert Memorial, **7**

Brompton Oratory, **2**

Commonwealth Institute, **14**

Harrods, **1**

Kensington Palace, **11**

Kensington Palace Gardens, **12**

Kensington Square, **10**

Linley Sambourne House, **13**

National Sound Archive, **6**

Natural History Museum, **4**

Royal Albert Hall, **8**

Royal College of Art, **9**

Science Museum, **5**

Victoria and Albert Museum, **3**

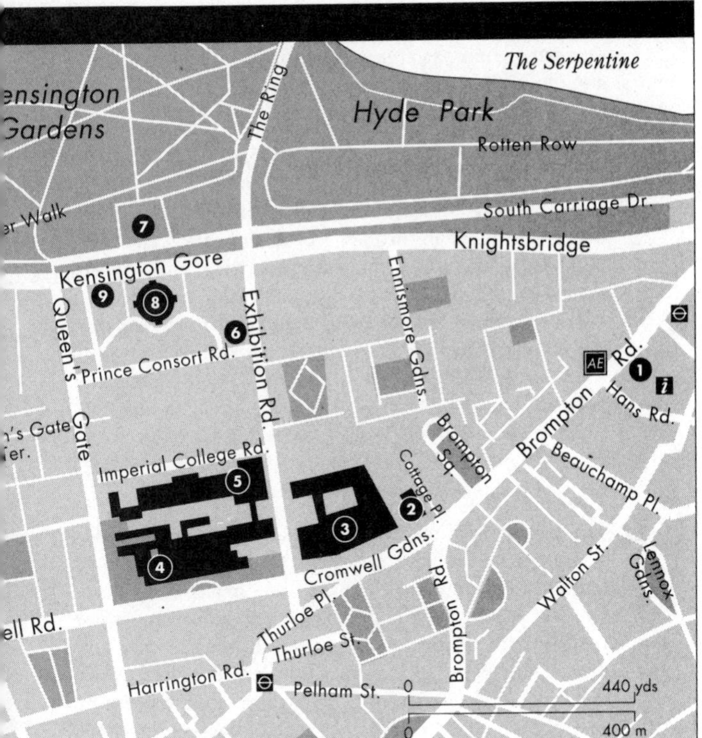

The Serpentine
Hyde Park
ensington
Gardens
The Ring
Rotten Row
South Carriage Dr.
er Walk
Knightsbridge
Kensington Gore
Ennismore Gdns.
Exhibition Rd.
Queen's Gate
Prince Consort Rd.
AE
Rd.
Brompton
Hans Rd.
Brompton Sq.
Cottage Pl.
Beauchamp Pl.
's Gate
Ter.
Imperial College Rd.
Cromwell Gdns.
Walton St.
Lennox Gdns.
Brompton Rd.
Thurloe Pl.
ell Rd.
Thurloe St.
Harrington Rd.
Pelham St.
0
440 yds
0
400 m

make essential viewing in a museum that realized it was getting crusty and has consequently invested millions overhauling itself in recent years.

The **Creepy Crawlies Gallery** features a nightmarish superenlarged scorpion, yet ends up making tarantulas cute (eight out of 10 animal species, one learns here, are arthropods). Other wonderful bits include the **Human Biology Hall,** which you arrive in through a birth-simulation chamber; the full-size blue whale; and in the east wing, once the separate Geological Museum, an earthquake machine (not for L.A. residents) in the **Earth Galleries.** Understandably, this place usually resembles grade-school recess. *Cromwell Rd.,* ☎ *0171/938–9123.* ☛ *£5 adults, £2.50 children under 17 and senior citizens, £13.50 family (2 adults, 4 children).* ☛ *Free weekdays 4:30–5:50, weekends 5–5:50. White Card accepted.* ⏲ *Mon.–Sat. 10–5:50., Sun. 11–5:50; closed Dec. 24–26, Jan. 1. Tube: S. Kensington.*

5 The last of the three big museums, the **Science Museum,** stands behind the Natural History Museum in a far plainer building. This one features even more hands-on exhibits, with entire schools of children apparently decanted inside to play with them; but it is, after all, painlessly educational. Highlights include the **Launch Pad** gallery, which demonstrates basic scientific principles (try the beautiful plasma ball, where your hands attract "lightning"—if you can get them on it); the **Computing Then and Now** show, which gets the most crowded of all; ***Puffing Billy,*** the oldest train in the world; and the actual **Apollo 10** capsule, which took U.S. astronauts around the moon in 1969 and now sits beside a mock-up moon-base in the space exploration segment. Food technology, medical history, flight, navigation, transport, meteorology—all these topics are explored, and the entire height of the museum is used for a **Foucault's Pendulum** that has been there, in perpetual motion thanks to the movement of the earth, from the start. *Exhibition Rd.,* ☎ *0171/938–8000.* ☛ *£4.50 adults, £2.40 children under 15 and senior citizens. White Card accepted.* ⏲ *Mon.–Sat. 10–6, Sun. 11–6; closed Dec. 24–26, Jan. 1. Tube: S. Kensington.*

Turn left to continue north up Exhibition Road, a kind of unfinished cultural main drag that was Prince Albert's conception, toward the road after which British moviemakers named their fake blood, Kensington Gore. Near the end on the left is the aural outpost of the British Library, the
6 **National Sound Archive,** in which you may listen to the queen who made this entire tour possible: The million recordings held here include one of Victoria speaking sometime in the 1880s, but you have to book in advance to hear her or anyone else. There's a small exhibit of early recording equipment and ephemera, too. *29 Exhibition Rd., ☎ 0171/589-6603. ☛ Free. ⏲ Weekdays 10–5 (Thurs. 10–9); closed public holidays, Dec. 24–26, Jan. 1. Tube: S. Kensington.*

Having heard Victoria, you can now see Albert, across Kensington Gore in the grandiose temple that his grieving widow had erected on the spot where his Great Exhibition had stood a mere decade before his early death from typhoid in
7 1861. To tell the truth, all you can actually see of the **Albert Memorial** is the world's tallest free-standing piece of scaffolding, since the intricate structure housing the 14-foot bronze statue of Albert is undergoing a £14m renovation—including a pure gold-leaf coat donated by an anonymous benefactor—not due to be finished until the year 2000.

Just opposite, on the south side of the street, stands a companion—and, this time, shriekingly visible—memorial, the
8 **Royal Albert Hall.** The Victorian public donated funds to build this domed, circular 8,000-seat auditorium (as well as the Albert Memorial), but more money was raised by selling 1,300 future seats at £100 apiece—not for the first night, but for every night for 999 years. (Some descendants of purchasers still use the seats.) The Albert Hall is best-known and best-loved for its annual July–September Henry Wood Promenade Concerts (the "Proms"). *Kensington Gore, ☎ 0171/589-3203. ☛ Varies according to event. Tube: S. Kensington.*

The building adjacent to the Albert Hall could hardly contrast more sharply with all this sentimental Victoriana: the
9 glass-dominated **Royal College of Art,** designed by Sir Hugh Casson in 1973. Famous in the '50s and '60s for process-

ing David Hockney, Peter Blake, and Eduardo Paolozzi, the RCA is still one of the country's foremost art schools, and there's usually an exhibition, lecture, or event here open to the public. *Kensington Gore,* ☎ *0171/584–5020.* ☛ *Free.* ⏲ *Weekdays 10–6; phone first to check exhibition details. Tube: S. Kensington.*

Kensington

You've already entered Kensington, but now you're drawing closer to the heart of it. It first became the *Royal* Borough of Kensington (and Chelsea) by virtue of a king's asthma. William III, who suffered terribly from the Thames mists over Whitehall, decided in 1689 to buy Nottingham House in the rural village of Kensington so that he could breathe more easily; besides, his wife and co-monarch, Mary II, felt confined by water and wall at Whitehall. Courtiers and functionaries and society folk soon followed where the crowns led, and by the time Queen Anne was on the throne (1702–14), Kensington was overflowing. In a way, it still is, since most of its grand houses, and the later, Victorian ones of Holland Park, have been divided into apartments, or else are serving as foreign embassies.

10 Begin with a stroll around the covetable houses of **Kensington Square,** laid out around the time William moved to the palace up the road, and therefore one of London's oldest squares. A few early 18th-century houses remain, with Nos. 11 and 12 the oldest. Return to Kensington High Street up Derry Street and follow Kensington High Street east until
11 you reach Kensington Gardens, where **Kensington Palace** stands close to the western edge. It did not enjoy a smooth passage as royal residence. Twelve years of renovation were needed before William and Mary could move in; it continued to undergo all manner of refurbishment during the next three monarchs' times. By coincidence, these monarchs happened to suffer rather ignominious deaths. First, William III fell off his horse when it stumbled on a molehill, and succumbed to pleurisy in 1702. Then, in 1714, Queen Anne (who, you may recall, was fond of brandy) suffered an apoplectic fit brought on by overeating. Next, George I, the first of the Hanoverian Georges,

had a stroke as a result of "a surfeit of melons"—admittedly not at Kensington, but in a coach to Hanover, in 1727. Worst of all, in 1760, poor George II burst a blood vessel while on the toilet (the official line was, presumably, that he was on the throne).

The best-known royal Kensington story, though, concerns the 18-year-old Princess Victoria of Kent, who was called from her bed in June 1837, by the Archbishop of Canterbury and the Lord Chamberlain. Her uncle, William IV, was dead, they told her, and she was to be queen. The **state rooms** where Victoria had her ultrastrict upbringing are currently being renovated, and will reopen in spring 1997, depicting the life of the royal family through the past century. *Kensington Gardens,* ☎ *0171/937–9561. Closed for renovation.*

Behind the palace runs one of London's rare private roads,
guarded and gated both here and at the Notting Hill Gate
12 end, **Kensington Palace Gardens.** If you walk it, you will
see why it earned the nickname "Millionaires' Row"—it
is lined with palatial white-stucco houses designed by a selection of the best architects of the mid-19th century. The
novelist William Makepeace Thackeray, author of *Vanity
Fair,* died in 1863 at No. 2—a building that now houses
an embassy (Israeli), as do most of the others. **Kensington
Church Street** also leads up to Notting Hill Gate, with the
little 1870 St. Mary Abbots Church on its southwest corner and a cornucopia of expensive antiques in its shops all
along the way.

Rather than walk the traffic-laden Kensington High Street,
take the longer, scenic route, first turning left off Kensington Church Street into Holland Street and admiring the sweet
18th-century houses (Nos. 10, 12–13, and 18–26 remain).
Turn left before Holland Park into Phillimore Gardens, then
13 left again into Stafford Terrace to reach **Linley Sambourne
House.** The Victorian Society has perfectly preserved this
1870s home of the political cartoonist Edward Linley Sambourne, complete with William Morris wallpapers and il-
lustrations from the (recently deceased) satirical magazine
Punch, including many of Sambourne's own, adorning the
walls. *18 Stafford Terr.,* ☎ *0181/994–1019.* ☛ *£3 adults,*

£1.50 children under 16. ⏲ *Mar.–Oct., Wed. 10–4, Sun. 2–5. Tube: High St. Kensington.*

14 Step back to Kensington High Street, turn right, pass the gates of Holland Park, and you'll see one of London's more eccentric structures—the swimming-pool-blue walls and asymmetric copper tent roof of the **Commonwealth Institute.** A wander around the open-plan walkways of this lovable museum is like a trip around the world, or at least around the 50 Commonwealth nations, with lifestyles and histories of other continents captured in dioramas and displays that are more like art than education, although education is an important part of the work done at this vibrant institute (it hosts a lot of music, art, and film events, too). Work should be well underway by now on the new first floor "Wonders of the World" exhibit, which owes more to Disneyworld than to the world of museum curators—passenger cars travel through simulations of a coral reef, a Caribbean storm, an African safari, underground volcanic eruptions, and the like. This is due to open in spring 1996 (at which point, expect a sharp increase in price). *230 Kensington High St.,* ☎ *0171/603–4535.* ☛ *£1 adults, 50p children.* ⏲ *Mon.–Sat. 10–5, Sun. 2–5; closed Good Fri., Dec. 24–26, Jan. 1. Tube: High St. Kensington.*

HYDE PARK AND KENSINGTON GARDENS

Numbers in the margin correspond to points of interest on the Hyde Park and Kensington Gardens map.

Many Londoners, not to mention visitors, love the city above all for its huge chunks of green, which cut right through the middle of town. The two we visit here together form by far the biggest of central London's royal parks. It's probably been centuries since any major royal had a casual stroll here, but the parks remain the property of the Crown, and it was the Crown that saved them from being devoured by the city's late-18th-century growth spurt.

★ Hyde Park, along with the smaller St. James's and Green Parks to the east, started as Henry VIII's hunting grounds.

He had no altruistic intent but—you could say—stole the land for his pleasure, from the monks at Westminster at the 1536 Dissolution of the Monasteries. James I was more generous and allowed the public in at the beginning of the 17th century, as long as they were "respectably dressed." Nowadays, as summer visitors can see, you may wear whatever you like—a bathing suit will do.

Hyde Park

Where else would you enter Hyde Park but at Hyde Park
Corner? The most impressive of the many entrances is here,
beside Apsley House (*see* Piccadilly *in* St. James's and Mayfair, *above*). Officially it's the Hyde Park Screen, but it's usu-
1 ally called **Decimus Burton's Gateway** because it was he who
designed this triple-arched monument in 1828. The next gate
along to the north was a 90th-birthday gift to Queen Elizabeth the Queen Mother (who is as old as the century), and
we don't know what she thought of it. Public reception of
2 the gaudy unicorns-and-lions-rampant **Queen Mother's
Gate,** wrought in scarlet-, cobalt-, white-, and gold-painted
metal, was derisive, but see what you think.

Your first landmark in all the greenery is a sand track that
3 runs along the south perimeter, called **Rotten Row.** It was
Henry VIII's royal path to the hunt—hence the name, a cor-
ruption of *route du roi.* Contemporary horses still use it,
ridden by the rich who own them, the fairly well-heeled who
hire them or the Household Cavalry who ride for the queen.
4 You can see the latter's **Knightsbridge Barracks**—a high rise
and a long, low, ugly red block—to the left. This is the
brigade that mounts the guard at the palace, and you can
see them leave to perform this duty, in full regalia, plumed
helmet and all, at around 10:30, or await the return of the
exhausted ex-guard about noon.

You can follow either Rotten Row or Serpentine Road
west, or you can stray over the grass, but the next landmark to find is the long, narrow, man-made (in 1730) lake,
5 the **Serpentine.** It is a beloved lake, much frequented in summer, when the south shore **Lido** resembles a beach and the
water is dotted with hired rowboats. If you rise very early,
you might catch the Serpentine Swimming Club—a band

Hyde Park and Kensington Gardens

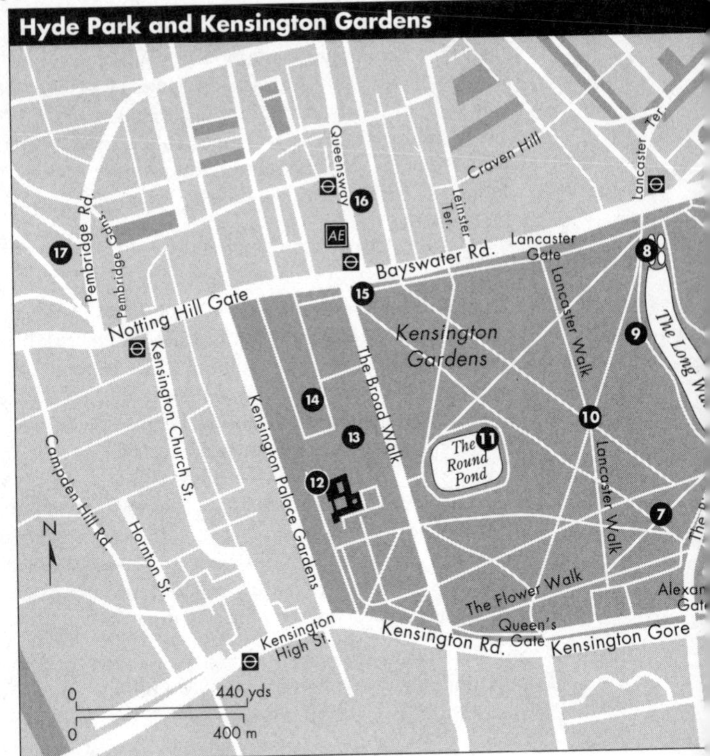

Black Lion Gate, **15**

Decimus Burton's Gateway, **1**

Elfin Oak, **14**

The Fountains, **8**

Kensington Palace, **12**

Knightsbridge Barracks, **4**

Peter Pan, **9**

Physical Energy, **10**

Portobello Road, **17**

Queen Mother's Gate, **2**

Queensway, **16**

Rotten Row, **3**

Round Pond, **11**

Serpentine, **5**

Serpentine Bridge, **6**

Serpentine Gallery, **7**

Sunken Garden, **13**

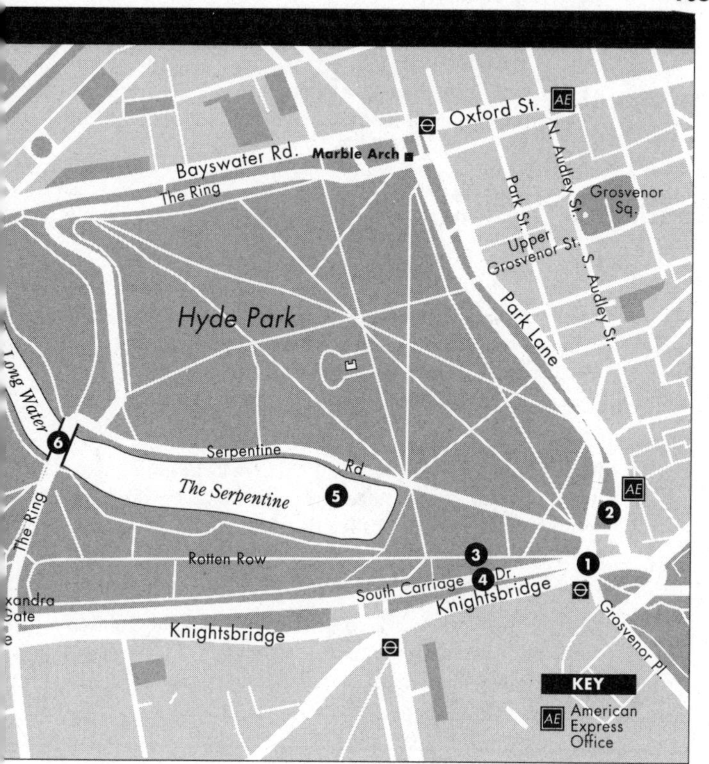
Oxford St.
Bayswater Rd.
Marble Arch
The Ring
N. Audley St.
Park St.
Grosvenor Sq.
Upper Grosvenor St.
S. Audley St.
Hyde Park
Park Lane
Long Water
Serpentine Rd.
The Serpentine
The Ring
Rotten Row
South Carriage Dr.
Knightsbridge
xandra Gate
Knightsbridge
Grosvenor Pl.
KEY
American Express Office

of eccentrics guaranteed to appear on TV at the first hard
frost each winter, since they dive in here at 6 AM every single day of the year, breaking the ice first if necessary. Walk
6 the bank and you will soon reach the picturesque stone **Serpentine Bridge,** built in 1826 by George Rennie.

Kensington Gardens

In passing the bridge, you leave Hyde Park and enter **Kens-
7 ington Gardens.** On the south side of the bridge is the **Serpentine Gallery,** which hangs several exhibitions of modern
work a year, often very avant-garde indeed, and always
worth a look. *Kensington Gardens,* ☎ *0171/402–6075.* ☛
Free. ⏲ *Daily 10–6; closed Christmas wk. Tube: Lancaster Gate.*

Kensington Gardens is more formal than its neighbor, since
it was first laid out as palace grounds. Continue along the
south bank of the lake, called the Long Water on this side
of the bridge, to the top, to reach the formal, paved Ital-
8 ian garden called, for obvious reasons, **The Fountains.**

On your way, you will have passed a statue that children
have loved since George Frampton cast it in 1912—a bronze
of the boy who lived on an island in the Serpentine and never
9 grew up, **Peter Pan.** His creator, J. M. Barrie, lived at 100
Bayswater Road, not 500 yards from here. There's another statue worth seeking southwest of Peter at the intersection of several paths: George Frederick Watts's 1904
10 bronze of a muscle-bound horse and rider, entitled **Physical Energy.**

Next on your westward stroll comes another water feature,
11 the **Round Pond,** a magnet for model-boat enthusiasts and
duck feeders. You may happen onto an exciting remote-con-
trolled shipwreck, or ice thick enough for skating, which
12 is allowed here. Next you reach **Kensington Palace** (*see* Kensington *in* Knightsbridge and Kensington, *above*), with an
13 early 19th-century **Sunken Garden** north of it, complete with
a living tunnel of lime trees and golden laburnam. **The
Broad Walk** between the pond and the palace runs south-
to-north, from the bottom to the top of the park. Following it all the way north to the Bayswater Road, you'll see,

on the left, a **playground** full of the kind of children who have nannies and whose nannies take them to the remains of a tree carved with scores of tiny woodland creatures, Ivor
14 Innes's **Elfin Oak.**

15 Leaving the park by **Black Lion Gate,** you are almost op-
16 posite Bayswater's main drag, **Queensway,** a rather peculiar, cosmopolitan street of ethnic confusion, late-night cafés and restaurants, a skating rink, and the Whiteleys shopping-and-movie mall. As you walk west, the Bayswater Road turns into **Notting Hill Gate,** the start of a happening neighborhood, a trendsetting square mile of multi-ethnicity, music, and markets, with lots of see-and-be-seen-in restaurants and the younger, more egalitarian and adventurous versions of the Cork Street commercial modern-art galleries.

17 The famous **Portobello Road** starts soon on the left and runs about a mile north. What it's famous for is its Saturday antiques market, which begins around Chepstow Villas and is lined by dozens of antiques shops and indoor markets, open most days. There's a strong West Indian flavor to Notting Hill, with a Trinidad-style **Carnival** centered along Portobello Road on the August bank-holiday weekend. *Tube: Notting Hill Gate, Ladbroke Grove.*

OTHER ATTRACTIONS

★ **The British Museum,** one of the world's greatest museums, is a monumental, severely Greek edifice, built in the first half of the 19th century. The vast collection of treasures here includes Egyptian, Greek, and Roman antiquities; Renaissance jewelry, pottery, coins, glass; and drawings from virtually every European school since the 15th century. It's best to concentrate on one area that particularly interests you or, alternatively, take one of the museum's guided tours, which cost £6 per person and last 1½ hours. Some of the highlights are the Elgin Marbles, sculptures from the Parthenon in Athens; the Rosetta Stone, which helped archaeologists decipher Egyptian hieroglyphics; and the Mildenhall Treasure, a cache of Roman silver found in East Anglia in 1842. *Great Russell St.,* ☎ *071/636-1555* *or 071/580-1788 (recorded information).* ☛ *Free.* ⏲ *Mon.–Sat. 10–5, Sun. 2:30–6.*

The Gardens of the Zoological Society of London, known simply as the Zoo, were founded over 150 years ago, absorbing over the years other collections, such as the royal menagerie, which used to be housed in the Tower of London. One fascinating exhibit is the Moonlight World, in the Charles Clore Pavilion. Here night conditions are simulated so that visitors can watch nocturnal animals during the day. *Regent's Park,* ☎ *071/722–3333.* ☛ *£6 adults, £4 children under 16, £5 senior citizens.* ⏲ *Summer, daily 9–6; winter, daily 10–4.*

Hampstead Heath in North London is a superb place for a walk. Join the kite-flyers on Parliament Hill Fields on the southern slopes of the heath throughout the year, and if there's snow get your hands on a toboggan—this is one of London's best tobogganing spots.

The London Planetarium, beside Madame Tussaud's, brings the night sky to life. There are also displays of holography and interactive videos. *Marylebone Rd.,* ☎ *071/486–1121.* ☛ *£3.80 adults, £2.40 children under 16, £2.95 senior citizens. Joint ticket with Madame Tussaud's, see above. Shows every 40 min; weekends 10:40–5:20, weekdays 12:40–4:40; extra shows during school vacations.*

Lincoln's Inn Fields is the capital's largest and oldest square—more like a small park—surrounded by handsome buildings. The magnificent 1806 portico on the south side fronts the Royal College of Surgeons. The square's great attraction, however, is **Sir John Soane's Museum,** one of the most idiosyncratic and fascinating museums in London. Sir John Soane, who lived here from 1790 to 1831, was a gifted architect and an avid collector. The exhibits include Hogarth's series of paintings *The Rake's Progress,* and the sarcophagus of the Egyptian emperor Seti I, which Soane bought for £2,000 after the British Museum refused it. *13 Lincoln's Inn Fields,* ☎ *071/405–2107.* ☛ *Free.* ⏲ *Tues.–Sat. 10–5; closed national holidays.*

Madame Tussaud's still maintains its position as one of London's most sought-after attractions, with an ever-changing parade of wax celebrities. Get there early to avoid the huge lines. *Marylebone Rd.,* ☎ *071/935–6861.* ☛ *£6.40 adults, £4.15 children under 16, £4.80 senior citizens. Joint ticket with Planetarium, £8.30 adults, £5.35 children, £6.40 senior citizens.* ⏲ *Easter–Sept., daily 9:30–5:30; Oct.–Easter, daily 10–5:30.*

3 Shopping

Shopping Districts

Camden Town

Crafts and vintage clothing markets and shops cluster in and around picturesque but over-renovated canalside buildings in this frenetic mecca for Generation X. Things are quieter midweek. It's a good place for boots and T-shirts, cheap leather jackets, ethnic crafts, antiques, and recycled trendywear.

Chelsea

Chelsea centers on the King's Road, which is no longer synonymous with ultra-fashion but still harbors some designer boutiques, plus antiques and home furnishings emporia.

Covent Garden

A something-for-everyone neighborhood. The restored 19th-century market building features mainly high-class clothing chain stores, plus good quality crafts stalls and design shops, with additional stalls selling vintage, army-surplus, and ethnic clothing around it. Neal Street and the surrounding alleys offer amazing gifts of every type—bikes, kites, tea, herbs, beads, hats . . . you name it. Floral Street and Long Acre have designer and chain-store fashion in equal measure. Good for people-watching, too.

Hampstead

For picturesque peace and quiet with your shopping, stroll around here midweek. Upscale clothing stores and representatives of the better chains share the half-dozen streets with cozy boutique-size shops for the home and stomach.

Kensington

Kensington Church Street features expensive antiques, plus a little fashion. The main drag, Kensington High Street, is a smaller, less crowded, and classier version of Oxford Street, with some good-quality mid-price clothing shops and larger stores at the eastern end.

Knightsbridge

Harrods dominates Brompton Road, but there's plenty more, especially for the well-heeled and fashion-conscious. Harvey Nichols is the top clothes stop, with many expensive designers' *boites* along Sloane Street. Walton Street and narrow Beauchamp (pronounced "beecham") Place offer more of the same, plus home furnishings and knickknacks, and Brompton Cross, at the start of Fulham Road, is the most design-conscious corner of London, with the Conran Shop and Joseph leading the field.

Mayfair

Here is Bond Street, Old and New, with desirable dress designers, jewelers, plus fine art (old and new) on Old Bond Street and Cork Street. South Molton Street has high-priced high-style fashion—especially at Browns—and the tailors of Savile Row are of worldwide repute.

Oxford Street

Crowded Oxford Street is past its prime and lined with tawdry disccunt shops. There are some good stores, however—particularly Selfridges, John Lewis, and Marks and Spencer—and interesting boutiques secreted in little St. Christopher's Place and Gees Court.

Piccadilly

Though the actual number of shops is small for a street of its length (Green Park takes up a lot of space), Piccadilly manages to fit in several quintessentially British emporia. Fortnum and Mason is its star, and the arcades are an elegant experience even for shop-phobics.

Regent Street

At right angles to Oxford Street, this wider, curvier version has another couple of department stores, including what is possibly London's most pleasant, Liberty's. Hamley's is the capital's toy center; other shops tend to be chain stores, or airline offices, though there are also shops selling china and bolts of English tweed. "West Soho," around Carnaby Street, stocks designer youth paraphernalia.

St. James's

Where the English gentleman shops. Here are hats, handmade shirts and shoes, silver shaving kits and hip flasks, as well as the Prince of Wales's aftershave supplier and possibly the world's best cheese shop. Nothing is cheap, in any sense.

Specialty Stores

Antiques

Antiquarius (131–141 King's Rd., SW3, ☎ 0171/351-5353), at the Sloane Square end of the King's Road, is an indoor antiques market with more than 200 stalls offering a wide variety of collectibles, including things that won't bust your baggage allowance: Art Deco brooches, meerschaum pipes, silver salt cellars . . .(*See* map B.)

Gray's Antique Market (58 Davies St., W1, ☎ 0171/629-7034) and **Gray's Mews** (1–7 Davies Mews, W1, ☎ 0171/629–7034) around the corner are conveniently central. Both assemble dealers specializing in everything from Sheffield plates to Chippendale furniture. Bargains are not impossible, and proper pedigrees are guaranteed. (*See* map A.)

China and Glass

English Wedgwood and Minton china are as collectible as they ever were, and most large department stores carry a selection, alongside lesser varieties with smaller price tags. Regent Street has several off-price purveyors, and, if you're in search of a bargain, Harrods's sale can't be beat.

Clothing

GENERAL

Aquascutum (100 Regent St., W1, ☎ 0171/734–6090) is known for its classic raincoats, but also stocks the garments to wear underneath, for both men and women. Style keeps up with the times but is firmly on the safe side, making this a good bet for solvent professionals with an antifashion attitude. (*See* map A.)

Burberrys (161–165 Regent St., W1, ☎ 0171/734–4060 and 18–22 The Haymarket, SW1, ☎ 0171/930–3343) have done their best to evoke an English Heritage ambience, with mahogany closets full of the trademark "Burberry Check" tartan. (*See* map A.)

Kensington Market (49–53 Kensington High St., W8, no general phone) is the diametric opposite of sober British stiff-upper-lip anti-fashion. For more than two decades it has been a principal purveyor of the constantly changing, frivolous, hip London street style. Hundreds of stalls—some shop-size, others tiny—are crammed into this build-

Shopping A (Mayfair, Soho, and Covent Garden)

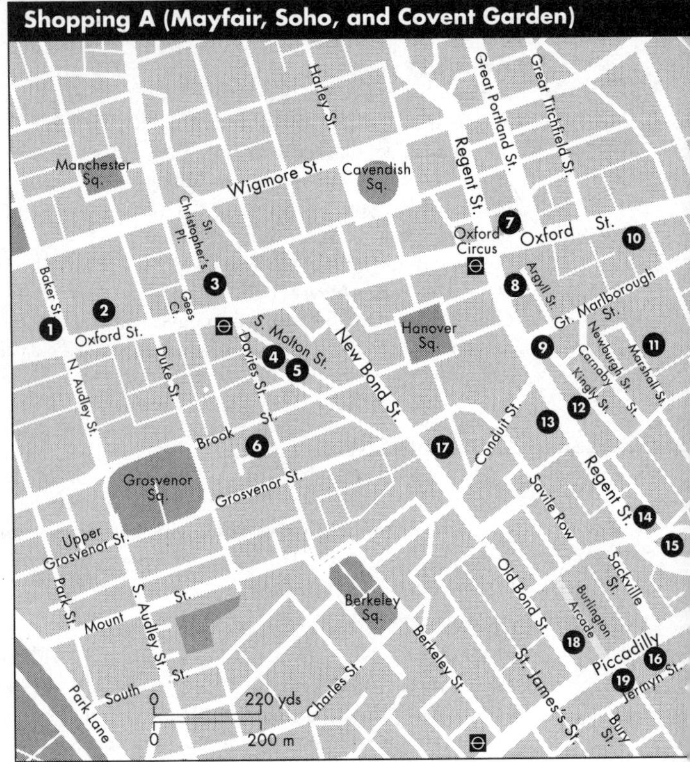

Aquascutum, **15**
Asprey's, **17**
Browns, **4**
Burberrys, **13, 21**
Butler and Wilson, **5**
Contemporary Applied Arts, **27**
Craftsmen Potters Shop, **11**
Fortnum & Mason, **19**
Garrard, **14**
Gray's Antique Market, **6**
Grosvenor Prints, **26**
Hamleys, **12**
The Irish Linen Co., **18**
Jigsaw, **29**
Liberty, **9**
The Linen Cupboard, **7**
Marks & Spencer, **1, 10**
Naturally British, **22**
Nicole Farhi, **3**
The Outlaws Club, **30**
Paul Smith, **28**
Penhaligon's, **24**
Selfridges, **2**
Simpson, **20**
The Tea House, **25**
Turnbull & Asser, **16**
Warehouse, **8**
Whistles, **23**

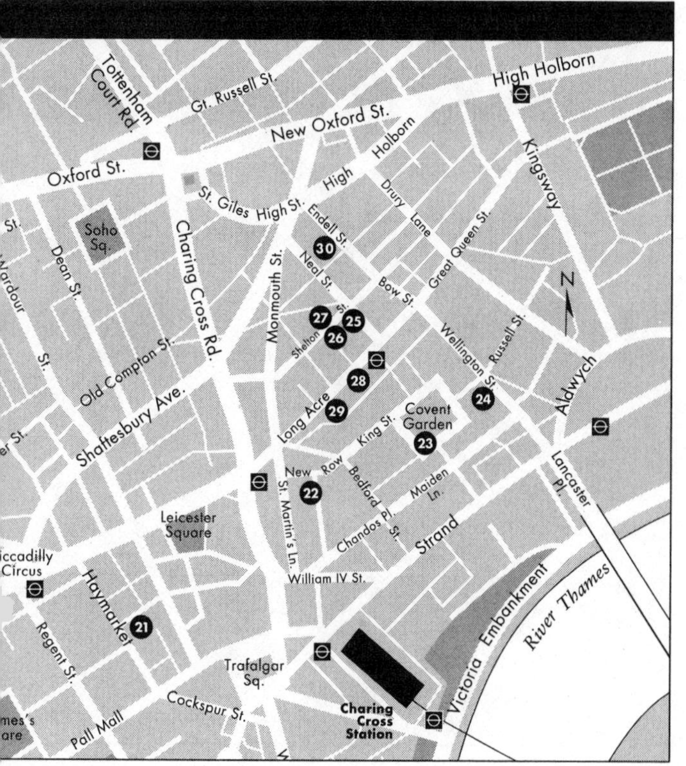

Tottenham Court Rd.
Gt. Russell St.
High Holborn
New Oxford St.
Oxford St.
High Holborn
St. Giles High St.
Drury Lane
Kingsway
Endell St.
Great Queen St.
Soho Sq.
Dean St.
Charing Cross Rd.
Monmouth St.
Neal St.
Bow St.
Wardour St.
Shelton St.
Wellington St.
Russell St.
Old Compton St.
Long Acre
Covent Garden
Aldwych
Shaftesbury Ave.
King St.
New Row
Bedford St.
Maiden Ln.
Lancaster Pl.
Leicester Square
St. Martin's Ln.
Chandos Pl.
Strand
Piccadilly Circus
William IV St.
Haymarket
Regent St.
Victoria Embankment
River Thames
Trafalgar Sq.
Cockspur St.
Charing Cross Station
Pall Mall
N
21
22
23
24
25
26
27
28
29
30

Shopping B (Kensington, Knightsbridge, and Chelsea)

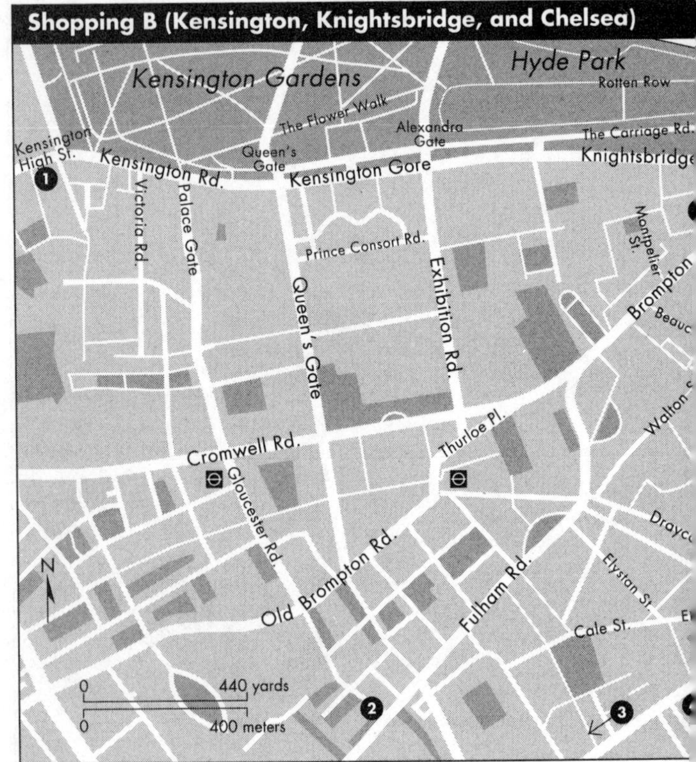

Antiquarius, **4**
Browns, **6**
Butler and Wilson, **2**
Hackett, **3**
Harrods, **5**
Harvey Nichols, **7**
Kensington Market, **1**
Warehouse, **8**

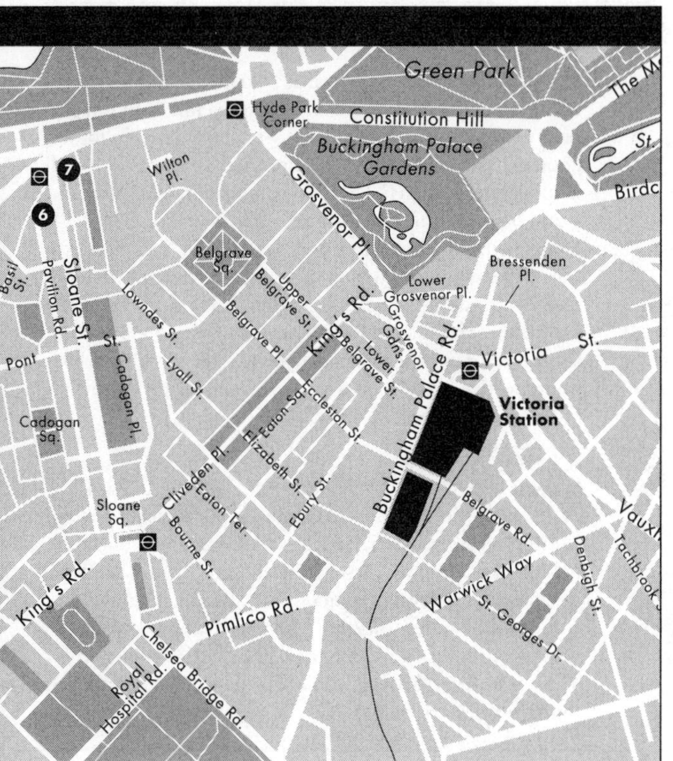
Green Park
Hyde Park Corner
Constitution Hill
Buckingham Palace Gardens
Wilton Pl.
7
6
Grosvenor Pl.
Belgrave Sq.
Basil St.
Pavilion Rd.
Sloane St.
Lowndes St.
Upper Belgrave St.
Lower Grosvenor Pl.
Bressenden Pl.
Belgrave Pl.
King's Rd.
Grosvenor Gdns.
Lower Belgrave St.
Buckingham Palace Rd.
Victoria St.
Pont St.
Cadogan Pl.
Lyall St.
Eaton Sq.
Eccleston St.
Victoria Station
Cadogan Sq.
Elizabeth St.
Cliveden Pl.
Eaton Ter.
Ebury St.
Sloane Sq.
Bourne St.
Belgrave Rd.
Denbigh St.
Tachbrook
Warwick Way
St. Georges Dr.
King's Rd.
Pimlico Rd.
Chelsea Bridge Rd.
Royal Hospital Rd.

ing, where you can get lost for hours trying to find the good bits. (*See* map B.)

Marks & Spencer (458 Oxford St., W1, ☎ 0171/935–7954, and branches) is a major chain of stores that's an integral part of the British way of life—sturdy practical clothes, good materials and workmanship, and basic accessories, all at moderate, though not bargain basement, prices. All of England buys their underwear here. (*See* map A.)

Simpson (203 Piccadilly, W1, ☎ 0171/734–2002) is a quiet, pleasant store with a thoughtful variety of designer and leisure wear, luggage, and gifts. It is the home of the Daks' brand of classic British design. There are a barbershop, restaurant, and wine bar here, plus the most disturbing nonreflective glass in its windows on Piccadilly. It's just a block west of Piccadilly Circus. (*See* map A.)

WOMEN'S WEAR

Browns (23–27 South Molton St., W1, ☎ 0171/491–7833) was the first notable store to populate the South Molton Street pedestrian mall, and seems to sprout more offshoots every time you see it. Well-established, collectible designers (Jean Muir, Donna Karan, Romeo Gigli, Jasper Conran, Jil Sander) rub shoulder pads here with younger, funkier names (Dries Van Noten, Jean Paul Gaultier, Yohji Yamamoto), and Browns also has its own label. Its July and January sales are famed. Also at 6C Sloane St., SW1 (☎ 0171/493–4232). (*See* both maps.)

Jigsaw (21 Long Acre, Covent Garden, WC2, ☎ 0171/240–3855, and other branches) is popular for its separates that don't sacrifice quality to fashion, are reasonably priced, and suit women in their twenties to forties. (*See* map A.)

Nicole Farhi (25–26 St. Christopher's Pl., W1, ☎ 0171/486–3416; also at 27 Hampstead High St., NW3, ☎ 0171/435–0866 and other branches), suits the career woman who requires quality, cut, *and* style in a suit, plus weekend wear in summer linens and silks, or winter hand-knit woolens. Prices are on the high side, but there is some affordable wear as well, especially the sporty, casual Diversion range. Farhi offers an equally desirable men's line. (*See* map A.)

Warehouse (19 Argyll St., W1, ☎ 0171/437–7101, and other branches) stocks practical, stylish, reasonably priced separates in easy fabrics and lots of fun colors. The finishing isn't so hot, but style, not substance, counts here, and the shop's youthful fans don't seem to mind. The stock changes very quickly, so it always presents a new face to the world. (*See* both maps.)

Whistles (The Market, Covent Garden, WC2, ☎ 0171/379–7401; also at Heath St., Hampstead, ☎ 0171/431–2395, and other branches) is a small chain stocking its own high-fashion, mid-price label, plus sever1al European (mostly French) designers. Clothes are hung color-coordinated in shops like designers' ateliers. (*See* map A.)

MEN'S WEAR

Hackett (65B New King's Rd., SW6, ☎ 0171/371–7964, and branches) started as a posh thrift store, recycling cricket flannels, hunting pinks, Oxford brogues, and similar Britishwear. Now they make their own, and they have become a genuine—and very good—gentlemen's outfitters. (*See* map B.)

Paul Smith (41 Floral St., WC2, ☎ 0171/379–7133) is your man if you don't want to look outlandish but you're bored with plain pants and sober jackets. His well-tailored suits have a subtle quirkiness, his shirts and ties a sense of humor, and his jeans and sweats a good cut. (*See* map A.)

Turnbull & Asser (70 Jermyn St., W1, ☎ 0171/930–0502) is *the* custom shirtmaker. Unfortunately for those of average means, the first order must be for a minimum of six shirts, from around £100 each. But there's a range of less expensive, still exquisitely made ready-to-wear shirts, too. (*See* map A.)

Crafts

Some of the best British potters joined to found the **Craftsmen Potters Shop** (7 Marshall St., W1, ☎ 0171/437–7605) as a cooperative venture to market their wares. The result is a store that carries a wide spectrum of the potter's art, from thoroughly practical pitchers, plates, and bowls to ceramic sculptures. Prices range from the reasonable to way up. (*See* map A.)

At **Contemporary Applied Arts** (43 Earlham St., WC2, ☎ 0171/836–6993), a mixed bag of designers and craftspeople displaying their wares over two floors. Anything from glassware and jewelry to furniture and lighting can be found here. (*See* map A.)

The Glasshouse (21 St. Albans Pl., N1, ☏ 0171/359–8162. Tube: Angel) is off our map, but for indigenous glassware it's about the only place, and you could drop in while visiting nearby Camden Passage. See glass being blown, by several artists, then buy it.

Naturally British (13 New Row, WC2, ☏ 0171/240–0551) stocks the traditional end of the crafts spectrum, with items made by woodcarvers and leather toolers and silversmiths and knitters across the British Isles. Here you can find Aran sweaters, Celtic silver, Dorset cream fudge, and Welsh woolen blankets without leaving town. (*See* map A.)

Gifts

Investigate the possibilities in the shops attached to the major museums, most of which offer far more than racks of souvenir postcards these days. Some of the best are at the **British Museum,** the **V&A,** the **Royal Academy,** and the **London Transport Museum.**

Fortnum & Mason (181 Piccadilly, W1, ☏ 0171/734–8040), the queen's grocer, is, paradoxically, the most egalitarian of gift stores, with plenty of irresistibly packaged luxury foods, stamped with the gold "by appointment" crest, for under £5. Try the teas, preserves, blocks of chocolate, tins of pâté, or a box of Duchy Originals oatcakes—like Paul Newman, the Prince of Wales has gone into the retail food business with these. (*See* map A.)

Hamley's (188–196 Regent St., W1, ☏ 0171/734–3161) has six floors of toys and games for both children and adults. The huge stock ranges from traditional teddy bears to computer games and all the latest technological gimmickry. Try to avoid it at Christmas, when police have to rope off a section of Regent Street for Hamleys customers. (*See* map A.)

Penhaligon's (41 Wellington St., WC2, ☏ 0171/836–2150; also at 16 Burlington Arcade, W1, ☏ 0171/629–1416, and branches) was established by William Penhaligon, court barber at the end of Queen Victoria's lengthy reign. He blended perfumes and toilet waters in the back of his shop, using essential oils and natural, often exotic ingredients, and you can buy the very same formulations today, along with soaps, talcs, bath oils, and accessories, with the strong whiff of Victoriana both inside and outside the pretty bottles and boxes. (*See* map A.)

The Tea House (15A Neal St., WC2, ☎ 0171/240–7539) purveys everything to do with the British national drink; you can dispatch your entire gift list here. Alongside every variety of tea—including strange or rare brews like orchid, banana, Japanese Rice, and Russian Caravan—are teapots in the shape of a British bobby or a London taxi, plus books, and what the shop terms "teaphernalia"—strainers, trivets, and infusers, and other gadgets that need explaining. (*See* map A.)

Jewelry

Asprey's (165–169 New Bond St., W1, ☎ 0171/493–6767) has been described as the "classiest and most luxurious shop in the world." It offers a range of exquisite jewelry and gifts, both antique and modern. If you're in the market for a six-branched Georgian candelabrum or a six-carat emerald-and-diamond brooch, you won't be disappointed. (*See* map A.)

Butler and Wilson (20 South Molton St., W1, ☎ 0171/409–2955; 189 Fulham Rd., SW3, ☎ 0171/352–8255) is designed to set off its irresistible costume jewelry to the very best advantage—against a dramatic black background. It has some of the best displays in town, and keeps very busy marketing silver, diamanté, French gilt, and pearls by the truckload. (*See* both maps.)

Garrard (112 Regent St., W1, ☎ 0171/734–7020) has connections with the royal family going back to 1722 and are still in charge of the upkeep of the Crown Jewels. But they are also family jewelers, and offer an enormous range of items, from antique to modern. (*See* map A.)

Outlaws Club (49 Endell St., WC2, ☎ 0171/379–6940) stocks the work of around 100 designers, with prices ranging from a few pounds up to £200. The dominant style is avant-garde, meaning that this shop has been a favorite with fashion writers for a decade. (*See* map A.)

Linen

Irish Linen Co. (35–36 Burlington Arcade, W1, ☎ 0171/493–8949) is a tiny store bursting with crisp, embroidered linen for the table, the bed, and the nose. Exquisite handkerchiefs should be within reach of everyone's pocket. (*See* map A.)

Linen Cupboard (21 Great Castle St., W1, ☎ 0171/629–4062) is stacked with piles of sheets and towels of all sorts and has by far the lowest-priced fine Irish linens and Egyptian cottons in town. (*See* map A.)

Prints

Grosvenor Prints (28–32 Shelton St., WC2, ☎ 0171/836–1979) sells antiquarian prints, but with an emphasis on views and architecture of London—and dogs! It's an eccentric collection, and the prices range widely, but the stock is so odd that you are bound to find something interesting and unusual to meet both your budget and your taste. (*See* map A.)

Department Stores

You will recognize **Liberty** (200 Regent St., W1, ☎ 0171/734–1234) by its wonderful black-and-white mock-Tudor facade, a peacock among pigeons in humdrum Regent Street. Inside, it is a labyrinthine building, full of nooks and crannies, all stuffed with goodies like a dream of an eastern bazaar. Famous principally for its fabrics, it also has an Oriental department, rich with color; men's wear that tends to the traditional; and women's wear that has lately been spiced up with extra designer ranges. It is a hard store to resist, where you may well find an original gift—especially one made from those classic Liberty prints. (*See* map A.)

Selfridges (400 Oxford St., W1, ☎ 0171/629–1234) was started earlier this century by an American. This giant, bustling store is London's upscale version of Macy's. If this all-rounder has an outstanding department, it has to be its Food Hall, onto which attention has lately been lavished—or else its frenetic cosmetics department, which seems to perfume the air the whole length of Oxford Street. In recent years, Selfridges has made a specialty of high-profile popular designer fashion. Even more important for the visitor to town, there's a branch of the London Tourist Board on the premises, a theater ticket counter, and a branch of Thomas Cook, the travel agent, in the basement. (*See* map A.)

Harrods (87 Brompton Rd., SW1, ☎ 0171/730–1234), being the only English department store classed among monuments and museums on every visitor's list, hardly needs an introduction. In fact, its Englishness is tentative these days, since it is owned by the Egyptian Al Fayed brothers—but who cares? It is swanky and plush and deep-carpeted as ever, its spectacular food halls alone are worth the trip, and it stands out from the pack for fashion these days, too. You can forgive the store its immodest motto, *Omnia, omnibus, ubique* ("everything, for everyone, everywhere"), since there are more than 230 departments, including a pet shop rumored to supply aardvarks to zebras on request, and the toy department—sorry, *kingdom*—which does the same for plush versions. During the pre-Christmas period and the sales, the entire store is a menagerie. (*See* map B.)

Harvey Nichols (109 Knightsbridge, SW1, ☎ 0171/235–5000) is just a few blocks from Harrods, but is not competing on the same turf, since its passion is fashion, all the way. There are five floors of it, including departments for dressing homes and men, but the woman who invests in her wardrobe is the main target. Accessories are strong suits, especially jewelry, scarves, and make-up—England's first MAC (a trendy brand of make-up) counter here was 10-deep for months. The Fifth Floor restaurant is a serious dining option too. (*See* map B.)

Street Markets

Camden Lock Market (NW1). Visit the lock on a sunny August Sunday if you want your concept of a crowd redefined. Camden is actually several markets gathered around a pair of locks in the Regent's Canal, and was once very pretty. Now that further stalls and a new faux warehouse have been inserted into the surrounding brick railway buildings, the haphazard charm of the place is largely lost, although the variety of merchandise is mind-blowing—vintage and new clothes (design stars have been discovered here), antiques and junk, jewelry and scarves, candlesticks, ceramics, mirrors, toys . . . But underneath it's really a meat market for hip teens. The neighborhood is bursting with shops and cafés, and further markets, and is a whole lot calmer, if stall-free, midweek. *Take the tube or Bus 24 or 29 to Camden Town. Shops open Tues.–Sun. 9:30–5:30, stalls weekends 8–6.*

Petticoat Lane (Middlesex St., E1). Actually, Petticoat Lane doesn't exist, and this Sunday clothing and fashion market centers on Middlesex Street, then sprawls in several directions, including east to Brick Lane. Between them, the crammed streets turn up items of dubious parentage (CD players, bikes, car radios), alongside clothes (vintage, new, and just plain tired), jewelry, books, underwear, antiques, woodworking tools, bed linens, jars of pickles, and outright junk in one of London's most entertaining diversions. *Liverpool St., Aldgate, or Aldgate East tubes are the closest.* ⏲ *Sun. 9–2.*

Portobello Market (Portobello Rd., W11). London's most famous market still wins the prize for the all-round best. It sits in a most lively and multicultural part of town, the 1,500-odd antiques dealers don't rip you off, and it stretches over a mile, changing character completely as it goes. The top (Notting Hill Gate) end is antiques-land (with shops midweek); the middle is where locals buy fruit and veg, and hang out in trendy restaurants; the section under the elevated highway called the Westway boasts the best flea market in town; and then it tails off into a giant rummage sale among record stores, vintage clothing boutiques, and art galleries. *Take Bus 52 or the tube to Ladbroke Grove or Notting Hill Gate. Fruit and vegetables Mon.–Wed. and Fri. 8–5, Thurs. 8–1; antiques Fri. 8–3; both on Sat. 6–5.*

VAT Refunds

To the eternal fury of Britain's storekeepers, who struggle under cataracts of paperwork, Britain is afflicted with a 17½% Value Added Tax. Foreign visitors, however, need not pay VAT if they take advantage of the Personal Export Scheme. Of the various ways to get a VAT refund, the most common are **Over the Counter** and **Direct Export.** Note that though practically all larger stores operate these schemes, information about them is not always readily forthcoming, so it is important to ask. Once you have gotten on the right track, you'll find that almost all of the larger

DURING THE PAST, OH, EIGHT YEARS, London has undergone an incredible transformation. The city is now—and absentees must suspend disbelief here—among the ·s in the world for dining out. A new generation ıas emerged, weaned in restaurants and familiar :uisines of six continents. They watch each other's ı cross-pollinate. Collectively they've precipitated yle of cooking, which you could call "London," ıost have dubbed it "Modern British."

ıre the current healthy restaurant scene crystallized, e waves of immigrants had done their best to help ıut. There are a handful still extant of the vener- ch and Italian places that were once the last word and there are still the thousands of (mostly north- an restaurants that have long ensured that Lon- see a good tandoori as their birthright. -Cantonese, mostly—places in London's tiny Chi- ıave been around a long time, too, as have Greek Thai restaurants are the latest to proliferate. ı, Spanish, a hint of Japanese, Russian, and Ko- :s have also been opening. After all this, traditional ıod, lately revived from its deathbed, appears as exotic cuisine in the pantheon.

ɔst, the democratization of restaurants means ıecks than during the '80s, with many experi- fixed-price menus, but still London is not an in- : city. Damage-control methods include making ır main meal—the very top places often have bar- h menus, halving the price of evening à la carte— ring a second appetizer instead of an entrée, to ȷ places should object. Seek out fixed-price menus, h for hidden extras on the check: "cover," bread :ables charged separately, and service.

taurants exclude service charges from the menu ıe law obliges them to display outside), then add % to the check or else stamp SERVICE NOT IN- long the bottom, in which case you should add -15% yourself. Don't pay twice for service—un-

stores have export departments that will be able to give you all the help you need.

The easiest and most usual way of getting your refund is the **Over the Counter** method. There is normally a minimum of £75, below which VAT cannot be refunded. You must also be able to supply proof of your identity—your passport is best. The salesclerk will then fill out the necessary paperwork, Form 407 VAT. (Be sure to get an addressed envelope as well.) Keep the form and give it to customs when you leave the country. Lines at major airports are usually long, so leave plenty of time, and pack the goods you have purchased in your carry-on bags—you'll need to be able to produce them. The form will then be returned to the store and the refund forwarded to you, minus a small service charge, usually around $3. You can specify how you want the refund. Generally, the easiest way is to have it credited to your charge card. Alternatively, you can have it in the form of a sterling check, but your bank will charge a fee to convert it. Note also that it can take up to eight weeks to receive the refund.

The **Direct Export** method—whereby you have the store send the goods to your home—is more cumbersome. You must have the VAT Form 407 certified by customs, police, or a notary public when you get home and then send it back to the store. They, in turn, will refund your money.

If you are traveling to any other European Union country from Britain, the same rules apply, except in France, where you can claim your refund as you leave the country.

However, in 1988 the **Tourist Tax-Free Shopping** service came into operation. This service, which uses special VAT refund vouchers, rather than Form 407, expedites your refund, provided that you make your purchases at a store (identified by the red, white, and blue Tax-Free for Tourists sign) offering the service. If you are going on from Britain to the Continent, you can even get cash refunds. Full details and a list of stores offering the Tax-Free service are available from the British Tourist Authority (40 W. 57th St., New York, NY 10019, ☎ 800/452–2748) and the British Travel Centre (12 Regent St., London SW1Y 4PQ).

Clothing Sizes

Men

Suit and shirt sizes in the United Kingdom and the Republic of Ireland are the same as U.S. sizes.

Women

DRESSES/COATS

U.S.	4	6	8	10	12	14	16
U.K./ Ireland	6	8	10	12	14	16	18

BLOUSES/SWEATERS

U.S.	30	32	34	36	38	40	42
U.K./ Ireland	32	34	36	38	40	42	44

SHOES

U.S.	4	5	6	7	8	9	10
U.K./ Ireland	2	3	4	5	6	7	8

4 Res
anc

longtim
top pla
of chefs
with the
work a
a fresh
though

Even be
successi
the city
able Fre
in fancy
ern) In
doners
Chinese
natown
taverna
Malaysi
rean pla
British
one mo

As for
lighter
ments i
expensi
lunch y
gain lur
and or
which f
and wa
and veg

Most re
(which
10%–1
CLUDED
the 10%

scrupulous restaurateurs may add service, then leave the total in the credit card slip blank, hoping for more.

One final caveat: beware of Sunday. Many restaurants are closed on this day, especially in the evening; likewise public holidays. Over the Christmas period, London shuts down completely—only hotels will be prepared to feed you. When in doubt, call ahead.

CATEGORY	COST*
$$$$	over £45
$$$	£30–£45
$$	£15–£30
$	under £15

**per person for a three-course meal, excluding drinks, service, and VAT*

Mayfair

French

$$$$ ★ **Le Gavroche.** Albert Roux has handed the toque to his son, Michel, but many still consider this London's finest restaurant. The excellent service and the discreetly sumptuous decor complement the positively Lucullan *haute cuisine*—seafood velouté with champagne, lobster roasted with cépes and rosemary. The basement dining room is comfortable and serious, hung with oil paintings, its darkness intensified by racing-green walls. Yet again, the set lunch is relatively affordable at £36 (for canapés and three courses, plus mineral water, a half-bottle of wine, coffee, and petit fours, service). In fact, it's the only way to eat here if you don't have a generous expense account at your disposal—as most patrons do. ✕ *43 Upper Brook St., W1,* ☎ *0171/408–0881. Reservations advised at least 1 wk in advance. Jacket and tie. AE, DC, MC, V. Closed weekends, 10 days at Christmas, national holidays. Tube: Marble Arch.*

Mediterranean

$$ **Zoe.** Handy for West End shopping, this two-level place serves two-level food—proper dinners downstairs in a sunlit basement of jazzy colors; and posh cocktails, coffee, and sandwiches ("hot spicy pork with prunes and crispy bacon" is typical) upstairs. It's another Antony Worrall Thompson place (*see* Bistrot 190 in South Kensington, *below*) and so features the trademark heartiness. The schizophrenic restaurant menu is half smart "City" dishes (corn crab cakes, poached eggs, hollandaise, and wilted greens), half huge "Country" ensembles (poached ham, parsley sauce, pease pudding, and hot potato salad), most offered in two sizes, rendering decisions impossible. ✕ *St. Christopher's Pl., W1,* ☏ *0171/224–1122. Reservations advised. AE, DC, MC, V. Closed Sat. lunch, Sun. (bar open 7 days), Christmas. Tube: Bond St.*

Mexican

$ **Down Mexico Way.** Many of London's proliferating Mexican joints serve horrid food, but this one's good. The fine lumpy guacamole is fresh, not factory-packed, and amongst the usual tortillas and burritos are a few adventurous numbers like fish in almond-chili sauce, with sides of cheese and jalapeño muffins or spiced spinach. Look for the beautiful Spanish ceramic tiles and avoid evenings if you want a quiet night out—the place is often taken over by party animals. ✕ *25 Swallow St., W1,* ☏ *0171/437–9895. Reservations advised. AE, MC, V. Closed Dec. 25–26. Tube: Piccadilly Circus.*

Modern British

$$$ ★ **Le Caprice.** Secreted in a small street behind the Ritz, Caprice may command the deepest loyalty of any London restaurant, because it gets everything right: The glamorous, glossy black Eva Jiricna interior, the perfect pitch of the informal but respectful service, the food, halfway between Euro-peasant and fashion plate. This food—crispy duck and watercress salad; seared scallops with bacon and sorrel; risotto nero; Lincolnshire sausage with bubble-and-squeak (potato-and-cabbage hash); grilled rabbit with black olive polenta; and divine desserts too—is superb, but the other reason everyone comes here is for the best people-watching in town. (Also try sister restaurant, the Ivy; *see* Covent Garden, *below.*) ✕ *Arlington House, Arlington St., SW1,* ☏ *0171/629–2239. Reservations required. AE, DC, MC, V. Closed Sat. lunch. Tube: Green Park.*

$$$ **Quaglino's.** Sir Terence Conran—of Bibendum, Conran Shop, Cantina del Ponte, and Pont de la Tour fame (*see below*)—lavished £2.5 million doing up this famous

pre–World War II haunt of the rich, bored, and well-connected. Now in its fourth year, "Quags" is *the* out-of-towners' post-theater or celebration destination, while Londoners like its late hours. The gigantic sunken restaurant boasts a glamorous staircase, "Crustacea Altar," large bar, and live jazz music. The food is fashionably pan-European with some Oriental trimmings—crab with mirin and soy; noodles with ginger, chili and cilantro; rabbit with prosciutto and herbs; roast crayfish; plateaux de fruits de mer. Desserts come from somewhere between the Paris bistro and the English nursery (raspberry sablé pastry, parkin pudding with butterscotch sauce), and wine from the Old World and the New, some bottles at modest prices. ✕ *16 Bury St., SW1,* ☎ *0171/930–6767. Reservations required. AE, DC, MC, V. Closed Christmas. Tube: Green Park.*

$$$ **The Square.** For sublime dining in St. James's, here's your third opportunity. Young chef Philip Howard's sophisticated food is matched by an understated tall white room, punctuated with gold and primary-colored squares. The menu changes every five minutes, but features a lot from the sea, and game fowl, all with its soul mate on the side: Sweet and sour scallops and spiced squid; saddle of rabbit and *tarte fine* of onions; then roast Tuscan pigeon paired with *trompettes* and balsamic vinegar; sautée of john dory with pesto noodles and sauce *vierge*. Desserts are subtle—vanilla cream with red fruit compote, or a pile of crème brûlée with its sugar crust balanced on top, in a perfect square. Worldwide wines are grouped by grape and are not overpriced; wait staff is knowledgeable, likeable, and efficient. ✕ *32 King St., SW1,* ☎ *0171/839–8787. Reservations required. AE, MC, V. Closed weekend lunch, Dec. 24, 25. Tube: Green Park.*

$ ★ **Criterion.** This palatial neo-Byzantine mirrored marble hall, which first opened in 1874, is now back on the map. When the huge blue-lit glass clock says 2:30, it's teatime; otherwise you can choose from a commendably unpretentious "nouveau Brit" menu of appetizers like grilled squid on spinach with lemon vinaigrette, or penne and mussels in a fennel cream, then entrées such as cod and crab cakes, or grilled tuna with mushroom chutney. More London restaurants should copy the Criterion's generous attitude toward set-price dining: About half the dishes on the main menu

Dining in Mayfair, St. James's, Soho, Covent Garden, and

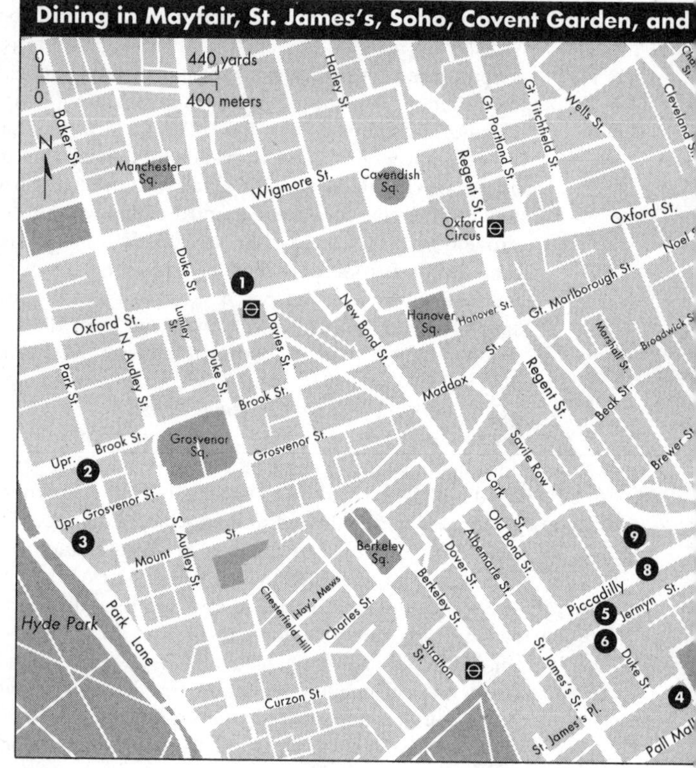

Alastair Little, **11**
Bahn Thai, **12**
Bertorelli's, **24**
Bistrot Bruno, **13**
Café Flo, **20**
Criterion, **7**
dell'Ugo, **10**
Down Mexico Way, **9**
Fatboy's Diner, **22**
Food for Thought, **16**
The Fountain, **5**
Fung Shing, **14**
Green's Restaurant and Oyster Bar, **6**
The Ivy, **15**
Joe Allen's, **23**
Le Gavroche, **2**
Le Palais du Jardin, **3**
Mandeer, **18**
Maxwell's, **25**
Mulligans, **11**
Quaglino's, **8**
Rules, **21**
The Square, **4**
Wagamama, **19**
White Tower, **17**
Zoe, **1**

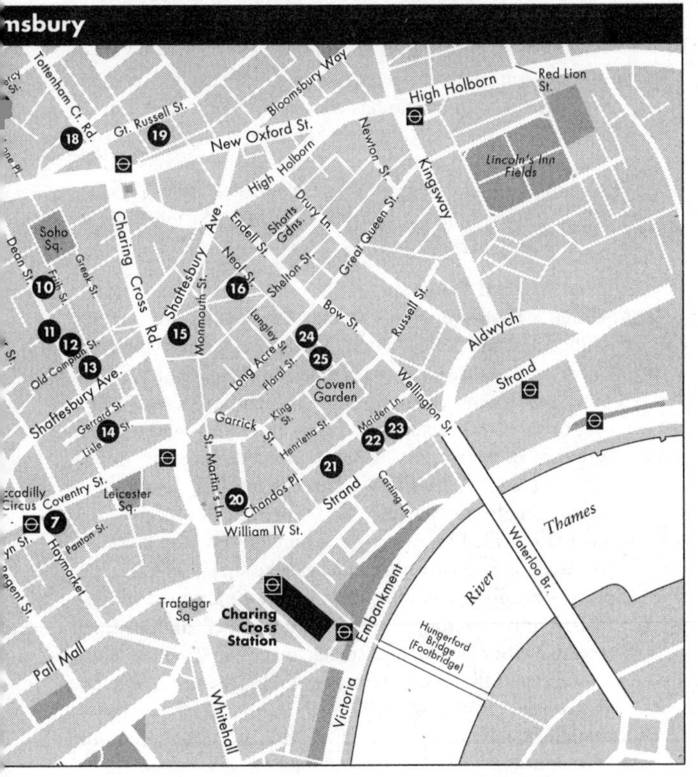

msbury
Tottenham Ct. Rd.
Gt. Russell St.
Bloomsbury Way
High Holborn
Red Lion St.
New Oxford St.
Newton St.
Kingsway
Lincoln's Inn Fields
High Holborn
Drury Ln.
Shorts Gdns.
Endell St.
Charing Cross Rd.
Shaftesbury Ave.
Soho Sq.
Dean St.
Frith St.
Greek St.
Neal St.
Shelton St.
Great Queen St.
Monmouth St.
Langley
Bow St.
Russell St.
Aldwych
Old Compton St.
Long Acre St.
Floral St.
Covent Garden
Wellington St.
Strand
Shaftesbury Ave.
Gerrard St.
Lisle St.
Garrick St.
King St.
Henrietta St.
Maiden Ln.
St. Martin's Ln.
Chandos Pl.
Strand
Carting Ln.
Piccadilly Circus
Coventry St.
Leicester Sq.
Haymarket
Panton St.
William IV St.
Thames
Waterloo Br.
River
Regent St.
Trafalgar Sq.
Charing Cross Station
Embankment
Hungerford Bridge (Footbridge)
Pall Mall
Victoria
Whitehall

are offered at £10 for two courses, any time (desserts like sticky toffee pudding or lemon tart are an extra £4.50 or so). Cooking and service, though not seamless, are certainly more assured than one has a right to expect at the price, and this is a pretty setting to while away a wet Sunday over the noon-to-5:30 brunch. Altogether a welcome oasis in the Piccadilly desert. ✕ *Piccadilly Circus, W1,* ☏ *0171/925–0909. Reservations advised. AE, DC, MC, V. Closed Christmas. Tube: Piccadilly Circus.*

Traditional English

$$$$ **Green's Restaurant and Oyster Bar.** The oyster side of things and the comfy-wood-paneled-restaurant angle are in equal balance at this reliable purveyor of the British dining experience, complete with the whiff of public (meaning private and exclusive) school, and its former inmates. Oysters, of course, are served (and they're not only in season whenever there's an "R" in the month), in two varieties, "small" or "large," alongside smoked fish, lobster cocktail, grilled sole, fish cakes, and so on, but there are comforting English unfishy dishes, like shepherd's pie, too, and—the proper ending to a nanny-sanctioned meal—warm and fattening "nursery puddings," like steamed sponge with custard, and treacle tart. The wine list is notable, especially in the champagne region. ✕ *36 Duke St., St. James's, SW1,* ☏ *0171/930–4566. Reservations required. Jacket and tie. AE, DC, MC, V. Closed Sun. dinner, national holidays. Tube: Green Park.*

$ ★ **The Fountain.** At the back of Fortnum & Mason is this old-fashioned restaurant, frumpy and popular as a boarding school matron, serving delicious light meals, toasted snacks, sandwiches, and ice-cream sodas. During the day, go for the Welsh rarebit or cold game pie; in the evening, a no-frills fillet steak is a typical option. Just the place for afternoon tea and ice-cream sundaes after the Royal Academy or Bond Street shopping, or for pre-theater meals. ✕ *181 Piccadilly, W1,* ☏ *0171/734–4938. Reservations accepted for dinner only. AE, DC, MC, V. Closed Sun., national holidays. Tube: Green Park.*

Soho

Chinese

$$ ★ **Fung Shing.** This comfortable, cool green restaurant is a cut above the Lisle/Wardour Street crowd in both service and ambience, as well as in food. The usual Chinatown options are supplemented by some exciting dishes. Salt-baked chicken, served on or off the bone with an accompanying bowl of intense broth, is essential, and the adventurous might try intestines—deep-fried cigarette-shaped morsels, far more delicious than you'd think. ✕ *15 Lisle St., WC2,* ☎ *0171/437–1539. Reservations suggested. AE, DC, MC, V. Closed Dec. 25. Tube: Leicester Sq.*

French

$$ ★ **Bistrot Bruno.** Bruno is Bruno Loubet, who won acclaim at the Four Seasons, opened L'Odeon in Regent Street too late for us to check out, and who is one of London's most dedicated and original chefs. Though Loubet doesn't cook here, the menu is unmistakably his work, dotted with bits of animals you wouldn't want in your freezer, which in his hands become balanced, beautiful *cuisine du terroir* dishes. His *fromage de tête*, or brawn (a pâté from the Lorraine made from pig's head in aspic), or tripes niçoise (cow's stomach, frankly) may not sound appetizing, but on the plate, they are irresistible. Cowards can order smoked fish cannelloni; sautéed rabbit with Swiss chard, olives and rosemary; salt cod on ministrone vegetables, then an iced meringue and cherry slice. Coffee arrives with mini-sorbets encased in chocolate. Next door is the bargain Café Bruno. ✕ *63 Frith St., W1,* ☎ *0171/734–4545. Reservations required. MC, V. Closed Sat. lunch, Sun., Christmas. Tube: Leicester Sq.*

Mediterranean

$$ **dell'Ugo.** A three-floor Mediterranean café-restaurant from the stable of Antony Worrall Thompson (*see* Bistrot 190 in South Kensington, *below*). You can choose light fare—bruschetta loaded with marinated vegetables, mozzarella, Parmesan etc., Tuscan soups, and country bread—or feast on wintry, warming one-pot ensembles and large platefuls of sunny dishes like spicy sausages and white bean casserole with onion confit. The place gets overrun with hor-

mone-swapping youth some weekends, but trendiness, on the whole, doesn't mar pleasure. ✕ *56 Frith St., W1,* ☎ *0171/734–8300. Reservations required for restaurant, not taken for café. AE, MC, V. Closed Sun., Christmas. Tube: Leicester Sq.*

Modern British

$$$ ★ **Alastair Little.** Little is one of London's most original chefs, drawing inspiration from practically everywhere—Thailand, Japan, Scandinavia, France—and bringing it off brilliantly. His restaurant is starkly modern, so all attention focuses on the menu, which changes not once but twice daily in order to take advantage of the best ingredients. There will certainly be fish, but other than that it's hard to predict. Anyone truly interested in food will not be disappointed. ✕ *49 Frith St., W1,* ☎ *0171/734–5183. Reservations advised. No credit cards. Closed weekends, national holidays, 2 wks at Christmas, 3 wks in Aug. Tube: Leicester Sq.*

Thai

$$ **Bahn Thai.** Many people find this the best of London's many Thai restaurants (you can see at least four others from the door), better still now that its ancient, gloomy decor has been excised. An immensely long menu features little chili symbols for the nervous of palate, plus easy options like char-grilled *poussin* (fish) marinated in honey and spices with a plum dipping sauce. Other Thai dishes are well explained. ✕ *21A Frith St., W1,* ☎ *0171/437–8504. Reservations advised for dinner. AE, MC, V. Closed Dec. 25–26. Tube: Leicester Sq.*

Covent Garden

American

$$ ★ **Joe Allen's.** Long hours (thespians flock after the curtain falls in theaterland) a welcoming, if loud, brick-walled interior mean New York Joe's London branch is still swinging after nearly two decades. The fun, California-inflected menu helps: Roast stuffed poblano chili, or black bean soup are typical starters; entrées feature barbecue ribs with black-eyed peas and London's only available corn muffins, or roast monkfish with sun-dried-tomato salsa. There are the perennial egg dishes and huge salads, too, and Yankee

desserts like grilled banana bread with ice cream and hot caramel sauce. It can get chaotic, with long waits for the cute waiters, but at least there'll be famous faces to ogle in the meantime. ✕ *13 Exeter St., WC2,* ☎ *0171/836–0651. Reservations required. No credit cards. Closed Easter, Dec. 25–26. Tube: Covent Garden.*

$ **Fatboy's Diner.** One for the kids, this is a 1941 chrome trailer transplanted from the banks of the Susquehanna in Pennsylvania and now secreted, unexpectedly, in a backstreet, complete with Astroturf "garden." A '50s jukebox accompanies the dogs, burgers, and fries. ✕ *21 Maiden La., WC2,* ☎ *0171/240–1902. No reservations. No credit cards. Closed Christmas. Tube: Covent Garden.*

$ **Maxwell's.** London's first-ever burger joint, 21 in '93, cloned itself and then grew up. Here's the result, a happy place under the Opera House serving the kind of food you're homesick for: quesadillas and nachos, Buffalo chicken wings, barbecue ribs, Cajun chicken, chef's salad, a real NYC Reuben, and a burger to die for. ✕ *8–9 James St., WC2,* ☎ *0171/836–0303. Reservations advised weekends. AE, DC, V. Closed Christmas. Tube: Covent Garden.*

French

$$ **Le Palais du Jardin.** This does a fair imitation of a Parisian brasserie, complete with a seafood bar offering lobsters for a tenner, though there's plenty else—duck confit with apples and prunes; coq au vin; tuna with a black olive potato cake. It's not as chic nor as expensive as it looks, and always busy. ✕ *136 Long Acre, WC2,* ☎ *0171/379–5353. Reservations advised. AE, DC, MC, V. Closed Christmas. Tube: Covent Garden.*

$ **Café Flo.** This useful brasserie serves the bargain "Idée Flo"—soup or salad, *steak-frites* or *poisson-frites,* and coffee—a wide range of French café food, breakfast, wines, *tartes,* espresso, fresh orange juice, simple set-price weekend menus . . . everything for the Francophile on a budget. There are branches in Hampstead, Islington, Fulham, and Kensington. ✕ *51 St. Martin's La., WC2,* ☎ *0171/836–8289. Reservations advised. MC, V. Closed Dec. 25, Jan. 1. Tube: Covent Garden.*

International

$$$ ★ **The Ivy.** This seems to be everybody's favorite restaurant—everybody who works in the media or the arts, that is. In a Deco dining room with blinding white tablecloths, and Hodgkins and Paolozzis on the walls, the celebrated and the wannabes eat Caesar salad, roast grouse, shrimp gumbo, braised oxtail, and rice pudding with Armagnac prunes or sticky toffee pudding. ✕ *1 West St., WC2,* ☎ *0171/836–4751. Reservations advised. AE, DC, MC, V. Closed Christmas. Tube: Covent Garden.*

Italian

$$ ★ **Bertorelli's.** Right across from the stage door of the Royal Opera House, Bertorelli's is quietly chic, the food better than ever now that Maddalena Bonnino (formerly of 192) is in charge. Poached *cotechino* sausage with lentils; monkfish ragout with fennel, tomato and olives; and *garganelli* with French beans, cob nuts, and Parmesan are typical dishes. Downstairs is a very relaxed, inexpensive wine bar serving a simpler menu of pizza, pasta, salads, and a few big dishes and daily specials. ✕ *44A Floral St., WC2,* ☎ *0171/836–3969. Reservations required for restaurant; advised downstairs for dinner. AE, DC, MC, V. Closed Christmas. Tube: Covent Garden.*

Traditional English

$$$ **Rules.** A London institution—an Edwardian restaurant that was a great favorite of Lily Langtry's, among others. After decades the restaurant remains interesting for its splendid period atmosphere, but annoying for its slow service. For a main dish, try the seasonal entrées on the list of daily specials, which will, in season, include game from Rules's own Scottish estate (venison is disconcertingly called "deer"). It is more than a little touristy, but that's because it's so quaint. ✕ *35 Maiden La., WC2,* ☎ *0171/836–5314. Reservations advised at least 1 day in advance. AE, DC, MC, V. Closed Christmas. Tube: Covent Garden.*

Vegetarian

$ ★ **Food for Thought.** This simple basement restaurant (no liquor license) seats only 50 and is extremely popular, so you'll almost always find a line of people down the stairs. The menu—stir-fries, casseroles, salads, and desserts—

changes every day, and each dish is freshly made; there's no microwave. ✕ *31 Neal St., WC2,* ☎ *0171/836–0239. No reservations. No credit cards. Closed after 8* PM, *2 wks at Christmas, national holidays. Tube: Covent Garden.*

Bloomsbury

Greek

$$$ **White Tower.** Barely changed in six decades, the White Tower is quite different from the average London Greek, its three Georgian stories lined with antique pistols and prints (and a portrait of that most famous Hellenist, Lord Byron), and its verbose menu listing many unusual dishes, like the cracked wheat–, fruit-, and nut-stuffed duck you must order in advance, or the chicken Paxinou, served with fried banana and aubergine (eggplant). The *taramasalata*—cod's roe dip, which all too often resembles Pepto-Bismol—is the best in town, was the first in town, and is always ordered by the many establishment types who love this place. ✕ *1 Percy St., W1,* ☎ *0171/636–8141. Reservations required. Jacket and tie. AE, DC, MC, V. Closed weekends, national holidays, 3 wks in Aug., 1 wk at Christmas. Tube: Goodge St.*

Indian Vegetarian

$ **Mandeer.** Buried in a basement, with tiled floors, brick walls, and temple lamps, the Mandeer is useful for being central (off Tottenham Court Road, where there's nothing much else), and extremely cheap at lunchtime, when you help yourself to the buffet. ✕ *21 Hanway Pl., W1,* ☎ *0171/580–3470. No reservations at lunch. AE, DC, MC, V. Closed Sun., national holidays, 2 wks over New Year. Tube: Tottenham Court Rd.*

Japanese

$ ★ **Wagamama.** London's gone wild for Japanese noodles in this big basement. It's high-tech (your order is taken on a hand-held computer), high-volume—there are always crowds, with which you share wooden refectory tables—and high-turnover, with a fast-moving line always at the door. You can choose ramen in or out of soup, topped with sliced meats or tempura; or "raw energy" dishes—rice, curries, tofu, and so on—all at give-away prices and doggy-bag sizes. So successful has this formula proved, there is now an entire range of clothing so that grateful diners can now *wear* Wagamama. By now, at least one of the planned offshoots ought to have opened too. ✕ *4 Streatham St., WC1,* ☏ *0171/323–9223. No reservations. No credit cards. Closed Christmas. Tube: Tottenham Court Rd.*

South Kensington

Mediterranean

$$ Bistrot 190. Chef-restaurateur and popular guy Antony Worrall Thompson dominates this town's medium-priced eating scene with his happy, hearty food from Southern Europe and around the Mediterranean rim in raucous hardwood-floor-and-art settings. The identifiable feature of an AWT menu is its lists of about a hundred loosely related ingredients (pork chop with rhubarb compote, cheese, and mustard mash, for instance), which when read all at once force you to salivate. Country bread and smoked haddock butter is always on the table, oftentimes served with tapenade; char-grilled squid with red and green salsa, and a great lemon tart are always in favor. This place, which was his first, is handy to museum or Albert Hall excursions. ✕ *190 Queen's Gate, SW7,* ☏ *0171/581–5666. No reservations. AE, DC, MC, V. Closed Sat. lunch, Sun., Dec. 25–26, Jan. 1. Tube: Gloucester Rd.*

Polish

$ Daquise. This venerable and well-loved Polish café by the tube station is incongruous in this neighborhood, since it's neither style-conscious nor expensive. Fill your stomach without emptying your pocketbook (or, it must be said, overstimulating your taste buds) on *bigos* (sauerkraut with garlic sausage and mushrooms), stuffed cabbage and cucumber salad, or just coffee and cakes. ✕ *20 Thurloe St., SW7,* ☏ *0171/589–6117. Reservations advised weekend dinner. No credit cards. Closed Christmas. Tube: S. Kensington.*

Knightsbridge

French

$$ St. Quentin. A very popular slice of Paris, frequented by French expatriates and locals alike. Every inch of the Gal-

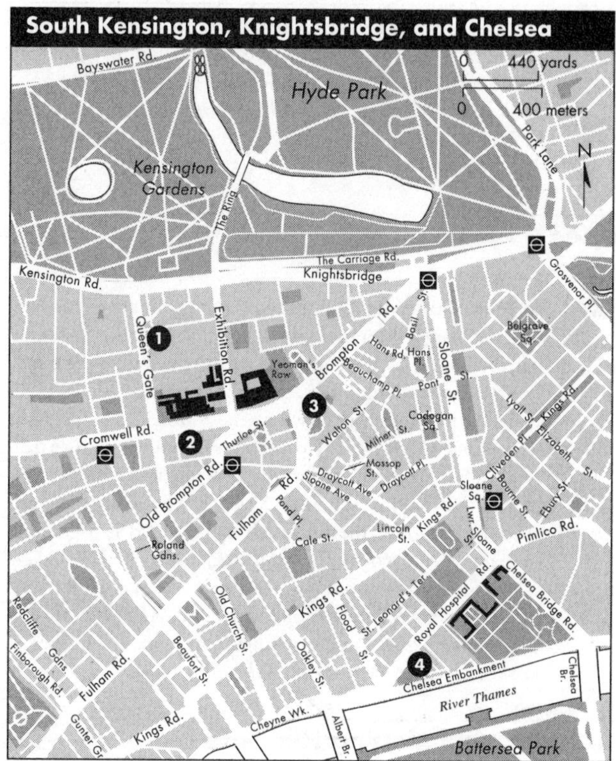

Bistrot 190, **1**
Daquise, **2**
La Tante Claire, **4**
St. Quentin, **3**

lic menu is explored—gruyere quiche, escargots, cassoulet, lemon tart—in the bourgeois provincial comfort so many London chains (the Dômes, the Cafés Rouges) try hard for, yet fail to achieve. ✕ *243 Brompton Rd., SW3,* ☎ *0171/589–8005. Reservations advised. AE, DC, MC, V. Tube: S. Kensington.*

Chelsea

French

$$$$ ★ La Tante Claire. Justly famous, but cripplingly expensive. The decor is light and sophisticated, the service impeccable, the French wine list impressive, but the food is the point. From the *carte,* you might choose hot pâté de foie gras on shredded potatoes with a sweet wine and shallot sauce, roast spiced pigeon, or Pierre Koffmann's famous signature dish of pig's feet stuffed with mousse of white meat with sweetbreads and wild mushrooms. As every gourmet expense-accounter knows, the set lunch menu (£25) is a genuine bargain. ✕ *68 Royal Hospital Rd., SW3,* ☎ *0171/352–6045. Reservations advised 3–4 wks in advance for dinner, 2–3 days for lunch. Jacket and tie. AE, DC, MC, V. Closed weekends, 2 wks at Christmas, Jan. 1, 10 days at Easter, 3 wks in Aug.–Sept. Tube: Sloane Sq.*

Kensington and Notting Hill Gate

Mediterranean

$$ The Belvedere. There can be no finer setting for a summer supper or a sunny Sunday brunch than a window table—or a balcony one if you luck out—at this stunning restaurant in the middle of Holland Park. The menu is big on shaved Parmesan, sun-dried tomatoes, and arugula, which suits the conservatory-like room, but both food and service do occasionally miss the target. Still, with a view like this, who cares about water glasses or bland chicken? ✕ *Holland Park, off Abbotsbury Rd., W8,* ☎ *0171/602–1238. Reservations required weekends. AE, DC, MC, V. Closed Sun. dinner, Christmas. Tube: Holland Park.*

Modern British

$$$ ★ **Kensington Place.** A favorite among the local glitterati, always packed and noisy. A huge plate-glass window and mural are backdrops to fashionable food—grilled foie gras with sweet-corn pancake and baked tamarillo with vanilla ice are perennials—but it's the buzz that draws the crowds. ✕ *201 Kensington Church St., W8,* ☎ *0171/727–3184. Reservations advised. MC, V. Closed Aug. bank holiday, Christmas. Tube: Notting Hill Gate.*

$$ ★ **192.** A noisy, buzzy wine bar/restaurant just off the Portobello Road, this is as much a social hangout for the local media mafia as anywhere. Food likes to keep ahead of fashion, and is best on the appetizer list—many people order two of these instead of an entrée. Try the risottos, the seasonal salad (perhaps romanesco, broccoli, anchovy, and gremolata), the fish (sea bass with fennel, lemon, and rosemary; scallop, chickpea, chorizo, and clam casserole), or whatever sounds unusual. ✕ *192 Kensington Park Rd., W11,* ☎ *0171/229–0482. Reservations advised. AE, MC, V. Closed Mon., lunch, public holidays. Tube: Notting Hill Gate.*

Polish

$$ ★ **Wódka.** This smart, modern Polish restaurant is the only one in the world, as far as we know, to serve smart, modern Polish food. It is popular with elegant locals plus a sprinkling of celebs and often has the atmosphere of a dinner party. Alongside the smoked salmon, herring, caviar, and eggplant *blinis,* you might also find venison sausages or roast duck with krupnik (honey-lemon vodka). Order a carafe of the purest vodka in London (and watch the check inflate . . .); it's encased in a block of ice and hand-flavored (with bison grass, cherries, rowanberries . . .) by the owner, who, being an actual Polish prince, is uniquely qualified to do this. ✕ *12 St. Albans Grove, W8,* ☎ *0171/937–6513. Reservations required for dinner. AE, DC, MC, V. Closed weekend lunch, public holidays. Tube: High St. Kensington.*

Seafood

$ ★ **Geales.** This is a cut above your typical fish-and-chips joint. The decor is stark but the fish will have been swimming just hours beforehand, even the ones from the Caribbean (fried swordfish is a specialty). Geales is popular with the rich and famous, not just loyal locals. ✕ *2 Farmer*

The Belvedere, **2**
Geales, **3**
Kensington Place, **4**
192, **1**
Wódka, **5**

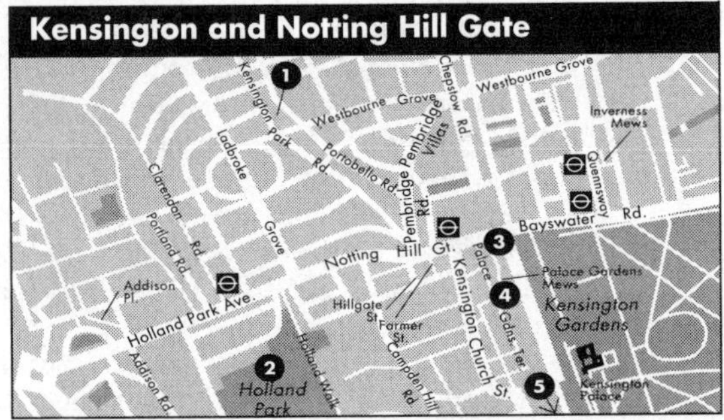

St., W8, ☎ 0171/727–7969. No reservations. MC. Closed Sun., Mon., 2 wks at Christmas, 3 wks in Aug., national holidays. Tube: Notting Hill Gate.

The City

French

$$$ ★ Le Pont de la Tour. Sir Terence Conran's other pièce de résistance (in addition to Quaglino's and Bibendum) lies across the river, overlooking the bridge that gives it its name, and so comes into its own in summer, when the outside tables are heaven. Inside the "Gastrodrome" (his word) there's a vintner and baker and deli, a seafood bar, a brasserie, and this '30s diner-style restaurant, smart as the captain's table. Fish and seafood (lobster salad; Baltic herrings in crème fraîche; roast halibut with aioli), meat and game (venison fillet, port and blueberry sauce; roast veal, caramelized endive) feature heavily—vegetarians are out of luck. Prune and Armagnac tart or chocolate terrine could finish a glamorous—and expensive—meal. By contrast, an impeccable *salade niçoise* in the brasserie is about £8. ✕ *36D Shad Thames, Butler's Wharf, SE1, ☎ 0171/403–8403. Reservations required for lunch, weekend dinner. MC, V. Closed Christmas. Tube: Tower Hill.*

Traditional English

$$ Quality Chop House. This was converted from one of the most gorgeous "greasy spoon" caffs in town, retaining the solid Victorian fittings (including pew-like seats, which you often have to share). It is not luxurious, but the food is wonderful. It's almost a parody of caff food—bangers and mash turns out to be home-made herbed veal sausage with rich

Le Pont de la Tour, **3**
Quality Chop House, **1**
St. John, **2**

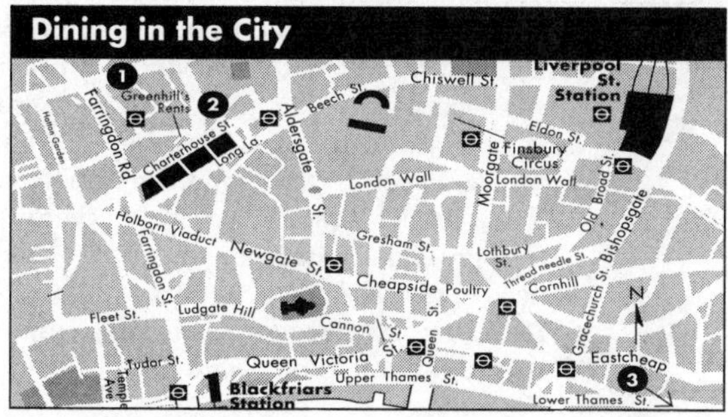

gravy, light, fluffy potato, and vegetables *à point;* egg and chips (fries) are not remotely greasy. There are also posh things like salmon fishcakes and steak, and desserts that change with the seasons. ✕ *94 Farringdon Rd., EC1,* ☏ *0171/837–5093. Reservations required. No credit cards. Closed Sat. lunch, Sun. dinner, public holidays. Tube: Farringdon.*

$$ ★ **St. John.** This former smokehouse (ham, not cigars), converted by erstwhile architect owner/chef Fergus Henderson, has wowed the town since opening night. Soaring white walls, schoolroom lamps, stone floors, iron railings, and plain wooden chairs would be bleak, but for the nattering crowds. Some find Henderson's chutzpah scary: One infamous early appetizer was carrots and egg (a bunch of carrots with green tops intact, and a boiled egg), although the imaginativeness of others—roast bone marrow and parsley salad; smoked eel, beetroot, and horseradish—excuses this silliness. Entrées (roast lamb and parsnip; smoked haddock and fennel; deviled crab) can appear shockingly nude and lumpen on the plate, then you take a bite, and find that beauty is within—usually. There are failures, but they're heroic failures. An all-French wine list has plenty of affordable bottles, service is efficiently matey, and the pastry chef's chocolate slice belongs in the brownie hall of fame. ✕ *26 St John St., EC1,* ☏ *0171/251–0848. Reservations required. AE, MC, V. Closed Sunday dinner, Christmas. Tube: Farringdon.*

Camden Town and Hampstead

Belgian

$$ ★ **Belgo.** To enter what must be London's least normal restaurant, you pass the wavy concrete facade and cross the

spotlit "drawbridge" over the brushed-steel open kitchen. Inside, wait staff in maroon monks' habits sweep over to your refectory-like table to take your order of moules-frites (steamed mussels in various sauces with fries), waterzooi (a whitefish stew), wild boar sausages, and other authentic Belgian dishes. Try the Kriek, cherry beer brewed by Trappist monks. Improbably, it's enormous fun—and the food's great. ✕ *72 Chalk Farm Rd., NW1,* ☏ *0171/267–0718. Reservations required, same day only. AE, MC, V. Closed Christmas. Tube: Chalk Farm.*

Brunch and Afternoon Tea

It is sometimes suggested that among Londoners, brunch is catching on while the afternoon ritual (often mistakenly referred to as "high tea") is dying out. Tea, the drink, however, is so ingrained in the national character, that tea, the meal, will always have a place in the capital, if only as an occasional celebration, a children's treat, or something you do when your American friends are in town. Reserve for all these, unless otherwise noted.

Brunch

Christopher's. Imagine you're in Manhattan at this superior Covent Garden purveyor of American food, from pancakes to steak, eggs and fries, via salmon fishcakes and a caesar. Two courses are £12. ✕ *18 Wellington St., WC2,* ☏ *0171/240–4222. AE, DC, MC, V. Brunch served Sun. noon–3:30.*

Joe Allen's is where to take refuge from the lovely British weather, down some Bloody Marys, and maybe a grilled chicken sandwich with swiss, or a salad of spicy sausage, shrimp, and new potato. Three brunch courses are a bargain £10—half the usual price. ✕ *Brunch served Sat., Sun. noon–4* PM. *(*See *Covent Garden,* above.*)*

The Room at the Halcyon. The Halcyon is favored by stars of Hollywood and rock, and is secreted in the leafy neighborhood of Holland Park. An excellent modern British kitchen. ✕ *129 Holland Park Ave., W11,* ☏ *0171/221–5411. AE, DC, MC, V. Brunch served Sun. noon–3:30.*

Afternoon Tea

Claridges is the real McCoy, with liveried footmen proffering sandwiches, a scone, and superior patisseries (£12.50) in the palatial yet genteel Foyer, to the sound of the resident "Hungarian orchestra" (actually a string quartet). ✕ *Brook St., W1,* ☎ *0171/629–8860. Tea served daily 3–5.*

Fortnum & Mason. Upstairs at the queen's grocer's, three set teas are ceremoniously offered: standard Afternoon Tea (sandwiches, scone, cakes, £9.50), old-fashioned High Tea (the traditional nursery meal, adding something more robust and savoury, £11.50), and Champagne Tea (£13). ✕ *St. James's Restaurant, fourth floor, 181 Piccadilly, W1,* ☎ *0171/734–8040. Tea served Mon.–Sat. 3–5:20.*

The Ritz. The Ritz's new owners have put the once-peerless Palm Court tea back on the map, with proper tiered cake stands and silver pots, a harpist, and Louis XVI chaises, plus a leisurely four-hour time slot. A good excuse for a glass of champagne. Reservations are taken only to 50% capacity. ✕ *Piccadilly, W1,* ☎ *0171/493–8181. Tea served daily 2–6.*

Savoy. The glamorous Thames-side hotel does one of the pleasantest teas, its triple-tiered cake stands packed with goodies, its tailcoated waiters thrillingly polite. ✕ *The Strand, WC2,* ☎ *0171/836–4343. Tea served daily 3–5:30.*

Pubs

Black Friar. A step from Blackfriars tube, this pub has an arts-and-crafts interior that is entertainingly, satirically ecclesiastical, with inlaid mother-of-pearl, wood carvings, stained glass, and marble pillars all over the place, and reliefs of monks and friars poised above finely lettered temperance tracts, regardless of which there are six beers on tap. ✕ *174 Queen Victoria St., EC4,* ☎ *0171/236–5650.*

Crown and Goose. The possible shape of pubs to come is exemplified by this sky-blue-walled, art-bedecked Camden Town local, where armchairs augment the tables, coffee and herb tea the beers, and great food (steak in baguette, smoked chicken salad with honey vinaigrette, baked and stuffed mushrooms) is served to the crowds. ✕ *100 Arlington Rd., NW1,* ☎ *0171/485–2342.*

Dove Inn. Read the list of famous ex-regulars, from Charles II and Nell Gwynn (mere rumor, but a likely one) to Ernest Hemingway, as you queue ages for a beer at this very popular, very comely 16th-century riverside pub by Hammersmith Bridge. If it's *too* full, stroll upstream to the Old Ship or the Blue Anchor. ✕ *19 Upper Mall, W6,* ☏ *0181/748–5405.*

Freemason's Arms. This place is supposed to have the largest pub garden in London, with two terraces, a summerhouse, country-style furniture, and roses everywhere. Try your hand at the 17th-century game of pell mell—a kind of croquet—or at skittles. It's a favorite Hampstead pub, and popular with local young people. ✕ *32 Downshire Hill, NW3,* ☏ *0171/435–2127.*

French House. In the pub where the French Resistance convened during World War II, Soho hipsters and eccentrics rub shoulders now. More than shoulders, actually, because this tiny, tricolor-waving, photograph-lined pub is always full to bursting. ✕ *49 Dean St., W1,* ☏ *0171/437–2799.*

Lamb and Flag. This 17th-century pub was once known as "The Bucket of Blood," because the upstairs room was used as a ring for bare-knuckle boxing. Now, it's a trendy, friendly, and entirely bloodless pub, serving food (at lunchtime only) and real ale. It's on the edge of Covent Garden, off Garrick Street. ✕ *33 Rose St., WC2,* ☏ *0171/836–4108.*

Mayflower. An atmospheric 17th-century riverside inn, with exposed beams and a terrace, this is practically the very place from which the Pilgrims set sail for Plymouth Rock. The inn is licensed to sell American postage stamps alongside its superior pub food. ✕ *117 Rotherhithe St., SE16,* ☏ *0171/237–4088.*

Museum Tavern. Across the street from the British Museum, this gloriously Victorian pub makes an ideal resting place after the rigors of the culture trail. With lots of fancy glass—etched mirrors and stained glass panels—gilded pillars, and carvings, the heavily restored hostelry once helped Karl Marx to unwind after a hard day in the Library. He could have spent his kapital on any one of six beers available on tap. ✕ *49 Great Russell St., WC1,* ☏ *0171/242–8987.*

Pheasant and Firkin. David Bruce single-handedly revived the practice of serving beer that's been brewed on the premises (then sold the thriving business), and this is one

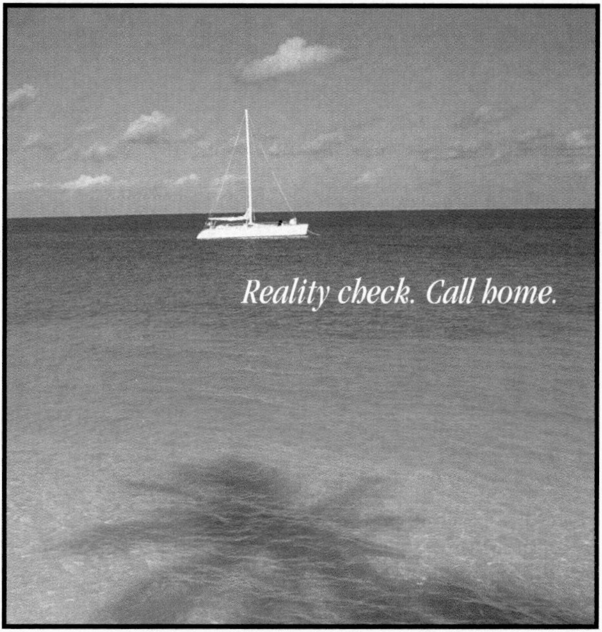

of his jolly microbrewery/pubs, all named the something and Firkin (a small barrel), serving beers called "dogbolter" or "rail ale," and selling T-shirts printed with *bons mots* like "I had a Pheasant time at the Firkin pub." Students like this a lot. ✕ *166 Goswell Rd., EC1,* ☏ *0171/235–7429.*

Spaniards Inn. This is another historic, oak-beamed pub on Hampstead Heath, boasting a gorgeous rose garden, scene of the tea party in Dickens's *Pickwick Papers*. Dick Turpin, the highwayman, used to frequent the inn; you can see his pistols on display. Romantic poets—Shelley, Keats, Byron—hung out here, and so, of course, did Dickens. It's extremely popular, especially on Sunday when Londoners take to the Heath in search of fresh air. ✕ *Spaniards Rd., NW3,* ☏ *0171/455–3276.*

Windsor Castle. One to rest at on a Kensington jaunt, and sample the traditional sort of pub food (steak and kidney pudding is good here), which you order from a Cruikshank-illustrated menu, in keeping with the general Dickensian ambience. In winter there are blazing fires; in summer, an exquisite walled patio garden. ✕ *114 Campden Hill Rd., W8,* ☏ *0171/727–8491.*

Ye Olde Cheshire Cheese. Yes, it is a tourist trap, but this most historic of all London pubs (it dates from 1667) deserves a visit anyway, for its sawdust-covered floors, low wood-beamed ceilings, the 14th-century crypt of Whitefriars' monastery under the cellar bar, and the set of 17th-century pornographic tiles upstairs. This was the most regular of Dr. Johnson's and Dickens's *many* locals. ✕ *145 Fleet St., EC4,* ☏ *0171/353–6170.*

5 Lodging

MAKE NO MISTAKE, London hotels are expensive. The city has a peculiar dearth of the pleasant medium-priced hotels that other European capitals have no difficulty in supplying. Grand hotels London has got (and, at the other end of the scale, seedy lodging houses which you will not find in these pages), but modest, family-run hotels tend to inflate their rates a few notches above what one would expect in, say, Paris or Madrid. Our gradings are based simply on price, and you should note that in some establishments, especially those in the $$$$ category, you could pay considerably more—well past the £200 mark in some cases. Like hotels in most other European countries, British hotels are obliged by law to display a tariff at the reception desk. If you have not prebooked, you are strongly advised to study this carefully.

Be sure to make reservations well in advance, as seasonal events, trade shows, or royal occasions can fill hotel rooms for sudden brief periods. However, if you arrive in the capital without a room, the **London Tourist Board Information Centres** at Heathrow and Victoria Station Forecourt can help; or call the **LTB Accommodation Sales Service** (☎ 0171/824–8844, weekdays 9:30–5:30) for prepaid credit-card bookings (MC, V).

CATEGORY	COST*
$$$$	over £180
$$$	£120–£180
$$	£70–£120
$	under £70

**cost of a double room; VAT included; add service*

Mayfair to Regent's Park

$$$$ Athenaeum. This well-loved baby grand opposite Green Park came back from the brink a couple years ago when it went to independent owners (it had been a Rank Hotel—almost literally). The welcome here is in the details: From Donald, the super-concierge at his door-side desk, to the disposable camera, Japanese rice crackers, and teddy bear (twee, but they get away with it) in the minibar, to the compact Health Spa with whirlpool, steam and sauna, cardio and free-weight equipment, and masseuse. Rooms retain the distinctive custom-made leather-topped mahogany and yew furniture, now set against navy-and-cream checkered drapes, Wedgewood green walls, and thick, thick cream carpets. Without getting out of bed, you can control lighting and temperature, order free videos and CDs, pick up your voice mail from your two phone lines. Also—hallelujah—there's a *real* hair dryer, and an outlet by the mirror (there's also a US voltage outlet). In glittering grey marble bathrooms are power showers, mirrors angled to get the back of your head, and old-fashioned Bronnley smellies; downstairs, there's the cozy Whisky Bar, famed for its 70 single malts, and the not too formal Bullochs restaurant. Rooms 201–205 face Green Park view; others have a bay which affords a partial, angled view. ⊞ *116 Piccadilly, W1V OBJ,* ☎ *0171/499–3464,* FAX *0171/493–1860. 123 rooms. Restaurant, bar, lounge, in-room VCR and CD players, health club. AE, DC, MC, V. Tube: Green Park.*

$$$$ **Brown's.** Founded in 1837 by Lord Byron's "gentleman's gentleman," James Brown, Forte Hotels' Victorian country house in central Mayfair occupies 11 Georgian houses and is occupied by many Anglophile Americans—a habit that was established by the two Roosevelts (Teddy while on honeymoon). A fairly recent refurbishment enlarged 100 bedrooms but didn't besmirch the oak-paneled, chintz-laden, grandfather-clock-ticking-in-the-parlor ambience. Bedrooms feature thick carpets, soft armchairs, sweeping drapes, brass chandeliers, and moiré or brocade wallpapers, as well as, in the newly refitted ones, air-conditioning. On the doorstep are the boutiques and art galleries of Bond and Cork streets, while in the lounge, one of London's best-known afternoon teas is served from 3 to 6. ⊞ *34 Albemarle St., W1A 4SW,* ☎ *0171/493–6020,* FAX *0171/493–9381. 132 rooms. Restaurant, bar, lounge, writing room. AE, DC, MC, V. Tube: Green Park.*

$$$$ ★ **Claridges.** A hotel legend, with one of the world's classiest guest lists. The liveried staff are friendly and not in the least condescending, and the rooms are never less than luxurious. It was founded in 1812, but present decor is either 1930s Art Deco, or country-house traditional. Have

a drink in the Foyer lounge (24 hours a day) with its Hungarian mini-orchestra, or retreat to the reading room for perfect quiet, interrupted only by the sound of pages turning. The bedrooms are spacious, as are the bathrooms, with their enormous shower heads and bells (which still work) to summon either "maid" or "valet" from their station on each floor. Beds are handmade and supremely comfortable—the King of Morocco once brought his own, couldn't sleep, and ended up ordering 30 from Claridges to take home. The grand staircase and magnificent elevator are equally impressive. ☐ *Brook St., W1A 2JQ,* ☎ *0171/629–8860 or 800/223–6800,* FAX *0171/499–2210. 200 rooms. 2 restaurants, lounge, beauty salon, valeting. AE, DC, MC, V. Tube: Bond St.*

$$$$ ★ **The Dorchester.** A London institution since its 1931 inception (apart from a break in continuity for its recent complete refurbishment), the Dorchester appears on every "World's Best" list. The glamour level is off the scale: 1,500 square meters of gold leaf, 1,100 of marble, and 2,300 of hand-tufted carpet gild this lily, and bedrooms (some not as spacious as you might imagine) feature Irish linen sheets on canopied beds, brocades and velvets, Italian marble and etched glass bathrooms with Floris goodies, individual climate control, dual voltage outlets, and cable TV. There's a beauty spa (run by Elizabeth Arden) a nightclub, the Oriental and Terrace restaurants, plus the well-known power-dining Grill Room. Afternoon tea, drinking, lounging, and posing are all accomplished in the catwalk-shaped Promenade lounge, where you may spot one of the film-star types who will stay nowhere else. Probably no other hotel this opulent manages to be this charming. ☐ *Park La., W1A 2HJ,* ☎ *0171/629–8888,* FAX *0171/409–0114. 197 rooms, 55 suites. 3 restaurants, bar, lounge, air-conditioning, health club, nightclub, business services, meeting rooms, ballroom, theater ticket desk. AE, DC, MC, V. Tube: Marble Arch.*

$$$$ **Grosvenor House.** "The old lady of Park Lane" has settled happily back into top-dowager position, having thrown off her creeping frumpiness during a complete overhaul. It's not the kind of place that encourages hushed whispers or that frowns on jeans, despite the marble floors and wood-paneled "library," open fires, oils, and fine antiques, all in-

Lodging in Mayfair, St. James's, Soho, and Covent Garden

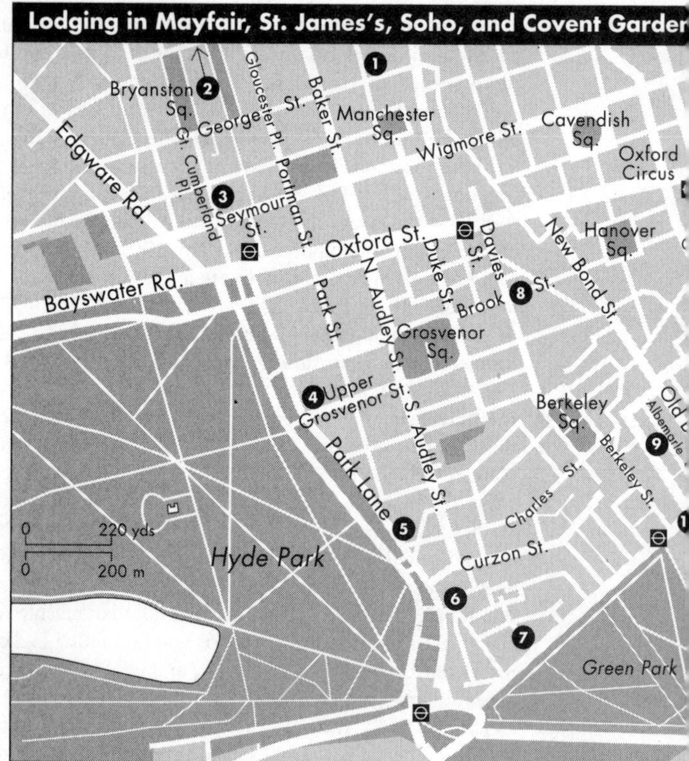

Athenaeum, **7**
Brown's, **9**
Claridges, **8**
The Dorchester, **5**
Dukes, **11**
Durrants, **1**
Edward Lear, **3**
Fielding, **13**
Grosvenor House, **4**
Hazlitt's, **12**
London Hilton on Park Lane, **6**
The Regent, **2**
The Ritz, **10**
The Savoy, **14**

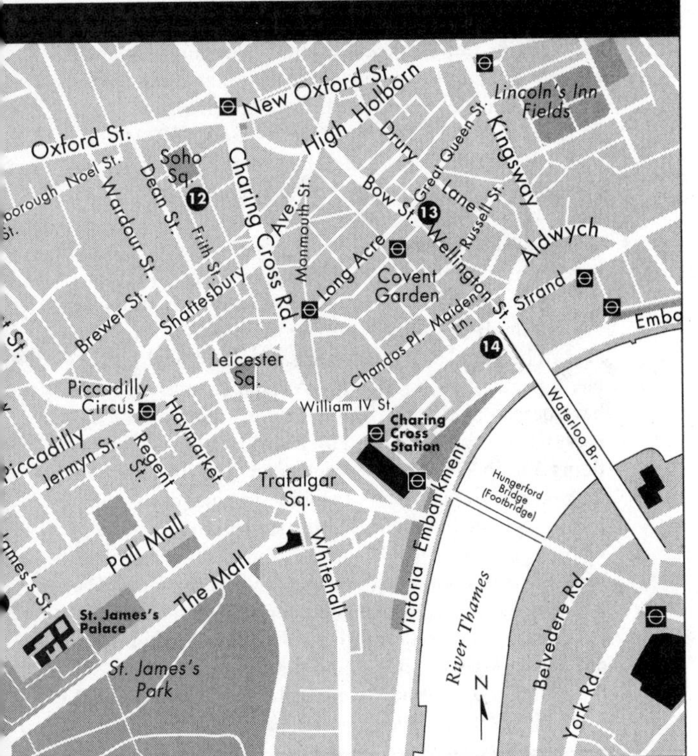

Oxford St.
New Oxford St.
High Holborn
Lincoln's Inn Fields
Drury Lane
Great Queen St.
Kingsway
Soho Sq.
Noel St.
Wardour St.
Dean St.
Frith St.
Charing Cross Rd.
Ave.
Monmouth St.
Bow St.
Wellington St.
Russell St.
Aldwych
Long Acre
Covent Garden
Strand
Shaftesbury
Brewer St.
Maiden Ln.
Chandos Pl.
Emba
Leicester Sq.
Piccadilly Circus
William IV St.
Charing Cross Station
Waterloo Br.
Piccadilly
Jermyn St.
Regent St.
Haymarket
Trafalgar Sq.
Victoria Embankment
Hungerford Bridge (Footbridge)
Pall Mall
Whitehall
The Mall
St. James's Palace
St. James's Park
River Thames
Belvedere Rd.
York Rd.
N

spired by the Earl of Grosvenor's residence, which occupied the site in the 18th century. The hotel health club is just about the best around. Bedrooms are spacious, and most of the freshly glamorized big marble bathrooms have natural light. ☎ *Park La., W1A 3AA,* ☎ *0171/499–6363,* FAX *0171/493–3341. 360 rooms, 70 suites. 3 restaurants, bar, lounge, indoor pool, health club, banquet suites, ballroom, theater ticket desk. AE, DC, MC, V. Tube: Marble Arch.*

$$$$ London Hilton on Park Lane. London's only major high-rise hotel offers fine views over Hyde Park—when you can see through the mist—and an impressive array of facilities, including the Fitness on Five center, with personal trainers at your beck and call. Public areas are glitzy in white marble, topped off by an oblong of crystal chandelier; suites have been recently redecorated to bring them out of *Dynasty* territory and into the '90s. Bedrooms, too (except for floors 20 and 21) have been renovated. They're a fair size, but you may forget which city they're in, since decor is uniform corporate Hiltonese. Hardly surprising in a hostelry whose guest list is 70% business travelers, for whom there is now a Clubroom on the designated Executive Floor. The top-floor Windows Roof Restaurant, known for the view, is making a culinary effort with a new French chef, but hokey old Trader Vic's on the ground floor is still cranking out those lurid, soup tureen-sized cocktails. ☎ *22 Park La., W1A 2HH,* ☎ *0171/493–8000,* FAX *0171/493–4957. 448 rooms. Restaurant, beauty salon, health club, doctor, baby-sitting, laundry service, business center, travel services, theater ticket desk. AE, DC, MC, V. Tube: Hyde Park Corner.*

$$$$ The Regent. A year older than the century, the onetime Great Central Hotel and former BritRail HQ is London's newest luxury hotel—and a most elegantly understated place it is, too. A palm-filled, eight-story glazed atrium "Winter Garden" forms the core, and odd-numbered rooms—somewhat surreally—overlook this. If size matters to you, note that even standard rooms here are among the largest in London and that this Hong Kong–based hotel group is famous for glamorous bathrooms—these are marble and chrome, complete with robe and hair dryer. Despite appearances, this is the only London grand hotel that doesn't force you to dress up—even jeans are okay. Unsurprisingly, the Regent is very near Regent's Park; the West End is a 15-

minute walk away. *222 Marylebone Rd., NW1 6JQ, 0171/631–8000, FAX 0171/631–8080. 309 rooms. Restaurant, 2 bars, indoor pool, health club, VCR and personal fax on request, business center. AE, DC, MC, V. Tube: Marylebone.*

$$ **Durrants.** A hotel since the late 18th century, Durrants occupies a quiet corner almost next to the Wallace Collection, a stone's throw from Oxford Street and the smaller, posher shops of Marylebone High Street. It's good value for the area, and if you like Ye wood-paneled, leather-armchaired, dark-red-patterned-carpeted style of olde Englishness, this will suit you. Bedrooms, by way of contrast, are wan and motel-like but perfectly adequate—a few have no bathrooms, though this disadvantage has the advantage of saving you £10 a night. Each landing harbors a communal minibar (a maxibar?) and ice machine. Best give the baron of beef-type restaurant a miss. *George St., W1H 6BH, 0171/935–8131, FAX 0171/487–3510. 96 rooms, 85 with bath. Restaurant, bar, dining rooms, lounges. AE, MC, V. Tube: Bond St.*

$ **Edward Lear.** This is a good-value, family-run hotel in a Georgian town house, a minute's walk from Oxford Street, which used to be home to writer/artist Edward Lear (famous for his nonsense verse). Rooms vary enormously in size, with some family rooms very spacious indeed and others barely big enough to get out of bed (avoid Room 14); rooms at the back are quieter. It's a friendly place with a lot of repeat customers, but there are no hotel-type facilities (although if you want a jacket pressed you're welcome to borrow the iron), except for a lounge and the light and pleasant brick-walled breakfast room. The management is very proud of the English breakfasts—they use the same butcher as the queen. *28–30 Seymour St., W1H 5WD, 0171/402–5401, FAX 0171/706–3766. 31 rooms, 15 with shower (no WC), 4 with full bath. Breakfast room, lounge. MC, V. Tube: Marble Arch.*

St. James's

$$$$ **Dukes.** This small, exclusive, Edwardian-style hotel, with its lantern-lit entrance, central but still quiet since it's set in its own silent cul-de-sac behind the Ritz, and close to the Stafford too. Though all three were once stablemates, this one is now run by the same upmarket management as the Franklin (*see* Knightsbridge, Chelsea, and Belgravia, *below*). Portraits of notable dukes hang on the walls, in a successful bid for a stately-home ambience, except for the deeper carpets and better climate control. The atmosphere continues in the bedrooms, with requisite marble bathrooms. ☷ *35 St. James's Pl., SW1A 1NY,* ☎ *0171/491–4840,* FAX *0171/493–1264. 62 rooms. Restaurant, dining room. AE, DC, MC, V. Tube: Green Park.*

$$$$ **The Ritz.** Management of the Ritz was assumed in 1994 by the enormously respected Mandarin Oriental Group, which had yet to break into Europe. Mandarin will not alter the palatial (as in Versailles) Belle Epoque decor: Not in the Palm Court, with its cranberry velvet chairs, statuary, fluted columns, and greenery, nor in the resplendent dining room which, with its frescoes, gilding, and Italian Garden, is generally thought the prettiest in town. Bedrooms, too, will stay as César Ritz prescribed—white pilasters and moldings on sorbet paint work; antique bureaus; specially commissioned brass beds (17 of these remain); reproduction bronze figurines on the mantle huge mirrors above it; heavy brocades, and linens embroidered with "R"—but they will get rigorous refreshment, and (especially where the original marble baths were tragically ripped out) new bathrooms. Big work starts early in 1996, including the addition of a much-needed health club. Until then, expect improved service, and check out the cozy, tiny, secret Rivoli Lounge up the curved staircase off Reception. ☷ *Piccadilly, W1V 9DG,* ☎ *0171/493–8181,* FAX *0171/493–2687. 129 rooms. Restaurant, bar, baby-sitting. AE, DC, MC, V. Tube: Green Park.*

Soho and Covent Garden

$$$$ ★ **The Savoy.** This historic, grand, late-Victorian hotel is beloved by the international influential, now as ever. Like the other Savoy Group hotels, it boasts handmade beds and staff who are often graduates of its exclusive training school. Its celebrated Grill Restaurant the premier power lunch tables; it hosted Elizabeth Taylor's first honeymoon in one of its famous river-view rooms; and it poured the world's first martini in its equally famous American Bar—

haunted by Hemingway, Fitzgerald, Gershwin, et al. And does it measure up to this high profile? Absolutely. The impeccably maintained, spacious, elegant, bright, and comfortable rooms are furnished with antiques and serviced by valets. A room facing the Thames costs an arm and a leg and requires an early booking, but there are few better views in London. Bathrooms have original fittings, with the same sunflower-size shower heads as at Claridges, and there's a compact new "Fitness Gallery" (with pool) secreted above the entrance. Though the Savoy is as grand as they come, the air is tinged with a certain naughtiness, which goes down well with Hollywood types. *Strand, WC2R 0EU, ☎ 0171/836–4343, FAX 0171/240–6040. 202 rooms. 3 restaurants, 2 bars, indoor pool, health club, hairdressing, theater ticket desk. AE, DC, MC, V. Tube: Aldwych.*

$$$ ★ Hazlitt's. The solo Soho hotel is in three connected early 18th-century houses, one of which was the essayist William Hazlitt's (1778–1830) last home. It's a disarmingly friendly place, full of personality, but devoid of such hotel features as elevators, room service (though if the staff aren't too busy, you can get ad-hoc take-outs), and porterage. Robust antiques are everywhere, assorted prints crowd every wall, plants and stone sculptures (by a father-in-law of one of the owners) appear in odd corners, and every room has a Victorian claw-foot bath in its bathroom. There are tiny sitting rooms, wooden staircases, and more restaurants within strolling distance than you could patronize in a year. Book way ahead—this is the London address of media people, literary types, and antiques dealers everywhere. *6 Frith St., W1V 5TZ, ☎ 0171/434–1771, FAX 0171/439–1524. 23 rooms. AE, DC, MC, V. Tube: Tottenham Court Rd.*

$$ Fielding. Tucked away in a quiet alley by the world's first police station (now Bow St. Magistrates' Court), and feeling far from the madding crowds of Covent Garden, this very small and pretty hotel is so adored by its regulars that you'd be wise to book well ahead. Cameron Mackintosh, the Broadway musical producer (who could no doubt afford Claridges), stays here—presumably for the homey atmosphere; the old London Town character; the continuity of a loyal, friendly staff who maintain the place as the two founders, now retired, kept it for over two decades; and, of course, for the convenience of having the Royal Opera

House, every theater, and half of London's restaurants within spitting distance. It is not uneccentric. The bedrooms are all different, shabby-homey rather than chic, and cozy rather than spacious, though you can have a suite here for the price of a chain-hotel double. There's no elevator; only one room comes with bath (most have showers); and only breakfast is served in the restaurant. Cute. ☎ *4 Broad Ct., Bow St., WC2B 5QZ, ☎ 0171/836–8305, FAX 0171/497–0064. 26 rooms, 1 with bath, 23 with shower. Bar, breakfast room. AE, DC, MC, V. Tube: Covent Garden.*

Kensington

$$$$ ★ **Blakes.** Blakes is another world—some would say a '70s rock-star era time-warp. It was designed by owner Anouska Hempel (a.k.a. Lady Weinberg), and each room is a fantasy packed with precious Biedermeier, Murano glass, and modern pieces inside walls of red lacquer and black, or dove-gray moire, or perhaps—like 007, the movie stars' favorite suite—pink. Cinematic mood lighting, featuring recessed halogen spots, compounds the impression that you, too, are a movie star living in a big-budget biopic. The foyer sets the tone with its piles of cushions, Phineas Fogg valises and trunks, black walls, rattan and bamboo, and a noisy parakeet under a gigantic Asian parasol. Downstairs, an equally dramatic, exorbitant black-and-white restaurant displays Thai warriors' costumes in glass cases. Stay away if you don't like Hollywood or the music biz; look out for The Hempel, Lady W's sister hotel, due in late 1995, if you do. ☎ *33 Roland Gardens, SW7 3PF, ☎ 0171/370–6701, FAX 0171/373–0442. 52 rooms. Restaurant. AE, DC, MC, V. Tube: Gloucester Rd.*

$$$ **The Cranley.** The pedigree of this small young Georgian town-house hotel is Ann Arbor, Michigan (where the owners hail from) out of South Ken (where it stands, near the big museums), and it looks the part. Anglo antiques, oils, and etchings are mixed with a lot of U.S.-style swagged drapery in assorted florals and vivid color schemes. Bedrooms have kitchenettes, and many are high-ceilinged and huge-windowed, while two of the apartments have Jacuzzis and cute patio gardens. The cheaper rooms here and at the nearby 10-room **One Cranley Place** (SW7 3AB, ☎ 0171/

589–7944, FAX 0171/225–3931), which operates March to October, belong in the $$ category. *10–12 Bina Gardens, SW5 0LA, ☎ 0171/373–0123, FAX 0171/373–9497. 26 rooms, 10 apartments. Breakfast room. AE, DC, MC, V. Tube: Gloucester Rd.*

$$$ ★ **The Gore.** Just down the road from the Albert Hall, this very friendly hotel is run by the same people who run Hazlitt's (*see* Soho and Covent Garden, *above*) and features a similar eclectic selection of prints, etchings, and antiques. Here, though, are spectacular folly-like rooms—Room 101 is a Tudor fantasy with minstrel gallery, stained glass, and four-poster bed, and Room 211, done in over-the-top Hollywood style, has a tiled mural of Greek goddesses in the bathroom. Despite all that, the Gore manages to remain most elegant. Bistrot 190 (*see* Chapter 4, Restaurants and Pubs) and Downstairs at 190 serve as dining rooms and bar. *189 Queen's Gate, SW7 5EX, ☎ 0171/584–6601, FAX 0171/589–8127. 54 rooms. Brasserie, lounge. AE, DC, MC, V. Tube: Gloucester Rd.*

$$ **Hotel 167.** This friendly little bed-and-breakfast (B&B) is a two-minute walk from the V&A, in a grand white-stucco Victorian corner house. The lobby is immediately cheering, with its round marble tables, wrought-iron chairs, palms, and modern paintings; it also does duty as lounge and breakfast room. Bedrooms have a hybrid antiquey/Ikea style, with Venetian blinds over double-glazed windows (which you need on this noisy road), plus cable TV and minibars. *167 Old Brompton Rd., SW5 0AN, ☎ 0171/373–0672, FAX 0171/373–3360. 19 rooms with bath or shower. Lounge/breakfast room. AE, DC, MC, V. Tube: Gloucester Rd.*

$$ **Kensington Close.** This large, fairly utilitarian hotel feels like a smaller one and boasts a few extras you wouldn't expect for the reasonable rate and convenient location (in a quiet lane off Kensington High Street. The main attraction is the health club, with an 18-meter pool, two squash courts, a steam room, and a beauty salon; there's also a secluded little water garden. Standard rooms are on the small side, with plain chain-hotel (this one has belonged to the British Forte Hotels for 50 years) built-in furniture. Some Executive rooms are twice the size. Good value. *Wrights La., W8 5SP, ☎ 0171/937–8170, FAX 0171/937–8289. 530 rooms.*

Lodging in Kensington, Knightsbridge, Chelsea and Belgrc

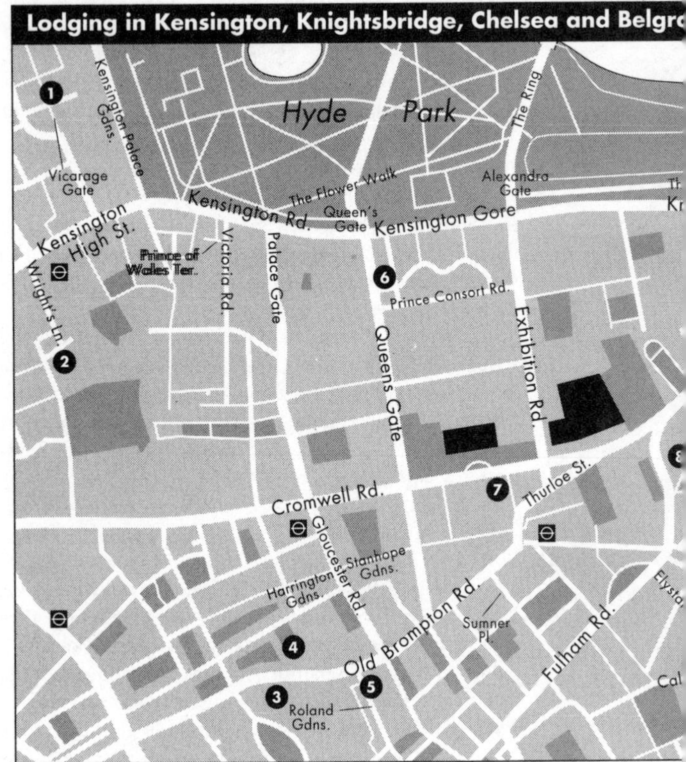

Basil Street, **13**
Beaufort, **10**
Blakes, **5**
Claverley, **9**
The Cranley, **4**
The Franklin, **8**
The Gore, **6**
Goring, **17**
The Halkin, **16**
Hotel 167, **3**
Hyde Park Hotel, **14**
Kensington Close, **2**
Knightsbridge Green, **12**
The Lanesborough, **15**
L'Hotel, **11**
The Pelham, **7**
Vicarage, **1**

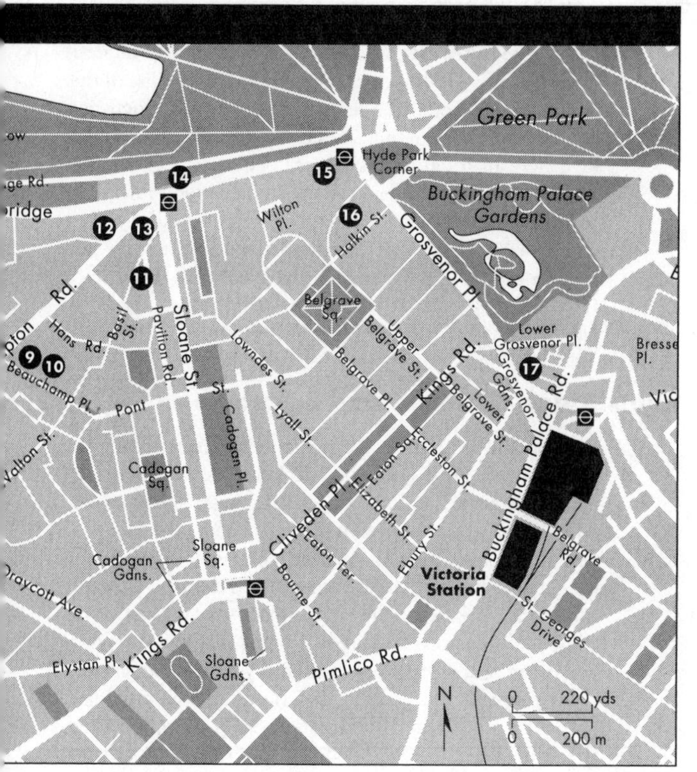
Green Park
Hyde Park Corner
Buckingham Palace Gardens
Wilton Pl.
Halkin St.
Grosvenor Pl.
Belgrave Sq.
Upper Belgrave St.
Lower Grosvenor Pl.
Bressenden Pl.
Grosvenor Gdns.
Lower Belgrave St.
Buckingham Palace Rd.
Kings Rd.
Belgrave Pl.
Lowndes St.
Lyall St.
Eaton Sq.
Eccleston St.
Elizabeth St.
Eaton Pl.
Cliveden Pl.
Eaton Ter.
Bourne St.
Ebury St.
Victoria Station
Belgrave Rd.
St. Georges Drive
Pimlico Rd.
Sloane St.
Pavilion Rd.
Basil St.
Hans Rd.
Beauchamp Pl.
Pont St.
Walton St.
Cadogan Sq.
Cadogan Pl.
Sloane Sq.
Cadogan Gdns.
Draycott Ave.
Elystan Pl.
Sloane Gdns.
N
0
220 yds
200 m

2 restaurants, 2 bars, lounge, indoor pool, health club, baby-sitting. AE, DC, MC, V. Tube: High St. Kensington.

$ ★ **Vicarage.** A great deal of care goes into the running of this family-owned hotel in a leaf-shaded big white Victorian house just off Kensington Church Street (spend the cash you save here in its antiques shops). The decor is sweetly anachronistic, full of heavy, dark-stained wood furniture, patterned carpets, and brass pendant lights, and there's a little conservatory. Six of the spotless bedrooms have just been redecorated, and many now have TVs. *10 Vicarage Gate, W8 4AG, ☎ 0171/229–4030. 19 rooms. Lounge. No credit cards. Tube: High St. Kensington.*

Knightsbridge, Chelsea, and Belgravia

$$$$ ★ **The Halkin.** If you can't take any more Regency stripes, English-country florals, or Louis XV chaises, this luxurious little place is the antidote. You could say its slickness doesn't belong in the '90s, or you could just enjoy the Milanese design: the clean-cut white marble lobby with its royal-blue leather bucket chairs, the arresting curved charcoal-gray corridors, the "diseased mahogany" veneers that darken as you climb, and the gray-on-gray bedrooms that light up when you insert your electronic key. Wealthy business and media types frequent the Halkin, and they can't breathe easy without a fax, Reuters, and two phone lines with conference-call. These are provided, along with two touch-control pads for all the gadgets, cable TV and video (library downstairs), room safe, and minibar. The bathrooms are palaces of shiny chrome, anti-mist mirrors, and marble that changes color according to which floor you're on. It might be like living in the Design Museum, except that this place employs some of the friendliest staff around—and they look pretty good in their white Armani uniforms, too. *Halkin St., SW1X 7DJ, ☎ 0171/333–1000, FAX 0171/333–1100. 41 rooms. Restaurant, Reuters news service. AE, DC, MC, V. Tube: Hyde Park Corner.*

$$$$ ★ **Hyde Park Hotel.** For just over 100 years, the Hyde Park has entertained lavishly, its banqueting rooms and ballroom regularly hosting royalty—including the current batch, who still have a designated Royal Entrance—its bedrooms housing assorted stars from Rudolph Valentino to Winston

Churchill. Forte Hotels owns it now, and has done a grand job restoring its eight-kinds-of-marble halls and strewing fine antiques and paintings throughout. Bedrooms are large and hushed. Some have gentle windowfuls of treetop; from others, you can preview your Harvey Nichols purchases, since the building stands on the cusp of Knightsbridge shops and Hyde Park itself. The 1993 opening of Marco Pierre White: The Restaurant did no harm to the Hyde Park's image—they've now got the chef with the biggest attitude, and one of the biggest talents, in London. The blinding white basement gym isn't bad, either. *66 Knightsbridge, SW1Y 7LA,* ☎ *0171/235–2000,* FAX *0171/235–2000. 160 rooms. 2 restaurants, bar, lounge, beauty salon, health club, theater ticket desk. AE, DC, MC, V. Tube: Knightsbridge.*

$$$$ **The Lanesborough.** This very grand hotel acts for all the world as though the Prince Regent took a ride through time and is about to resume residence. Royally proportioned public rooms (not lounges but "The Library" and "The Withdrawing Room") lead one off the other like an exquisite giant Chinese box in this multimillion-pound American-run conversion of the old St. George's Hospital opposite Wellington's house. Everything undulates with richness—brocades and Regency stripes, moiré silks and fleurs-de-lys in the colors of precious stones, magnificent antiques and oil paintings, reproductions of more gilded splendor than the originals, handwoven £250-per-square-yard carpet—as if Liberace and Laura Ashley had collaborated on the design. All you do to register is sign the visitors book, then retire to your room, where you are waited on by a personal butler. Full-size Lanesborough toiletries, umbrellas (take them home), robes (don't), a drinks tray (pay by the inch), and even business cards with your temporary fax (in every room) and phone numbers (two lines) are waiting. If you yearn for a bygone age and are very rich, this is certainly for you. Nonresidents can have lunch in the slightly self-conscious conservatory, invest £500 in a shot of "liquid history", or a sip of 1812 cognac from bar manager Salvatore Calabrese's eccentric collection. *1 Lanesborough Pl., SW1X 7TA,* ☎ *0171/259–5599,* FAX *0171/259–5606. 95 rooms. 2 restaurants, bar. AE, DC, MC, V. Tube: Hyde Park Corner.*

$$$ **Basil Street.** A gracious Edwardian hotel on a quiet street behind busy Brompton Road and off (rich) shoppers heaven,

Sloane Street. It's been family-run for three quarters of a century, and has always been popular with lone woman travelers, who get automatic membership at the Parrot Club—an enormous lounge, with copies of *The Lady* and *Country Life* among the coffee cups. All the bedrooms are different; many are like grandma's guest room, with overstuffed counterpanes and a random selection of furniture—some good pieces, some utilitarian. You can write letters home in the peaceful gallery, which has polished wooden floors and fine Turkish carpets underneath a higgledy-piggledy wealth of antiques. Americans with a taste for period charm like this place; some come back often enough to merit the title "Basilite"—a privileged regular offered a 15% discount. *Basil St., SW3 1AH, ☎ 0171/581–3311, FAX 0171/581–3693. 92 rooms, 72 with bath. Restaurant, lounge, wine bar. AE, DC, MC, V. Tube: Knightsbridge.*

$$$ ★ **Beaufort.** You can practically hear the jingle of Harrods's cash registers from a room at the Beaufort, the brainchild of ex–TV announcer Diana Wallis, who employs an all-woman team to run the hotel. Actually, "hotel" is a misnomer for this elegant pair of Victorian houses. There's a sitting room instead of Reception; guests have a front door key and the run of the drinks cabinet, and even their own phone number, with the customary astronomical hotel surcharges waived. The high-ceilinged, generously proportioned rooms are decorated in muted, sophisticated shades to suit the muted, sophisticated atmosphere—but don't worry, you're encouraged by the incredibly sweet staff to feel at home. The rates are higher than the top range for this category but include unlimited drinks, breakfast, and membership at a local health club. *33 Beaufort Gardens, SW3 1PP, ☎ 0171/584–5252, FAX 0171/589–2834. 29 rooms. Air-conditioning. AE, DC, MC, V. Tube: Knightsbridge.*

$$$ **The Franklin.** It's hard to imagine, while taking tea in this pretty hotel overlooking a quiet, grassy square, that you're an amble away from busy Brompton and Cromwell roads and the splendors of the V&A. A few of the rooms are small, but the marble bathrooms—in which Floris toiletries and heated towel racks are standard issue—are not; the large garden rooms and suites (which fall into the $$$$ category) are romantic indeed. Tea is served daily in the lounge, and there's also a self-service bar. The staff is friendly and ac-

commodating. If the Franklin is booked up, then consider its slightly older (1990) sister hotel, the **Egerton House** (☎ 0171/589–2412, FAX 0171/584–6540), just around the corner on Egerton Terrace. *28 Egerton Gardens, SW3 2DB, ☎ 0171/584–5533 or 800/473–9487, FAX 0171/584–5449. 40 rooms. Bar, lounge, air-conditioning, valet parking (fee). AE, DC, MC, V. Tube: S. Kensington.*

$$$ **Goring.** Useful if you have to drop in at Buckingham Palace, just around the corner. In fact, visiting VIPs use it regularly as a conveniently close, and suitably dignified, base for royal occasions. The hotel was built by Mr. Goring in 1910 and is now run by third-generation Gorings. The atmosphere remains Edwardian: Bathrooms are marble-fitted, and some of the bedrooms have brass bedsteads and the original built-in closets; many have been opulently redecorated. The bar/lounge looks onto a well-tended garden. *15 Beeston Pl., Grosvenor Gardens, SW1W 0JW, ☎ 0171/834–8211, FAX 0171/834–8211. 87 rooms. Restaurant, bar, lounge. AE, DC, MC, V. Tube: Victoria.*

$$$ ★ **L'Hotel.** An upscale B&B run by the same Levins who own the Capital next door. This is a plainer alternative—less pampering, unfussy decor. There's an air of provincial France around, with the white wrought-iron bedsteads, pine furniture, and delicious breakfast croissants and baguettes (included in the room rate) served on that chunky dark green and gold Parisian café china in Le Metro cellar wine bar (also open to nonresidents). This really is like a house—you're given your own front door key, there's no elevator, and the staff leaves in the evening. Reserve ahead—it's very popular. *28 Basil St., SW3 1AT, ☎ 0171/589–6286, FAX 0171/225–0011. 12 rooms. Restaurant, wine bar. AE, V. Tube: Knightsbridge.*

$$$ **The Pelham.** The second of three gorgeous hotels for husband and wife Tim and Kit Kemp, an architect and an interior designer; they opened it in 1989 and this one looks more the country house. There's 18th-century pine paneling in the drawing room, flowers galore, quite a bit of glazed chintz and antique lace bed linen, and the odd four-poster and bedroom fireplace. Everything is exquisite, including the nearby garden with its heated pool. The Pelham stands opposite the South Kensington tube stop, by the big museums, and close to the shops of Brompton Cross and

Knightsbridge, with Kemps restaurant supplying an on-site trendy menu. Lauren Bacall deserted the Athenaeum for this hotel. ☐ *15 Cromwell Pl., SW7 2LA,* ☎ *0171/589–8288,* FAX *0171/584–8444. 37 rooms. Restaurant, air-conditioning, outdoor pool. AE, MC, V. Tube: S. Kensington.*

$$ **Claverley.** Can't afford the Beaufort, but like the area? This B&B is on the same quiet street a moment from Harrods and makes a good alternative. The less expensive rooms have either bath or shower (not both); as you go up the scale, rooms get larger, decor (homey florals, either Victorian- or Edwardian-style) newer, and bathrooms better equipped; some top-rate rooms have four-poster beds. The service is friendly, everything's spotless, and breakfast is included. ☐ *13–14 Beaufort Gardens, SW3 1PS,* ☎ *0171/589–8541,* FAX *0171/584–3410. 36 rooms. AE, V. Tube: Knightsbridge.*

$$ **Knightsbridge Green.** There are more suites than bedrooms at this Georgian hotel that's a two-minute walk from Harrods. One floor is French-style, with white furniture, another English, in beech. Costing only £15 more than a double room, the suites are not overpriced, and all the rooms have trouser presses and tea-and coffee-makers. There's no restaurant, but there are plenty in the area; or if you ask they'll send the porter out to find you a sandwich. There's also coffee and cake left out in the lounge—a detail that exemplifies the friendliness of this place. ☐ *159 Knightsbridge, SW1X 7PD,* ☎ *0171/584–6274,* FAX *0171/225–1635. 13 rooms, 12 suites. Lounge. AE, MC, V. Closed 5 days over Christmas. Tube: Knightsbridge.*

Bayswater and Notting Hill Gate

$$$$ ★ **Halcyon.** Discretion, decadent decor, and disco divas (everyone from RuPaul and Simple Minds to Snoop Doggy Dogg) make this expensive, enormous, wedding-cake Edwardian on Holland Park Avenue desperately desirable. You want film stars? Johnny Depp and William Hurt and Julia Roberts, and there are usually local residents like Sting, John Cleese, and *Absolutely Fabulous* Joanna Lumley haunting the absolutely excellent restaurant. But that's all by the by, since it's for perfect service and gorgeous rooms you'd follow them here. Many hotels lie when they claim "individ-

ual" room decor; not this one. The Blue Room has moons and stars, the famous Egyptian Suite is canopied like a bedouin tent; one room has a Jacuzzi and mint green stripes, another has heraldic motifs, black and red walls, a four-poster, and creaky floorboards; the Halcyon Suite has its own conservatory. All rooms are very large, with the high ceilings and big windows typical of the grand houses here—here being a ten-minute tube ride to the West End, and steps from London's most exquisite park. 🏨 *81 Holland Park, W11 3RZ,* ☎ *0171/727–7288,* FAX *0171/229–8516. 44 rooms. Restaurant. AE, DC, MC, V. Tube: Holland Park.*

$$ **London Elizabeth.** Steps from Hyde Park, Lancaster Gate tube, and from rows of depressing cheap hotels, is this family-owned gem. Foyer and lounge are crammed with coffee tables and chintz drapery, lace antimacassars, and little chandeliers, and this country sensibility persists through the bedrooms. All will by now have been redone—in palest blue-striped walls, wooden picture rails and Welsh wool bedspreads, or in pink cabbage rose prints and mahogany furniture—and although they do vary in size, there's a thoughtful tendency here to make sure what you lose on the swings (small wedge-shaped room), you gain on the roundabouts (bigger, brand new bathroom, or a small balcony). You wouldn't expect 24-hour room service in a little place like this, but Chez Joseph, the "Continental" restaurant, provides it. Some rooms lack a full-length mirror, but they do have TV, direct dial phone, and hair dryer, and they're serviced by an exceptionally charming Anglo-Irish staff. 🏨 *Lancaster Terrace, W2 3PF,* ☎ *0171/402–6641,* FAX *0171/224–8900. 55 rooms. Restaurant, bar, lounge. AE, DC, MC, V. Tube: Lancaster Gate.*

$$ ★ **Pembridge Court.** A few doors down from the Abbey Court, in a similar colonnaded white-stucco Victorian row house, is Paul and Merete Capra's sweet home-away-from-home of a hotel, cozy with scatter cushions and books, quirky Victoriana, and framed fans from the neighboring Portobello Market—around which Merete gives private insider tours. Bedrooms have a great deal of swagged floral drapery, direct-dial phones, and satellite TV, and there's an elevator to the upper floors. Unusually for a small hotel, there's a restaurant, Caps, serving a French-bistro menu, plus the English breakfast that rates include (brought to your room

Abbey Court, **2**
Camelot, **7**
Columbia, **6**
Commodore, **5**
The Gate, **4**
Halcyon, **3**
London Elizabeth, **8**
Pembridge Court, **2**
Portobello, **1**

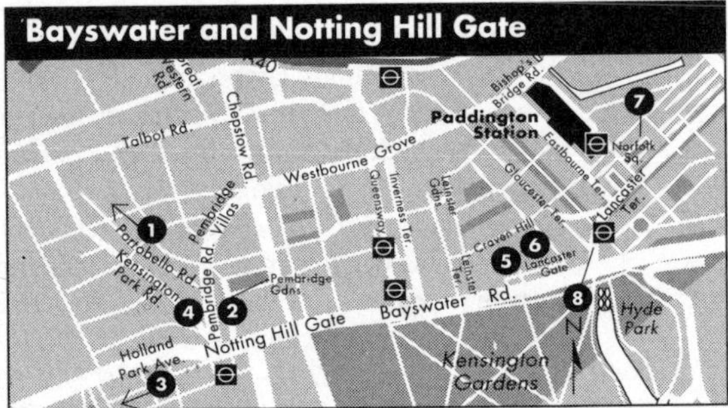

if you prefer)—take that into account when doing your sums, since only the half-size small twin rooms fall into the $$ category; larger ones are £10–£30 more. *34 Pembridge Gardens, W2 4DX, ☎ 0171/229–9977, FAX 0171/727–4982. 25 rooms. Restaurant, lounge. AE, DC, MC, V. Tube: Notting Hill Gate.*

$$ Portobello. This small, eccentric hotel consists of two adjoining Victorian houses which (as is common around here) back onto a beautiful large garden that is shared with the neighbors. It has long been the favorite of the arty end of the music biz and other media types. Some rooms are minute, others huge—you must book well ahead or depend on luck. Big mirrors, palms, and ferns are everywhere, as befits the fantasy Victorian decor. The naughty round-bedded suite is popular, though it falls in the top end of our $$$ category; only the small (some are *very* small) doubles are $$, but all rates include breakfast. The 24-hour basement bar/restaurant is one of many hangouts for locals in this very happening area. *22 Stanley Gardens, W11 2NG, ☎ 0171/727–2777, FAX 0171/792–9641. 25 rooms. Restaurant, bar. AE, DC, MC, V. Closed 10 days over Christmas. Tube: Ladbroke Grove.*

$ Camelot. This is an affordable hotel, just around the corner from Paddington Station, with bedrooms featuring utility pine furniture, TVs, tea/coffee makers, and attractive bathrooms. There's a lounge, and a very pretty breakfast room complete with exposed brick wall, large open fireplace, wooden farmhouse tables and floorboards, and a gallery of child guests' works of art. Everyone here is friendly beyond the call of duty. The few bathless single rooms are great bargains; the normal rate just busts the top of this category, but includes a breakfast of anything you want—full English or organic muesli, fruit, and herb tea. ☒ *45–47 Norfolk Sq., W2 1RX, ☎ 0171/723–9118, FAX 0171/402–3412. 44 rooms, 36 with bath. Lounge with VCR. MC, V. Tube: Paddington.*

$ ★ **Columbia.** If you're a sucker for '70s kitsch and like to stay out late, or alternatively, if you're a family on a tight budget, this unique paradox of a bargain hotel is worth a try. The public rooms in these five joined-up Victorians are as big as museum halls, painted in icy hues of powder blue and buttermilk, or panelled in dark wood. During the day, at one end they contain the most hip band du jour drinking alcohol; at the other, there are sightseers sipping coffee. However, the place is big enough and the walls thick enough that you'd not even know they were shooting sleazy clubwear for *The Face* magazine in room 100 while you use the hair dryer (provided) sipping tea (provided) and watching TV in room 101 (there's a direct-dial phone and a safe too). Rooms are clean and ceilings high, and some rooms are very large (especially those with three or four beds), with park views and balconies. It's just a shame that teak veneer, khaki-beige-brown color schemes, and avocado bathroom suites haven't made it back into the style bible yet. ☒ *95–99 Lancaster Gate, W2 3NS, ☎ 0171/402–0021, FAX 0171/706–4691. 103 rooms. Restaurant, bar, lounge, meeting rooms. AE, MC, V. Tube: Lancaster Gate.*

$ ★ **Commodore.** This peaceful hotel of three converted Victorians is close to the Columbia, deeper in the big leafy square known as Lancaster Gate. It's another independent, and another find, of a very different stripe, as you'd notice on entering the cozy, carpeted lounge with its muted colors and little fireplace. Try your best to get one of the amazing rooms—as superior to the regular ones (which usually go to package tour groups) as Harrods is to Woolworths, but priced the same. Twenty of these are split-level rooms with sleeping gallery, all large, all different, all with something special—like a walk-in closet with its own stained-glass window—and all with the full deck of tea/coffeemakers, hair dryers, and TV with pay movies. One (No. 11) is a duplex, entered through a secret mirrored door off a lemon yellow hallway with palms and Greek statuary, with a thick-carpeted *very* quiet bedroom upstairs and its toilet below. It's

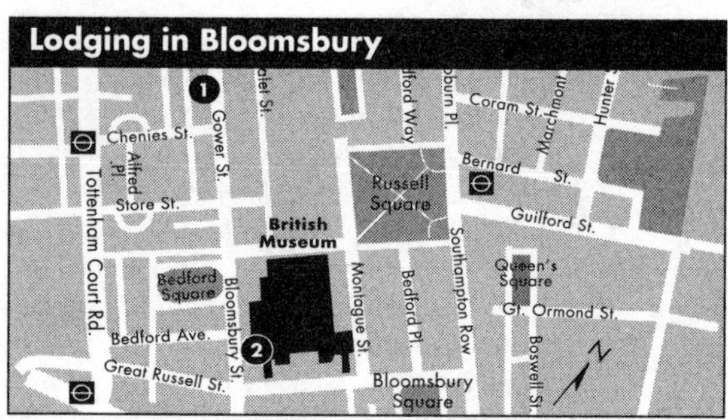

getting very popular here, so book ahead. 🏨 *50 Lancaster Gate W2 3NA, ☎ 0171/402–5291, FAX 0171/262–1088. 90 rooms. Bar, lounge, business services. AE, MC, V. Tube: Lancaster Gate.*

$ **The Gate.** It's absolutely teeny, the Gate, just a normal house at the very top of Portobello Road, off Notting Hill Gate. The plain bedrooms have fridges, TVs, direct-dial phones, and tea/coffee facilities, plus bath (unless you opt for a smaller, £10 cheaper, shower-only room), and you can have the inclusive Continental breakfast brought up to them, or take it in the first-floor lounge. 🏨 *6 Portobello Rd, W11 3DG, ☎ 0171/221–2403, FAX 0171/221–9128. 6 rooms. Lounge. AE, MC, V. Tube: Notting Hill Gate.*

Bloomsbury

$$ **Academy.** These three joined-up Georgian houses, boasting a patio garden and a wood-floored, mirrored basement bar/brasserie, supply the most sophisticated and hotel-like facilities in the Gower Street "hotel row." The comfortable bedrooms have TVs (no cable), direct-dial phones, and tea/coffee makers, and the two without en suite bathrooms are an entire £30/night cheaper. Like all the hotels in this section, the Academy neighbors the British Museum and University of London, a circumstance that appeals to culture vultures on a budget and the more affluent students. 🏨 *17–21 Gower St., WC1E 6HG, ☎ 0171/631–4115, FAX 0171/636–3442. 33 rooms, 25 with bath/shower. Restaurant/bar, lounge. AE, DC, MC, V. Tube: Russell Sq.*

$ ★ **Morgan.** This is a Georgian row-house hotel, family-run with charm and panache: Rooms are small and functionally furnished, yet friendly and cheerful overall, with phones and TVs. The five newish apartments are particularly pleasing: three times the size of normal rooms (and an extra £15/night, placing them in the $$ category), complete with eat-in kitchens (gourmet cooking sessions are discouraged) and private phone lines. The tiny paneled breakfast room (rates include the meal) is straight out of a doll's house. The back rooms overlook the British Museum. ⊞ *24 Bloomsbury St., WC1B 3QJ,* ☎ *0171/636–3735. 15 rooms with bath or shower, 5 apartments. Breakfast room. No credit cards. Tube: Russell Sq.*

6 The Arts and Nightlife

THE ARTS

WE'VE ATTEMPTED a representative selection in the following listings, but to find out what's showing now, the weekly magazine *Time Out* (it comes out every Wednesday—Tuesday in central London) is invaluable. The *Evening Standard* also carries listings, especially the Friday edition, as do the "quality" Sunday papers and the Friday and Saturday *Independent, Guardian,* and *Times.* You'll find racks overflowing with leaflets and flyers in most cinema and theater foyers, too, and you can pick up the free fortnightly "London Theatre Guide" leaflet from hotels and tourist information centers.

Theater

Of the 100 or so legitimate theaters in the capital, 50 are officially "West End," while the remainder go under the blanket title of "Fringe." Much like New York's Off- and Off-Off-Broadway, Fringe Theater encompasses everything from off-the-wall "physical theater" pieces to first runs of new plays and revivals of old ones.

Most theaters have matinees twice a week (Wednesday or Thursday and Saturday) and evening performances that begin at 7:30 or 8; performances on Sunday are rare, but not unknown. Prices vary, but in the West End you should expect to pay from £8 for a seat in the upper balcony to at least £20 for a good one in the stalls (orchestra) or dress circle (mezzanine). Ticket agents, such as **First Call** (☎ 0171/240–7941) or **TicketMaster** (☎ 0171/413–3321 or 800/775–2525 from the U.S.), usually do charge a booking fee. If you're coming from the United States and wish to book seats in advance, **Keith Prowse** has a New York office (234 W. 44th St., Suite 1000, New York, NY 10036, ☎ 212/398–1430 or 800/669–8687). Alternatively, the Half Price Ticket Booth (no ☎) on the southwest corner of Leicester Square sells half-price tickets on the day of performance for approximately 25 theaters (subject to availability). It's open Monday–Saturday from noon for matinees and

2:30–6:30 for evening performances; there is a £1.50 service charge, and only cash is accepted.

Warning: Be *very* careful of scalpers outside theaters; they have been known to charge £200 or more for a sought-after ticket.

The **Royal Shakespeare Company** and the **Royal National Theatre Company** perform at London's two main arts complexes, the **Barbican Centre** and **The Royal National Theatre** respectively. Both companies mount consistently excellent productions and are usually a safe option for anyone having trouble choosing which play to see. Fringe shows can be straight plays, circus, comedy, musicals, readings, or productions every bit as polished and impressive as those in the West End—except for their location and the price of the seat. All West End and fringe shows are listed in *Time Out.*

Concerts

The ticket prices to symphony-size orchestral concerts are fortunately still relatively moderate, usually ranging from £5 to £15. The London Symphony Orchestra is in residence at the **Barbican Centre,** although other top orchestras—including the Philharmonia and the Royal Philharmonic—also perform here. The **South Bank Arts Complex,** which includes the **Royal Festival Hall,** the **Queen Elizabeth Hall,** and the small **Purcell Room,** forms another major venue. For a different concert-going experience, as well as the chance to take part in a great British tradition, try the **Royal Albert Hall** during the Promenade Concert season: eight weeks lasting from July to September. Another summer pleasure is the outdoor concert series by the lake at **Kenwood** (Hampstead Heath, ☎ 0181/348–6684). Concerts are also part of the program at the open-air theater in **Holland Park** (no ☎).

You should also look for the lunchtime concerts that take place all over the city in smaller concert halls, the big arts center foyers, and churches; they usually cost under £5 or are free and will feature string quartets, singers, jazz ensembles, or gospel choirs. **St. John's, Smith Square** and **St. Martin-in-the-Fields** are two of the more popular locations. Performances usually begin about 1 PM and last an hour.

Opera

The main venue for opera in London is the **Royal Opera House** (Covent Garden), which ranks with the Metropolitan Opera House in New York. Prices range from £5 in the upper slips to well over £100 for the best seats.

English-language productions are staged at the **Coliseum,** home of the **English National Opera Company.** Prices here are lower than at the Royal Opera House, ranging from £8 to £45.

Ballet

The Royal Opera House is also the home of the world-famous **Royal Ballet.** The **English National Ballet** and visiting international companies perform at the Coliseum and the Royal Festival Hall from time to time. **Sadler's Wells Theatre** also hosts various other ballet companies and regional and international modern dance troupes.

Modern Dance

In addition to the many Fringe theaters that produce the odd dance performance, the following theaters showcase contemporary dance:

The Place (17 Duke's Rd., WC1, ☎ 0171/387–0031), **Riverside Studios** (Crisp Rd., W6 9RL, ☎ 0181/748–3354), and **Sadler's Wells** (Roseberry Ave., EC1R 4TN, ☎ 0171/278–8916).

Movies

Most of the major houses (Odeon, MGM, etc.) congregate in the Leicester Square/Piccadilly Circus area, where tickets average £4–£7. Mondays and matinees are sometimes better buys at £2–£4, and there are also fewer crowds.

One of the best repertory cinemas is the **National Film Theatre** (in the South Bank Arts Complex, ☎ 0171/928–3232), where the London Film Festival is based in the fall; there are also lectures and presentations. Daily memberships cost 40p. Also worth checking out are the **Everyman** (Hollybush Vale, Hampstead, ☎ 0171/435–1525; membership 60p/year) and the **Rio** (Kingsland High St., Hackney E8, ☎ 0171/254–6677), though it's a bit of a trek.

West End Theaters and Concert Halls

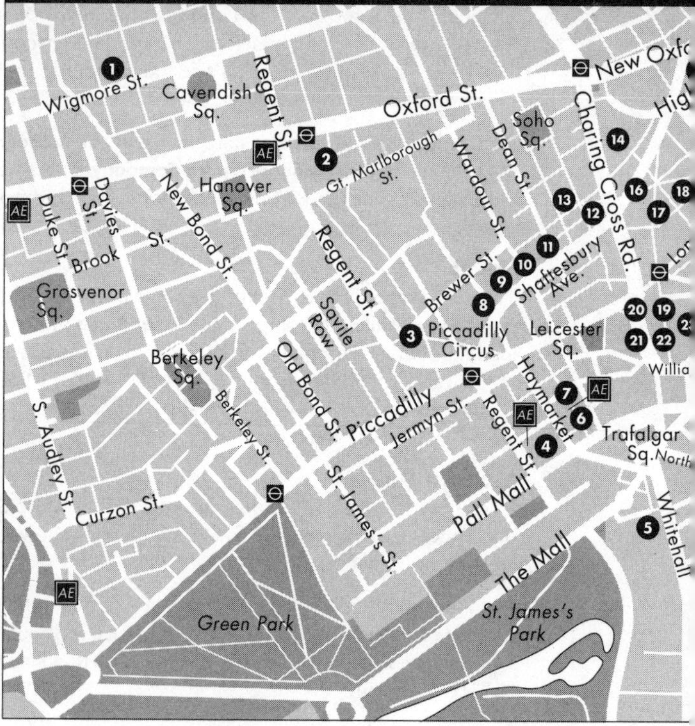

Adelphi, **33**
Albery, **19**
Aldwych, **28**
Ambassadors, **16**
Apollo, **9**
Barbican, **40**
Cambridge, **18**
Coliseum, **23**
Comedy, **7**
Drury Lane, **27**
Duchess, **30**
Duke of York's, **22**
Fortune, **26**
Garrick, **21**
Globe, **10**
Haymarket, **6**
Her Majesty's, **4**
London Palladium, **2**
Lyric, **8**
Mermaid, **39**
National Theatre, **36**
New London, **25**
Old Vic, **37**
Palace, **12**
Phoenix, **14**
Piccadilly, **3**
Playhouse, **34**
Prince Edward, **13**
Queen's, **11**
Royal Opera House, **24**
Sadler's Wells, **41**
St. Martin's, **17**
Savoy, **31**
Shaftesbury, **15**
South Bank Arts Complex, **35**
Strand, **29**
Vaudeville, **32**
Whitehall, **5**
Wigmore Hall, **1**
Wyndham's, **20**
Young Vic, **38**

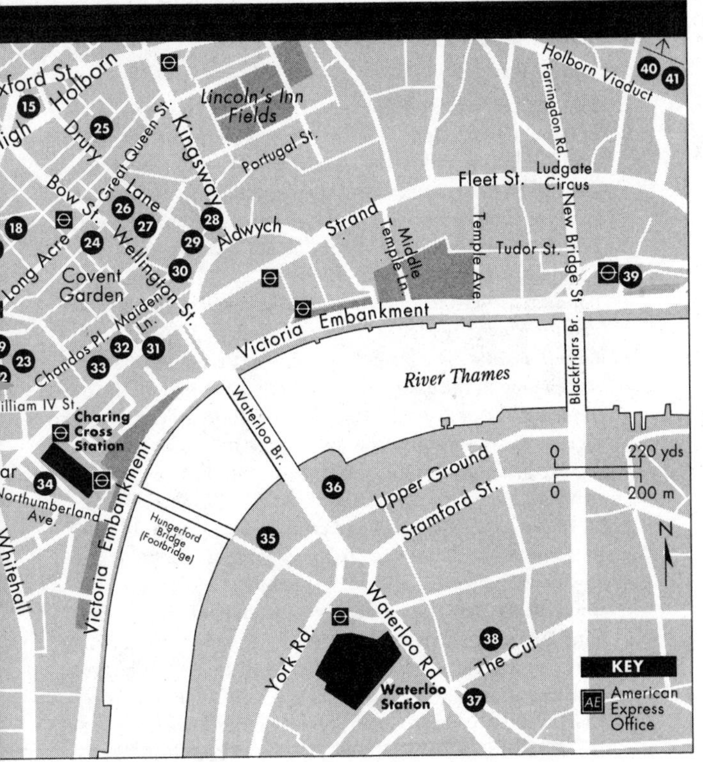
Holborn
Kingsway
Lincoln's Inn Fields
Portugal St.
Drury Lane
Great Queen St.
Bow St.
Long Acre
Covent Garden
Wellington St.
Aldwych
Strand
Fleet St.
Ludgate Circus
Holborn Viaduct
Farringdon Rd.
New Bridge St.
Middle Temple Ln.
Temple Ave.
Tudor St.
Maiden Ln.
Chandos Pl.
Victoria Embankment
River Thames
Blackfriars Br.
Waterloo Br.
Charing Cross Station
Northumberland Ave.
Whitehall
Hungerford Bridge (Footbridge)
Upper Ground
Stamford St.
0
220 yds
0
200 m
N
York Rd.
Waterloo Rd.
Waterloo Station
The Cut
KEY
AE
American Express Office

NIGHTLIFE

Jazz

Jazz Café. This palace of high-tech cool in a converted bank in bohemian Camden has its problems—you often have to stand in line, and there never seems to be enough seating—but still it remains an essential hangout for fans of the mainstream end of the repertoire and younger crossover performers. It's way north, but steps from Camden Town tube. *5–7 Pkwy., NW1, ☏ 0171/916–6000. ☛ £7–£12, depending on band. ⏲ Mon.–Sat. 7 PM–late (time varies). Reservations advised for balcony restaurant. AE, DC, MC, V.*

Ronnie Scott's. The legendary Soho jazz club which, since its opening in the early '60s, has been attracting all the big names. It's usually packed and hot, the food isn't great, service is slow—because the staff can't move through the crowds, either—but the atmosphere can't be beat, and it's probably still London's best. *47 Frith St., W1, ☏ 0171/439–0747. ☛ £10–£12 nonmembers. ⏲ Mon.–Sat. 8:30 PM–3 AM, Sun. 8–11:30 PM. Reservations advised; essential some nights. AE, DC, MC, V.*

South Bank. A certain kind of really big name (Carla Bley, Jan Garbarek, Richard Thompson . . .) ends up here, at the Royal Festival Hall, or the Queen Elizabeth Hall. What you lose in atmosphere, you gain in acoustical clarity, and you save wear and tear on the shoe leather. *Waterloo, ☏ 0171/928–8800. ☛ £7.50–£15. Jazz concerts usually start 7:30 PM; call for this week's events. Reservations essential. AE, MC, V.*

The Vortex. In the wilds of Stoke Newington, a very happening, liberal-arts neighborhood, with tons of vegetarian/Asian–type restaurants, is this showcase venue for the healthy British jazz scene, with the emphasis on advanced, free, and improvised work. *Stoke Newington Church St., N16, ☏ 0171/254–6516. ☛ £4–£6. ⏲ Most nights 8–11 PM. MC, V.*

Rock

The Forum. This ex-ballroom with balcony and dance floor packs in the customers and consistently attracts the best medium-to-big-name performers, too. Get the tube to Kentish Town, then follow the hordes. *9–17 Highgate Rd.,*

NW5, ☎ 0171/284–2200. ☛ Around £8–£12. ⌚ Most nights 7–11. AE, MC, V.

Rock Garden. Famous for the setting and for encouraging young talent to move on to bigger and better things. Talking Heads, U2, and The Smiths are just a few who made their London debuts here. Music is in the basement, where there is standing room only, so eat first. *6–7 The Piazza, Covent Garden, WC2, ☎ 0171/240–3961. ☛ £4–£7 depending on band. ⌚ Mon.–Sat. 7:30 PM–late (times vary); Sun. 8 PM–midnight. AE, DC, MC, V.*

Shepherd's Bush Empire. London's newest major venue was converted from the BBC TV theater, where Terry Wogan, the United Kingdom's Johnny Carson, recorded his show for years and years. Now it hosts the same kind of medium-big names as the north London Forum. *Shepherd's Bush Green, W12, ☎ 0181/740–7474. ☛ £8–£12. ⌚ 7:30–11. AE, MC, V.*

Subterania. Home of Notting Hillbillies everywhere—that is, the hip and cool bohemians of the neighborhood—this large, medium-tech balconied club never welcomes mainstream bands but books the top musicians in any alternative genre from all over the world. *12 Acklam Rd., W10, ☎ 0181/960–4590. ☛ £6–£8. Call for hours; bands play Tues.–Thurs. MC, V.*

Clubs

Always call ahead, especially to the dance and youth-oriented places, because the club scene changes constantly.

Café de Paris. This former gilt and red velveteen ballroom still looks like a disreputable tea-dance hall but hosts hot, hip nights for twenty-to-thirty-somethings who dress the part. *3 Coventry St., W1, ☎ 0171/287–3602. ☛ £5–£12. ⌚ Wed. 10 PM–4 AM, Thurs.–Sat. 11 PM–6 AM. No credit cards.*

Camden Palace. This is the student tourist's first stop, though some nights are hipper than others. Still, it would be difficult to find a facial wrinkle, even if you could see through the laser lights and find your way around the three floors of bars. There's often a live band. *1A Camden High St., NW1, ☎ 0171/387–0428. ☛ £3–£9. ⌚ Tues.–Sat. 9 PM–3 AM. No credit cards.*

The Gardening Club. Next door to the Rock Garden (*see* Rock, *above*), this club has different music, ambience, and groovers on different nights, but is consistently the place to be, especially if you're not yet 30. (*See* Queer Nation *in* The Gay Scene, *below.*) *4 The Piazza, WC2,* ☏ *0171/497-3154.* ☛ *£4–£12.* ⏲ *Mon.–Wed. 10 PM–3 AM, Fri. and Sat. 11 PM–6 AM. AE, MC, DC, V.*

Heaven. London's premier (mainly) gay club is the best place for dancing wildly for hours. A state-of-the-art laser show and a large, throbbing dance floor complement a labyrinth of quieter bars and lounges and a snack bar. (*See* The Gay Scene, *below.*) *Under the Arches, Villiers St., WC2,* ☏ *0171/839–2520.* ☛ *£4–£8. Call for opening times (Tues.–Sat. approx. 10 PM–3:30 AM). AE, DC, MC, V.*

Stringfellows. Peter Stringfellow's first London nightclub is not at all hip, but *is* glitzy, with mirrored walls, the requisite dance-floor light show, and an expensive art deco–style restaurant. Suburbanites and middle-aged swingers frequent it. *16–19 Upper St. Martin's La., WC2,* ☏ *0171/240–5534.* ☛ *Mon.–Wed. £8; Thurs. £10; Fri.–Sat. before 10, £10, after 10, £15.* ⏲ *Mon.–Sat. 8 PM–3:30 AM. AE, DC, MC, V.*

Bars

The Library. In this very comfortable, dress-code-free, but self-consciously "period" (doesn't matter which as long as it looks old) bar at the swanky Lanesborough Hotel, Salvatore Calabrese offers his completely eccentric collection of ancient cognacs, made in years when something important happened. A shot of this "liquid history" can set you back £500. Don't ask for brandy alexander. *Hyde Park Corner, SW1,* ☏ *0171/259–5599.* ⏲ *Mon.–Sat. 11–11, Sun. noon–2:30 PM and 7–10:30. AE, DC, MC, V.*

Cabaret

Comedy Café. Talent nights, jazz, and video karaoke, but mostly stand-up comedy, take place at this popular dive in the City. ☛ Charges are occasionally waived. There's food available in the evening and usually a late license (for alcohol). *66 Rivington St., EC2,* ☏ *0171/739–5706.* ☛ *Free–£7.* ⏲ *Wed.– Thurs. 7:30 PM–1 AM, Fri.–Sat. 7:30 PM–2 AM. MC, V.*

Comedy Store. This is the improv factory where the United Kingdom's funniest standups cut their teeth, now relocated to a bigger and better place. The name performers and new talent you'll see may be strangers to you, but you're guaranteed to laugh. *Haymarket House, Oxendon St., SW1,* ☎ *0171/344–4444, or 01426/914433 for information.* ☛ *£8–£9. Shows Tues.–Thurs., Sun. at 8, Fri.–Sat. at 8 and midnight. AE, MC, V.*

Casinos

The 1968 Gaming Act states that any person wishing to gamble *must* make a declaration of intent to gamble at the gaming house in question and *must* apply for membership in person. Membership usually takes about two days. In many cases, clubs prefer for the applicant's membership to be proposed by an existing member. Personal guests of existing members are, however, allowed to participate.

Charlie Chester Casino. The drawing cards here are an international restaurant and a modern casino with blackjack, roulette, craps, and Punto Banco. *12 Archer St., W1,* ☎ *0171/734–0255. Membership £5 for life.* ⏲ *Daily 2 PM–4 AM. Jacket and tie.*

Crockford's. This is a civilized club, established 150 years ago, with none of the jostling for tables that mars many of the flashier clubs. It has attracted a large international clientele since its move from St. James's to Mayfair. The club offers American roulette, Punto Banco, and blackjack. *30 Curzon St., W1,* ☎ *0171/493–7771. Membership £150 a year.* ⏲ *Daily 2 PM–4 AM. Jacket and tie.*

Sportsman Club. One of the few casinos in London to have a dice table as well as Punto Banco, American roulette, and blackjack. *3 Tottenham Court Rd., W1,* ☎ *0171/637–5464. Membership £3.45 a year.* ⏲ *Daily 2 PM–4 AM. Jacket and tie.*

The Gay Scene

Since February 1994, with the long-overdue lowering of the age of consent from 21, 18-year-old gay men in Britain have had the blessing of the law in doing together what they've always done together. (Westminster mooted 16, the boys-and-girls age, but British MPs could not quite deal with that). The change did not extend to lesbians, nor did it need to, since there has never been any legislation that so much as mentions gay women—a circumstance that, believe it or not, dates from Queen Victoria's point-blank refusal to believe that women did it with women. AIDS is, of course, a large issue, but the epidemic hasn't yet had quite as devastating an impact as it has on San Francisco and New York.

There are signs of a gay renewal in London. Soho, especially Old Compton Street, is acquiring a pre-AIDS Christopher Street atmosphere, with gay shops, bars, restaurants, and even beauty salons (get your chest waxed here) jostling for space. The lavender pound is a desirable pound. Though lesbians are included in the "Compton" scene (as are anyone's straight friends), it's predominantly men-for-men. The dyke scene certainly exists, and lesbian chic is as trendy in London as it is in New York or Los Angeles, but it has a lower profile, generally, than the male equivalent, and also tends to be more politically strident. Any women-only event in London attracts a large proportion of gay women.

Check the listings in *Time Out,* the weekly *MetroXtra* (*MX*), and the monthly *Gay Times* for events.

Bars, Cafés, Pubs

Comptons. This pub, which has been here forever, is run by Bass Charrington, one of the big U.K. breweries. It's a useful rendezvous for the Soho strip. *53 Old Compton St., W1,* ☎ *0171/437–4445.*

Crews Bar. As it sounds: a big West End pub with a swanky, New Yorky look, and testosterone on tap. *14 Upper St. Martin's La., W1,* ☎ *0171/379–4880.*

Drill Hall. A woman-centric arts center with a great program of theater/dance/art events and classes, plus a popular bar, which is women-only Monday. *16 Chenies St., WC1,* ☎ *0171/631–1353.*

The Edge. Poseurs welcome at this hip Soho hangout, where straight groovers mix in, and there are sidewalk tables in summer. Risk the vodkas infused with candy. *11 Soho Sq., W1,* ☎ *0171/439–1223.*

The Village. A cavern of a fashionable three-floored bar/restaurant/café/disco, whose name makes explicit the similarities between New York a decade back and London now. *81 Wardour St., W1,* ☎ *0171/434–2124.*

The Yard. This is Soho's best-looking and biggest bar/café, centered around the stunning Courtyard restaurant. *57 Rupert St., W1,* ☎ *0171/437–2652.*

Cabaret

Madame Jo Jos. By no means devoid of straight spectators, this place has long been one of the most fun drag cabarets in town—civilized of atmosphere, with bare-chested bar boys. *8 Brewer St., ☎ 0171/287–1414. ☛ Mon.–Thurs. £6, Fri. and Sat. £8. Doors open at 10 PM; shows at 12:15 and 1:15.*

Vauxhall Tavern. This venerable, curved pub had a drag cabaret before the Lady Bunny was born. Sometimes it's full of gay mafia, other times local media folk having a different night out, and Friday is the night for the lesbian cabaret, Vixens. *372 Kennington La., SE11, ☎ 0171/582–0833. ☛ Free. ⏲ Mon. 8 PM–1 AM, Tues., Thurs.–Sat. 8 PM–2 AM, Wed. 8 PM–midnight, Sun. 7–10:30 PM.*

Clubs

ONE-NIGHTERS

Some of the best gay dance clubs are held once a week in mixed clubs. The following are well-established, and likely still to be going, but it's best to call first.

Heaven. Aptly named, it has by far the best light show on any London dance floor, is unpretentious, *loud,* and huge, with a labyrinth of quiet rooms, bars, and live-music parlors. If you go to just one club, this is the one to choose. Thursday is straight night. *Under The Arches, Villiers St., WC2, ☎ 0171/839–2520. ☛ £4–£8. Call for opening times (Tues.–Sat. approx. 10:00 PM–3:30 AM.*

Queer Nation. This Sunday club is adorable for its laid-back, high-fashion friendliness, with hordes of gay and straight men and women recovering from the weekend together. *The Gardening Club, 4 The Piazza, Covent Garden, WC2, ☎ 0171/497–3153. ☛ £6. ⏲ 9 PM–2 AM.*

INDEX

✕ = *restaurant*, 🏨 = *hotel*

D

E

F

G

H

I

J

K

L

M

R

S

T

Fodor's Travel Publications

Available at bookstores everywhere, or call 1-800-533-6478, 24 hours a day.

Gold Guides

U.S.

Alaska
Arizona
Boston
California
Cape Cod, Martha's Vineyard, Nantucket
The Carolinas & the Georgia Coast
Chicago
Colorado
Florida
Hawaii
Las Vegas, Reno, Tahoe
Los Angeles
Maine, Vermont, New Hampshire
Maui
Miami & the Keys
New England
New Orleans
New York City
Pacific North Coast
Philadelphia & the Pennsylvania Dutch Country
The Rockies
San Diego
San Francisco
Santa Fe, Taos, Albuquerque
Seattle & Vancouver
The South
U.S. & British Virgin Islands
USA
Virginia & Maryland
Waikiki
Washington, D.C.

Foreign

Australia & New Zealand
Austria
The Bahamas
Barbados
Bermuda
Brazil
Budapest
Canada
Cancún, Cozumel, Yucatán Peninsula
Caribbean
China
Costa Rica, Belize, Guatemala
The Czech Republic & Slovakia
Eastern Europe
Egypt
Europe
Florence, Tuscany & Umbria
France
Germany
Great Britain
Greece
Hong Kong
India
Ireland
Israel
Italy
Japan
Kenya & Tanzania
Korea
London
Madrid & Barcelona
Mexico
Montréal & Québec City
Morocco
Moscow, St. Petersburg, Kiev
The Netherlands, Belgium & Luxembourg
New Zealand
Norway
Nova Scotia, New Brunswick, Prince Edward Island
Paris
Portugal
Provence & the Riviera
Scandinavia
Scotland
Singapore
South America
South Pacific
Southeast Asia
Spain
Sweden
Switzerland
Thailand
Tokyo
Toronto
Turkey
Vienna & the Danube

Fodor's Special-Interest Guides

Branson
Caribbean Ports of Call
The Complete Guide to America's National Parks
Condé Nast Traveler Caribbean Resort and Cruise Ship Finder
Cruises and Ports of Call
Fodor's London Companion
France by Train
Halliday's New England Food Explorer
Healthy Escapes
Italy by Train
Kodak Guide to Shooting Great Travel Pictures
Shadow Traffic's New York Shortcuts and Traffic Tips
Sunday in New York
Sunday in San Francisco
Walt Disney World, Universal Studios and Orlando
Walt Disney World for Adults
Where Should We Take the Kids? California
Where Should We Take the Kids? Northeast

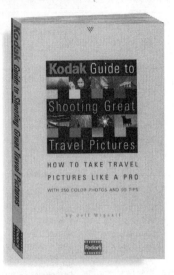